Wadewayę́stanih

A CAYUGA TEACHING GRAMMAR

Wadewayęstanih

A CAYUGA TEACHING GRAMMAR

third edition in the Henry orthography

Marianne Mithun and Reginald Henry

with revised spelling introduction by Carrie Dyck and Alfred Keye

WOODLAND CULTURAL CENTRE
Brantford, Ontario

JANUARY 2015

Copyright © 2015 Woodland Cultural Centre.

All rights reserved. No part of this publication may be reproduced, stored in a retrieval system, or transmitted in any form or by any means electronic, mechanical, photocopying, recording, or otherwise, without the prior written permission of the Woodland Cultural Centre.

Published by the Woodland Cultural Centre
184 Mohawk St, PO Box 1506
Brantford, ON, N3T 5V6, Canada

Third Edition – published 2015.

Watewayęstanih: A Cayuga teaching grammar, 1st Edition © 1982 Woodland Cultural Centre
Wadewayęstanih: A Cayuga teaching grammar, 2nd Edition © 2007 Woodland Cultural Centre

ISBN 978-1500820015

  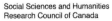 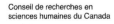

Table of Contents

PREFACE AND ACKNOWLEDGEMENTS xi

CH 1. INTRODUCTION 1
How to Use this Book

CH 2. THE SOUNDS OF CAYUGA 5

CH 3. SGĘ:NQ? 31
Greetings, Weather, Translation, Stress, Particles

CH 4. ĘYOSDÁQDI? 37
More Weather, Locations, Where Questions

CH 5. DĘ? HO?DĘ́? SYA:SQH? 43
Names, Origins, Iroquoian Communities, Thirst, Yes-no Questions, You and I

CH 6. SQ: HNE:? N?AHT TO:GYĘ́H? 57
Knowing People and Their Names, Delicious, Who questions, He and She

CH 7. OHSHÉ:DA? 73
Numbers and Ages

CH 8. EKSA?GÓ:WAH 81
Neighbours, Residence, Description of People, Plurals, Me, Him, Her, Them

CH 9. DÓ NIYOWIHSDÁ?E:?? 99
Time, Getting Up, Leaving the House

CH 10. GYA?DÁ?GEH 121
Body Parts, My and Your

CH 11. SATGĘH 135
Getting Up, Washing, Hurrying, Eating, Coat and Hat, Commands, Negation, More Yes-no Questions

CH 12. GYQDEHNÍ:NQH 151
Tools, Size, Price, Money, More, Most, Sort Of

CH 13. GATGWĘ́?DA? 179
Wallets, Purses, Baggage, Sickness, Seeing, Loss, Plurals, More Negation, I, She, He

CH 14. OHSÓHGWA? 189
   Colours

CH 15. AHGWĘ:NYA? 199
   Clothing, My and Your

CH 16. SATRǪ:NIH 211
   Getting Dressed and Undressed, Again, Commands, Repetition

CH 17. AGYA?DAWÍ?TRA? 221
   Too Big, Too Small, Underwear, Size, Shopping, Trying, Fitting, Buying, Which One, Too, Same

CH 18. DO: NIGA:GǪ:? 241
   Counting People

CH 19. GAHWAJIYÁ:DE? 251
   Relatives

CH 20. ǪDWĘNǪDÁHTA? 277
   Telephone Conversations, Current Activities, Approximate Time, Future Plans

CH 21. SEKSÁHǪ: 285
   Setting the Table

CH 22. DWADE:KǪ́:NIH 291
   Meal Conversation, Foods, Cooking, You/Me Yes-no Questions, More Future,
   More Negation, Don't

CH 23. SANAHSGWAĘ́? GĘ́H SGAHO?DĘ́:?ĘH? 313
   Pets, Animals, Feeding, Animal Body Parts, He, She, It, Counting Animals, Why Questions,
   Incorporation

CH 24. O?DRÉHDATGI? 337
   Cars, Car Parts, Mechanics, Giving a Ride, Knowing People, I/You, I/Him, I/Her, You/Me,
   You/Him, You/Her

CH 25. DĘH HO?DĘ́? NĘHSA:GYE:?? 347
   Future Plans, Summer Activities, Going To, Seasons, Days of the Week, Also, Hopes and Possibilities

CH 26. DEGAHENÁ?TRA?SE:? 363
   Toward, Away

CH 27. DAJǪH 373
   Dull, Sewing, Visiting

CH 28. GA̲HÁ:GǪ: 383
   The Forest, Past Events, Self

CH 29. ĘYAGWAHDĘ́:DIʔ 401
   Seasonal Activities, Future Plans, Here and There, They and I, You All

CH 30. ĘSWAYĘTOʔ GĘH? 415
   Gardening, Vegetables, Variety, Also, More Future, More Possibilities, They and I, You All

CH 31. DWĘNǪHSANÉKAHǪʔ 437
   Moving In, Baking, Running Out of Things, Borrowing, Being of a Kind, Looking Like,
   More Here and There, More Commands, Go and …

CH 32. OYĘ́HSRAʔ 455
   Quilt Making, Being Home, She and I, You Two, You All, When, He or She and I, They and I

CH 33. DĘDWAʔĘNÁĘʔ 477
   Snowsnake, Building a Track, Pushing, Pulling, You, You Two, You All, They and I, You and I

CH 34. ĘKNÍYĘTOʔ 493
   Planting, Doing Things for Someone Else, You and I, I for You, You for Me

CH 35. AʔǪHDĘGYǪ́HAʔ 503
   Travel, Means of Transportation, Duration, Days, Weeks, Months, Years, Women,
   Negative Questions, Where You Were

CH 36. TRANSLATIONS OF DIALOGUES 527

Preface and Acknowledgements

The first edition of *Wadewayęstanih*—then titled *Watewayęstanih*—was produced by linguist Marianne Mithun and Cayuga speaker Reginald Henry, through a National Endowment for the Humanities Research Tools grant, #RT-10038-80-1309 to Marianne Mithun. The original edition was in the 'linguistic' orthography. Simone Henry helped in preparing the English-Cayuga section of the glossary (which is found only in the first edition).

The second edition in the Henry orthography was funded by SSHRC grant #856-2004-1082 to co-investigators Dr. Carrie Dyck and Amos Key, Jr. The original manuscript in the linguistic orthography was not available in electronic form. For this reason, Hubert Buck, Jr. retyped the Cayuga portions, and Peggy-Ann Parsons of the Arts Faculty secretarial pool at Memorial University of Newfoundland retyped the English portions. Principal Investigator Carrie Dyck converted the 'linguistic' orthography into the 'Henry' orthography, and maintained the original drawings by Marianne Mithun (which lend great charm to the book). The spelling chapter was revised and expanded to reflect the change in orthography, and some of the end matter (including a grammatical description and glossary) was deleted.

Funding for the third edition was provided by a Social Sciences and Humanities Research Council of Canada *Community-University Research Alliance* grant entitled "COOL – Cayuga: Our Oral Legacy" (SSHRC #833-2009-1001) to co-investigators Dr. Carrie Dyck and Amos Key, Jr., and through in-kind contributions and grants to students provided by Memorial University of Newfoundland, the Woodland Cultural Centre, and Six Nations Polytechnical Institute. Students who worked on this revised edition include graduate students Sarah Knee, Ilia Nicoll, Stephanie Pile, Behak Rueentan, and Lana Williams and undergraduate student Sarah Dunbar. The following community members and teachers also contributed corrections and comment for the revised editions: Tom Deer, Tracy Deer, Joanne Longboat, and Angie Monture. Finally, Elders Lottie Keye, Frances Froman, Alfred Keye, Ruby Williams, and others also contributed corrections to the revised editions.

Nya:węh, swagwe:gǫh.

1

INTRODUCTION

HOW TO USE THIS BOOK

Learning a new language can be one of the most exciting things you can do. When you really learn a language, you discover a lot more than some strange sounds. You understand new ways of thinking, new ways of looking at the world, new ways of laughing. If you know any good Cayuga speakers, you may have heard them remark that a certain word does not really have an exact English equivalent, or that the joke that they were laughing so hard at just is not very funny in English. Although anything that can be said in one language can eventually be expressed in any other, different languages often prompt speakers to notice different things, to make different distinctions, to see different connections.

For a taste of one small way the languages differ, consider how a Cayuga speaker might say 'we'll eat'.

Ęgyadekǫ:niʔ.	'We'll eat.'
Ędwadekǫ:niʔ.	'We'll eat.'
Ęyagyadekǫ:niʔ.	'We'll eat.'
Ęyagwadekǫ:niʔ.	'We'll eat.'

Why does Cayuga need four different ways to say 'we'll eat'? (In fact, there are many more.) Cayuga speakers pay close attention to how many people they are talking about, and specify as well whether they mean to include the person they are talking to.

Ęgyadekǫ:niʔ.	'We two will eat (you and I).'
Ędwadekǫ:niʔ.	'We all will eat (yous and I).'
Ęyagyadekǫ:niʔ.	'We two will eat (he/she and I).'
Ęyagwadekǫ:niʔ.	'We all will eat (they and I).'

This can be a handy distinction when you are wondering whether you are being invited to dinner or subtly asked to leave. In fact, when Cayuga speakers say *ęyagwade:kǫ:niʔ*, they are actually saying 'we' (*yag-*) 'all' (*w-*) 'will' (*ę-*) 'make' (*-ǫ:niʔ*) 'ourselves' (*ade-*) 'a meal' (*-k-*). Does this mean that Cayuga speakers cannot generalize? Hardly. In English, if you want to discuss any object, you must specify whether you mean just <u>one</u>, or <u>more</u> than one.

I saw <u>a</u> car.	<u>A</u> car <u>is a</u> handy thing to have.
I saw (<u>some</u>) car<u>s</u>.	Car<u>s</u> <u>are</u> handy thing<u>s</u> to have.

You must also specify whether the cars in question are known to your listener.
I saw <u>a</u> car.
I saw <u>the</u> car. (Your listener can figure out which one you mean.)

In Cayuga, one word, *gʔadréhdaʔ*, can mean 'a car', 'cars', 'some cars', 'the car', or 'the cars'. In fact, it can even be used for other vehicles, such as trucks. (Of course Cayuga speakers can always add more words if they want to be more specific, just as we added 'two' and 'all' to the

Wadewayẹ́stanih

English translations of 'we'll eat'.) The point is, different languages <u>require</u> speakers to specify different distinctions. This word *gʔadréhdaʔ* is interesting in itself. One part, *-ʔdre-*, means 'drag', and another, *-hd-* means 'used for'. Cayuga speakers describe the most important feature of a vehicle, literally, 'it is used to drag things around'.

Cayuga is full of words like this. If you tell someone you are going fishing, *ẹgádahnyo:ʔ* you actually say 'I' (*g-*) 'will' (*ẹ-*) 'put in water' (*-o:ʔ*) a 'hook' (*-ahny-*) for 'myself' (*ad-*). To tell someone to put a shirt, dress, or coat on, you say *sagyáʔdawiʔt*, 'you' (*s-*) 'cause' (*-ʔd*) 'your' (*ag-*) 'body' (*-yaʔd-*) 'to be inside a tube' (*awi-*).

The purpose of learning a language like Cayuga is not just to be able to translate English thoughts into Cayuga sounds: it is to learn to think in Cayuga as much as possible. For this reason, we have tried to avoid direct translation whenever we could. New vocabulary is presented with pictures and in conversations so that students can learn to connect Cayuga words directly with objects and situations, not with other English words.

Often when people study a new language, they learn isolated words, but somehow never learn to put them together to say anything. They never learn to talk. The word-by-word approach can be especially frustrating with Iroquoian languages like Cayuga, because English and Cayuga words are not usually equivalent in size. One Cayuga word can correspond to a whole English sentence, as you saw on the last page. If you substitute English words directly for Cayuga words, one after the other, you can end up with English like this:

Ganagǫ́: haʔgeʔ.
it-town-in there-I-go   (literally, 'I am going to town.')

If you start with an English sentence and translate the words one at a time into Cayuga, the result sounds just as ridiculous. For this reason, the lessons in this book are mainly in the form of conversations. Instead of just learning isolated words, students should learn to use language appropriately in a variety of situations.

To speak a language, you must be able to do more than recite memorized sentences. You would like to be able to make up new sentences on your own, to fit new thoughts and new situations. The conversations in this book are not just random scraps of language: they are designed to teach patterns which students can absorb and use as models for new sentences, with as little conscious effort as possible. Instead of memorizing rules of grammar, such as how to form the future tense, students learn to talk about their plans for the coming summer, for example. Before they realize it, they should have a feeling for how the future is expressed, from firsthand experience. Some people learn better from explanations, and are curious about how and why things work. For them, each lesson has an explanation of the patterns used in the conversation. Some people learn better just by doing. These people should concentrate on memorizing and practicing the conversations until they are second nature, and not worry much about the explanations. With use, the patterns should seep in automatically. For this to happen, of course, it is necessary to know all words and conversations absolutely thoroughly.

The only way for anyone to really learn to speak a language is to imitate a good speaker. A book can be no substitute for the real thing. This book is meant to serve only as a guide through the working of this amazingly intricate language, pointing out what to watch for and how things fit together.

Wadewayęstanih

If you are studying Cayuga on your own, be sure to work closely with a speaker and tape recordings of the material, so you will learn to respond to the sound of the language, not just the sight of the written word. You want to understand and talk spontaneously. Reading and writing should take a back seat so they do not interfere with the link between a back room, in the car, doing dishes, in the shower, walking alone. If you have a dog or cat, he or she might love to hear what you have to say. This way you will get used to talking, and used to hearing the language. As you practice, visualize the objects and situations you are talking about, not their English translations. Once you have learned a word, such as *gʔadréhdaʔ* 'car', mentally (or loudly) name it each time you see one. Above all, learn each section <u>thoroughly</u> before you go on to the next one. Since each chapter is built on the one before, you really need to master each <u>inside out</u> to feel comfortable in the next. At first, memorizing new words might be difficult, because everything is new: new sounds, new rhythms, new structures, new ideas. After a while, the general sound and character of Cayuga will be familiar, and learning new words will be much, much easier.

If you are using the book in a class, you have quite an advantage. A good teacher can make it easier for students to learn to respond to spoken Cayuga quickly and to think in the language right from the start. Before students see a chapter at all, the teacher should teach the vocabulary pertaining to the topic of the day completely orally and <u>in</u> Cayuga. Instead of translation, the teacher should use objects, actions, and pictures to get the meaning across. For the lesson on greetings, for example, the teacher can move around greeting each student, as a group and individually. This should be continued until all students can return the greeting and exchange greetings with each other. They should not look at the book at all until after class, as a review. For the following class, all students should be able to take either part in the dialogue, perhaps with additional dramatic interpretation to liven things up. Each lesson should be taught this way, with the teacher teaching all new vocabulary orally and monolingually (that is, using only Cayuga, if possible) with props, until students can use the new expressions in sentences. Of course teachers should teach in natural statements and questions, rather than isolated words, since this is how they talk. Instead of saying the word for 'table' and pointing, for example, the teacher can touch the table and say something like 'this is a table' (in Cayuga, of course), and other similar simple but meaningful statements.

Teachers should of course feel free to add whatever vocabulary they please to any section. They will have a clear idea of what students would like to be able to say and which particular things they want to know. More clothing could be added to the trip to the dress shop, for example, more tools to the hardware store scene, more foods to the visits, more colors to the color section. Students could learn arithmetic in the number section. Teachers must of course read each chapter thoroughly before beginning to teach it, to be aware of the patterns being presented. Too many new patterns at once can be confusing to anyone.

An important element has been left mainly in the hands of the teacher: review. To set expressions into students' minds, it is necessary to refresh them every so often. This can be done by working old words into new conversations and by bringing up old topics. When talking about clothing, you can review colors and numbers (for prices and sizes), for example. You can always use greetings and talk about the weather.

Finally, any healthy language has variations. People living on different sides of a community, or even just coming from different families, will have slightly different styles of speaking. They may have slight differences in pronunciation on a few words, such as *onaʔnu:* vs. *onáʔno:*, 'it is cool', just like 'route' and 'either' in English. They may occasionally use different expressions, like 'bucket' vs. 'pail' in English. The variety of Cayuga used in this book is not meant to stand as <u>the</u> correct one. It is just one that is used among many. Anything said by a good Cayuga speaker in good faith is, of course, genuine, spoken Cayuga. Compared to the vast richness of the language as a whole, these kinds of differences are very small. Speakers are often not even aware of these differences until they think about teaching the language or writing it down. It is probably best for students to just learn the Cayuga spoken around them and to try to be reasonably consistent.

Incidentally, students should not expect Cayuga speakers to be able to explain the rules of their language. Being able to analyze how a language works actually has very little to do with being a good speaker. If a foreigner asked you the rules for constructing questions in your native language, could you leap into a clean, clear explanation? In a way, speakers know the rules thoroughly because they follow them every time they speak, but they do not necessarily know them consciously. As children, they absorbed them from the language they heard around them, without realizing it. The rules and patterns are there. Otherwise children could not learn to speak perfectly in such a short time. They do not learn all the sentences they will ever need. They just learn the rules for how to make them up as they need them. To an English speaker, Cayuga may seem complicated and irregular at first. It is, if you expect it to match English. Once you see it on its own terms, however, you cannot help but be amazed at its intricacy and harmony.

Re: Whispered and creaky-voiced syllables in Lower Cayuga

Von: Marianne Mithun (mithun@linguistics.ucsb.edu)

An: fritzforkel@yahoo.de

Datum: Samstag, 11. September 2021, 18:10 MESZ

Dear Fritz,

We're fine here. Hope you are as well.

Those voiceless syllables really are there, at least in the speech of people I worked with. They are there in the timing. I myself wouldn't have written those initial syllables with g, even in an English-based system. Of course in a system that fits the language, one would use only t and k, no d and g.

Best,
Marianne

> On Sat, Sep 11, 2021 at 5:56 AM Fritz Forkel <fritzforkel@yahoo.de> wrote:
>
> Dear Marianne,
>
> How are you? I hope you are in good health, and the Corona crisis has not affected you too much.
>
> My I ask a question about Cayuga, i.e. Lower Cayuga:
>
> I read about whispered vowels/syllables and "sounds like", but no exact phonetic and articulatory details.
>
> E.g. gihé:yõhs, "sounds like" kyé:yõhs, gadi'siha:? "sounds like" gadi'šha:? (gadišya:? in the book, but on the audio file I hear gadi'šha:?), sahsgá:ne:s "sounds like" sgá:ne:s.
>
> Are these words PRONOUNCED LIKE kyé:yõhs or do they just SOUND LIKE kyé:yõhs etc.? I feel there is a fundamental difference. I.e. do speakers pronounce these words fully, just whispering certain syllables, while hearers just don't hear those syllables, or do speakers really say e.g. sgá:ne:s (see above)? In the later case, the underlying form would be sahgá:ne:s (represented on the spelling, the first a being underlined) while the actual pronunciation would be sgá:ne:s - that would be like German "Bund" (underlying form and spelling) actual pronunciation /bunt/.
>
> Could you clarify that?
>
> Thank you!
>
> Best wishes,
>
> Fritz
>
> Dr. phil. Salomon Fritz Forkel
>
>> Am Mi., Sept. 18, 2019 at 14:19 schrieb Fritz Forkel <fritzforkel@yahoo.de>:
>>
>> Dear Marianne,
>>
>> Thank you! That answers my question.
>>
>> Warm regards,
>>
>> S. Fritz

Dr. phil. S. Fritz Forkel
Kastanienstr. 24
D-61352 Bad Homburg

Telefon (06172) 459338
Mobiltelefon 0163 8175898
fritzforkel@yahoo.de

Am Mittwoch, 18. September 2019, 11:04:20 MESZ hat Marianne Mithun <mithun@linguistics.ucsb.edu> Folgendes geschrieben:

Dear Fritz,

Yes, you got it right. Actually the only clitic there is the residential =hro:non'. There is a pronominal prefix ka-, but that is neuter, and refers to the place. You can use that word for any number of people. I think Onondagas would pretty much use the same term for Mohawks.

Best,
Marianne

On Mon, Sep 16, 2019 at 7:25 PM Fritz Forkel <fritzforkel@yahoo.de> wrote:
> Dear Marianne,
>
> May I ask you a question:
>
> Mohawk people collectively are referred to as
> Kanien'kehró:non (I hope I got it right) and similarly in other Iroquoian languages with the related clitic.
>
> How do you refer to one Mohawk (Onondaga etc.) person - and two or three, like I met a Mohawk, two/three Mohawks? Is there a special singular person clitic?
>
> Do you happen to know the probably related forms in other Iroquoian languages like e.g. Onondaga?
>
> Thank you!
> Warm regards,
>
> S. Fritz
>
> Dr. phil. S. Fritz Forkel

2

THE SOUNDS OF CAYUGA

1 About this version of the spelling manual

This spelling manual is a revised and expanded version of the description originally published in:

Mithun, Marianne and Reg Henry. 1984. *Watewayę́stanih. A Cayuga teaching grammar.* Brantford, Ontario: Woodland Indian Cultural Educational Centre.

This version of the spelling manual has been modified for the Henry orthography, and takes into account many comments provided by Cayuga speakers during spelling workshops that took place in the summer of 2005.

Learning a new language is more than just picking up a few new words; it also involves learning to hear and to pronounce some new sounds. Some Cayuga sounds are just about the same as English sounds, like N, R, W, and Y. Other Cayuga sounds are not used in English, so English speakers are not used to listening for them or pronouncing them. Because of this, the language can sound unclear or too fast at first. Once you have some practice in listening and pronouncing, however, you will find that speakers seem to speak much more clearly and slowly. The more Cayuga you listen to, the easier it will be to hear it and to imitate it.

The only way to learn a language really well is to imitate a native speaker. The explanations below are intended to point out what to listen for in Cayuga. If possible, ask a Cayuga speaker to go through this section with you, so that you can hear, firsthand, exactly how the language should sound. If no speaker is available, or if you exhaust the patience of your Cayuga speaking friend, you can find a version of this manual with sound files at this site: http://www.mun.ca/cayuga.

2 The Henry Orthography

The Henry orthography was created by the late Reg Henry (Śagohędéhtaʔ).[1] Reg was a fluent speaker of Cayuga, Onondaga, and English (among other languages), and was also a natural linguist.

The Henry orthography is widely used by Cayuga speakers at Six Nations. There is also a linguistic writing system, which is used in academic articles.

---

[1] The first sound in Reg Henry's name is an aspirated S ([sʰ]), which sounds like an S followed by an H. In the linguistic orthography, Reg's name would be spelled Shakohętéhtaʔ.

Example (1) shows the main differences between the Henry and linguistic writing systems.

1. The Henry and linguistic orthographies compared

Henry	Linguistic
t	th[2]
d	t
k	kh[2]
g	k
ś	sh
ts	tsh
j	ts, tsy

If you're familiar with other writing systems, you'll notice that the linguistic orthography has a lot in common with the Mohawk and Oneida writing systems, as the examples in (2) show.

2. Comparison of writing systems

Henry	Linguistic	Mohawk	
to:	tho:	e'tho	'that, there'
do:	to:	to	'how'

3 Some background notes about this manual

Sometimes, we need to make a distinction between letters (or written symbols) and how they are pronounced. For this reason, letters in the Henry orthography will be written as uppercase letters in the text; for example, D means 'the written letter D in the Henry orthography'. In contrast, to describe the exact pronunciation of a letter, symbols from the International Phonetic Alphabet (IPA) will be used. The letters from the IPA will be written between square brackets; for example, [ɑ] stands for 'the vowel sound in *lawn*'.

If you want to learn more about the IPA, you can go to the following website, which has interactive charts: http://www.paulmeier.com/ipa/charts.html. Or you can go to the website of the International Phonetic Association, which also has interactive charts and sound files illustrating what the letters of the IPA sound like: http://www.arts.gla.ac.uk/IPA/ipa.html.

---

[2] Word-finally, both the Henry and linguistic orthographies use a T or a K where appropriate.

4 Cayuga Letters

In this section, you'll find an overview of the letters and pronunciation markers used in the Henry orthography. In later sections, the pronunciation of each letter is described in greater detail.

The Cayuga vowel letters are listed in (3), and common vowel combinations are shown in (4).

3. Vowels

    i   ı̨
    e, ę   o, ǫ
         a

4. Common vowel combinations

    ai, ae, aę, ao, aǫ, ea, ei, ęi, ęǫ, ie, ię, iǫ, ia, oę, oi, ǫi

Vowels can be modified by two pronunciation markers or diacritics, which are shown in (5).

5. Vowel pronunciation markers or diacritics

Diacritic	Example	Name
´	é	acute accent (sometimes also called a stress marker, or stress point)
:	e:	lengthener
_	e̲	underlining (for devoiced or whispered vowels)

And finally, the Cayuga consonants are listed in (6).

6. Consonants

    t,d   k,g   ʔ (glottal stop)
    s   h
         ts,j
    n
    r
    w   y

Rules for pronouncing the Cayuga letters are provided in the following sections.

5 Cayuga vowel sounds

Cayuga vowels can occur alone (as in example 3) or in vowel combinations (as in example 4). When they are alone, each Cayuga vowel has one main pronunciation. The main pronunciation for each vowel is described below.

5.1 Single vowels

a [ɑ] sounds like the A in *father*

    sga:t   'one'
    Aha:k.   'He ate it.'
    Dasha:.   'Pass it here.'

e [e] sounds like the E in h*ey*, or like the AY in w*ay*, s*ay*

    é:ʔ   'again'
    ehswe:ʔ   'yous thought'

i [i] sounds like the I in pol*i*ce, or like the EA in *eat*

    i:ʔ   'I, myself'
    i:wi: 'I want'

o [o] sounds like the O in *so*, or like the OA in b*oa*t

    ó: 'oh'
    ó:nęh   'now'

u [u] sounds like the U in b*lu*e, or like the OO in b*oo*t

The [u] sound is rare; you are likely to hear it in just two words:

Niwú:ʔuh.   'It is small.'
Niwuʔdrugyé:ʔah. 'It is narrow.'

However, there's another case where you'll hear a [u] sound: some people pronounce the following words with a [u] sound, while other people use an [o] sound instead. (Perhaps this is the Cayuga version of "You say 'tomAYto', I say 'tomAHto'".)

swanóʔjʔageh, swanúʔjʔageh   'on your teeth (to two or more people)'
swayóʔtsaʔgeh, swayúʔtsaʔgeh   'on your chins (to two or more people)'
dago:s, dagu:s   'cat'

Cayuga also has two *nasal* vowels. The nasal vowels can sound fairly different, depending on who is speaking.

ę [ɛ̃] some speakers pronounce Ę like the E in English *en*counter, m*en*; or like the nasal vowel sound in French *frein* 'brake'.

ę [ʌ̃] other speakers pronounce Ę more like the O in English m*o*ney or like the U in English p*un*.

    ęhę:ʔ   'yes'
    gę́:s   'generally'

ǫ [õ] some speakers pronounce Ǫ like the O in English kn*ow*n, or like the nasal vowel sound in French *don* 'gift'.

ǫ [ũ] other speakers pronounce Ǫ more like the OO in English n*oo*n.

    ǫ́:dǫh   'she is saying'
    sǫ́:deʔ   'last night'

ę:, ǫ: After long Ę: and Ǫ:, you might sometimes hear an [n]-like sound; the sound is especially obvious when the nasal vowels are before T, D, K, G, TS, J. For example, the word *nę:dah* 'here, take it!' can sound a little bit like [nę:ⁿdah].

In contrast, you don't usually hear the same [n]-like sound when Ę and Ǫ are short.

a [ã]   There is one nasal vowel in Cayuga that doesn't have a special spelling because it is only heard in a few words. You can hear this sound in the word *hwaʔ* (as in the phrase *neʔ hwaʔ* 'this one this time, this one next').

5.2 *Vowels in combination*

When vowels are combined, they can sound different from the way they sound when they are alone. For example, both I and E sound nearly the same in the AI and AE vowel combinations: they sound like [ae].

7.   AI and AE sound nearly the same

   ái   hehsh**ái:**   'fox'
   áe   dakś**áe**ʔdohs[3]   'chicken'

Here are some more notes on how other vowel combinations are pronounced:

First, there is an I sound in the following vowel combinations, EI and ĘI. (It might be hard to hear but it's there!)

8.   Listen for the I sound

   ei   **ei**ʔgó:wah   'cherry'
   ęi   a:yets**ęi**ʔ[4]   'she might find it'

Next, some speakers use an AǪ vowel combination, while others use an ĘǪ combination instead:

9.   AǪ or ĘǪ

   aǫ, ęǫ   at**ęaǫ**ʔ, at**ęnęǫ**ʔ   'they raced (males only)'

As well, some speakers say IǪ where others would say IAǪ. Similarly, some speakers say IĘ while others would say IAĘ.

10.   Adding an A sound between two vowels

   iǫ, iaǫ   Had**iaǫ**hyaʔgéhó:nǫʔ.   'They are the heavenly kind (males only).'
   ię, iáę   god**iáę**naʔ   'their song (females or mixed)'

---

[3] The first S in this word stands for two sounds, [s] followed by [h].
[4] The first S in this word stands for two sounds, [s] followed by [h].

Finally, the following word is spelled *teá:ǫt* in the Cayuga Thematic Dictionary (Mithun and Henry 1984). However, it is also pronounced as *tí:aǫ:t*.

11. Muskrats

    í:a   tí:aǫ:t, teá:ǫt   'muskrat'

The remaining vowel combinations are relatively straightforward: they are pronounced as they are spelled. However, if the second Ę or I is unaccented, it can sound a bit more like a [y] sound.

12. Other vowel combinations

áo	gwáoh	'screech owl'
áę	gáęna'	'song'
áǫ	gáǫda'	'log'
oí	Hoího'de'.	'He's working.'
ǫi	Ęgǫihwę́hdę'.	'I will give you a significant message.'
oę	deyoęhda:hstá'[5] ahdáhgwa'	'running shoe'

5.3 Long versus short vowels

Long vowels take about twice as long to pronounce as short vowels. Long vowels are followed by a pronunciation marker called a COLON (some people call this a "lengthener").

In Cayuga the difference between long and short vowels is very important; in fact, sometimes length alone makes a difference in the meaning of a word.

13. Vowel length can make a difference in meaning

    E   ha'se'   'you are going'   E: ha'se:'   'you went'

    A   oyę́'gwa'   'tobacco'   A: oyę́'gwa:'   'smoke'

Here are a few more remarks about long vowels.

As mentioned earlier, after long Ę: and Ǫ:, you can sometimes hear an [n]-like sound; it is especially obvious when the nasal vowels are before T, D, K, G, TS, J. For example, the word *nę:dah* 'here, take it!' can sound a little bit like [nę:ⁿdah].

Cayuga speakers also like to write a lengthener after vowel combinations, such as after AE in the following example. This makes sense, since vowel combinations are twice as long as a single vowel.

    Satgǫhsoháe:.   'Wash your face.'

---

[5] This word is an exception to the accent rules described in §8.

Finally, long vowels are often accented. (Of course, the words presented earlier in example 13 are exceptions to this statement!) Section §8 describes the conditions under which accented vowels can be long.

6 Consonants

Cayuga consonants usually have two main pronunciations each; for example D can sound like [d] before regular vowels, but it can also sound like [t] before whispered vowels. The main pronunciation rules for consonants are described in this section. Section §7 provides details about when to expect pronunciations that are different from the spelling.

D   sounds like [d] in *dad* before regular (voiced) sounds:

    drę:na: 'skunk'
    dó:gaʔ.   'I don't know.'

D   sounds like [t] before whispered (devoiced) vowels:

    dehadí:hwahkwaʔ   'choir'

    ganǫhsagę́drahgǫh   'foundation'

    There are no D's word-finally: you will see T's instead:

    grahe:t   'tree'

T   sounds like [t] in *take*:

    Satǫ:.   'Lie down.'
    Sahsnęht.   'Get down.'

G   sounds like hard [g] before regular (voiced) sounds:

    degrǫʔ   'eight'
    agiʔ   'I said'

G   sounds like [k] before whispered (devoiced) vowels:

    gahsǫ́hdaʔ   'wire; nail; needle'
    grahe:t   'tree'

    There are no G's word-finally: you will see K's instead:

    Aha:k.   'He ate it.'

K   sounds like the [k] in *king*:

    knó:haʔ   'my mother'
    Odé:kaʔ.   'It is burning.'

S   sounds like the SH [ʃ] in *shirt* when it is before Y or R:

    Sahsyǫʔ.   'You returned.'
    Ęhsręʔ.   'You will set it on something.'

S   sounds like the [s] in *sing* almost everywhere else:

    só:wa:s   'dog'
    sgę́:nǫʔ   'hello'

S	sounds like a [z] in some words, especially when it's between vowels:

í:soʔ 'many, lots'

H	sounds like [h] in _hello_:

knó:haʔ 'my mother'
hahdo:s 'he dives'

H	is an important consonant in Cayuga, and it's important to pronounce any H's you see in the Cayuga spelling. Notice, for example, that Cayuga can have an H sound at the end of a word, as in *tsẹh* 'how'. In contrast, English never has an H sound at the end of the word.

For a more detailed description of pronunciation changes involving syllables with H, see §7.4 and §7.5.

SH	is a bit complicated. First, let's talk about what SH does not sound like: in English, the SH spelling stands for the first sound in the word _shirt_; in contrast, the SH spelling never stands for this sound in Cayuga.
SH	Next, let's talk about the linguistic orthography. (Recall from §2 that the linguistic orthography for Cayuga is a bit different from the Henry orthography.) The linguistic orthography has an SH spelling. It sounds like an [s] followed by an [h], as in the phrase _less heat_. For example, the following two words are spelled the linguistic way:

shẹh[6] 'how'
shehó:wi: 'tell her'

S	In contrast, the same sounds – the [s] sound followed by the [h] sound – are often just spelled with an S in the Henry orthography. The following two words are spelled the Henry way:

śẹh 'how'
śehó:wi: 'tell her'

As you can see, the Henry orthography has no way to spell the difference between a plain [s] sound and the sounds [s] followed by [h]. This isn't a bad thing, but if you're trying to sound out a Cayuga word that is spelled the Henry way, you will have to get a speaker to pronounce the word for you so that you can tell whether to pronounce just an [s], or an [s] followed by an [h].

J	can sound like the J [dʒ] in _judge_, or like the soft G in _Gerald_, especially before the vowels I and E. It can also sound like the [dz] sound in _adze_ or the DS in _leads_, especially before the vowels A and O. However, speakers will also use either one of the two J sounds with no difference in meaning. (Maybe this is another 'tomAYto/tomAHto' difference.)

onájagẹ:t 'rice'
hẹjéhehs 'birthdays'
Ẹhsnaʔjó:dẹʔ. 'You will boil something.'

---

[6] This word is also written as *tsẹh*, in which case it is pronounced as [tshẹh].

Wadewayę́stanih

J can sound like the CH [tʃ] in <u>ch</u>urch, or like the TS in ca<u>ts</u> before whispered vowels:

    joh̥sí?da:t   'one'
    joh̥sra:t   'one year'

TS is the spelling for three consonants, [t], [s], and [h], as in the phrase le<u>t's h</u>it:

    gadi:tsé:nę?   'farm animals'
    tsisédeh̥jih   'earlier this morning'

N sounds like the [n] in <u>n</u>od:

    ne?   'that'
    í:nǫh 'it is far'

N sounds like the N [n̥] in s<u>n</u>ore before H or whispered vowels:

    Gǫn̥he?.   'I am alive.'
    degan̥ohsá:ge: 'two houses'

R sounds like the [r] in <u>unr</u>est, <u>dr</u>ain, or <u>gr</u>ow:

    onráhda?   'leaf'
    gwadre:?   'my grandchild'
    o?gra?   'snow; snowflake'

R sounds like the R [ɹ̥] in <u>tr</u>ain in the TR spelling, or when DR is before a whispered vowel:

    atr̥iht   'you broke'
    hęnódr̥ahsta?   'they sprinkle on (males only)'

R sounds like the R [ɹ̥] <u>cr</u>eek in the KR spelling, or when GR is before a whispered vowel:

    Ękr̥ę?.   'I will set it.'
    gr̥ahe:t   'tree'

W sounds like the W in <u>w</u>ash:

    wa?ne:?   'today'
    Ǫ́:wi:.   'I think so.'

W sounds like the W [w̥] in s<u>w</u>ish, or like the sound you make when you blow out a candle, before whispered vowels:

    wah̥shę: 'ten'
    niyohw̥ih̥sdá?e: 'o'clock'

HW sounds like H followed by W (the same sounds you hear at the beginning of words such as <u>wh</u>at and <u>wh</u>ich in some varieties of British English):

    hwih̥s   'five'
    ganéhwa?   'hide; animal skin'

Y sounds like the Y in <u>y</u>es:

    í:yę: 'she wants, wishes'
    ó:ya?   'other'

Y	sounds like the Y [j] in the expression *Can I help you?* or like the [y] before the 'oo' sound in English *pure* or *cure*, when it's before whispered vowels:

gy̥ohdǫ: 'nine'
Dę:ˀ ni̥hságyéha??   'What are you doing?'

HY	sounds like [h] followed by [y]. You can also hear these sounds before the 'oo' sound in English *human* or *humour* in some types of English:

hyéi:ˀ   'six'
ohyaˀ   'fruit, berries'

ˀ	is the GLOTTAL STOP [ˀ] (some people call this a "slow marker"). This sound can be heard in English before the vowels in the words *uh-uh* (meaning 'no') and *uh-oh* (meaning 'oops'), but English does not spell the glottal stop. When you pronounce a glottal stop, you might be able to feel the vocal folds deliberately closing in your Adam's apple.

haˀnih   'my father'
onǫ́ˀa: 'a head'

ˀ	In Cayuga, the glottal stop is as important as any other consonant. For example, it can make the difference between a statement and a command:

satgǫhsoháe: 'wash your face' (command; no glottal stop at the end)

asatgǫhsóhae:ˀ   'you have washed your face' (statement; ends with a glottal stop)

Another language that uses glottal stop for a consonant is Hawai'ian.

For a more detailed description of pronunciation changes involving syllables with glottal stop, see §7.6 and §7.7.

7 Syllables with H or glottal stop

Syllables ending with H or glottal stop ˀ can sound quite different from the way they are spelled. Syllables ending with H can be whispered, while syllables ending with ˀ can undergo several types of pronunciation changes. To give one example, the glottal stop ˀ sound can disappear in such syllables.

In order to describe the sound changes, section §7.1 begins by describing what a syllable is. Then, section §7.2 describes where you can expect to hear syllables that are pronounced differently from the way they are spelled. Finally, sections §7.3 - §7.7 provide examples of how syllables with H or glottal stop ˀ are spelled and pronounced.

7.1 *What is a syllable?*

A syllable always contains a vowel, and can (but doesn't have to) begin or end with a consonant (or two). Example (14) lists some of the most common syllables of Cayuga.

14.   Common Cayuga syllables

i	e	a	o	u	ę	ǫ
di	de	da	do	du	dę	dǫ
gi	ge	ga	go	gu	gę	gǫ
hi	he	ha	ho	hu	hę	hǫ
ji	je	ja	jo	ju	ję	jǫ
ki	ke	ka	ko	ku	kę	kǫ
ni	ne	na	no	nu	nę	nǫ
ri	re	ra	ro	ru	rę	rǫ
si	se	sa	so	su	sę	sǫ
ti	te	ta	to	tu	tę	tǫ
wi	we	wa	wo	wu	wę	wǫ
yi	ye	ya	yo	yu	yę	yǫ
ʔi	ʔe	ʔa	ʔo	ʔu	ʔę	ʔǫ
dri	dre	dra	dro	dru	drę	drǫ
gri	gre	gra	gro	gru	grę	grǫ
kri	kre	kra	kro	kru	krę	krǫ
nri	nre	nra	nro	nru	nrę	nrǫ
sri	sre	sra	sro	sru	srę	srǫ
tri	tre	tra	tro	tru	trę	trǫ
dwi	dwe	dwa	dwo	dwu	dwę	dwǫ
gwi	gwe	gwa	gwo	gwu	gwę	gwǫ

kwi	kwe	kwa	kwo	kwu	kwę	kwǫ
nwi	nwe	nwa	nwo	nwu	nwę	nwǫ
swi	swe	swa	swo	swu	swę	swǫ
twi	twe	twa	two	twu	twę	twǫ
dyi	dye	dya	dyo	dyu	dyę	dyǫ
gyi	gye	gya	gyo	gyu	gyę	gyǫ
kyi	kye	kya	kyo	kyu	kyę	kyǫ
nyi	nye	nya	nyo	nyu	nyę	nyǫ
syi	sye	sya	syo	syu	syę	syǫ
sdi	sde	sda	sdo	sdu	sdę	sdǫ
sti	ste	sta	sto	stu	stę	stǫ
sgi	sge	sga	sgo	sgm	sgę	sgǫ
ski	ske	ska	sko	sku	skę	skǫ
shi	she	sha	sho	shu	shę	shǫ
sni	sne	sna	sno	snu	snę	snǫ
sgri	sgre	sgra	sgro	sgru	sgrę	sgrǫ
sgwi	sgwe	sgwa	sgwo	sgwu	sgwę	sgwǫ
sgyi	sgye	sgya	sgyo	sgyu	sgyę	sgyǫ
tsi	tse	tsa	tso	tsu	tsę	tsǫ

Cayuga has many more syllables than the ones listed in (14): for one thing, the table in (14) doesn't list any syllables <u>ending</u> with a consonant. You can add almost any consonant to the syllables listed in (14) in order to create more syllables. For example, you can create syllables such as DAʔ, DAH, DAK, DAHS, DAT, OR DAN[7] by adding consonants to end of the syllable DA.

7.2 *When do syllables sound different from the way they are spelled?*

Syllables <u>can</u> (but might not) sound different from the way they are spelled if all three of the following conditions are met:

- the syllable ends with H or glottal stop ʔ <u>and</u>
- the syllable is not accented <u>and</u>

---

[7] A syllable such as DAN will always be followed by an R or by a Y.

- the syllable is "odd-numbered". To find out if it is odd-numbered, count from the beginning of the word: the first, third, fifth, etc. syllable is odd-numbered.

Even if the above conditions are true, there are regular exceptions — cases where the syllable still sounds just the way it is spelled:

- The last syllable of the word always sounds the way it is spelled, even if it is odd-numbered.

- A syllable that <u>begins</u> with H or glottal stop ʔ sounds just the way it is spelled (even if it <u>ends</u> with H or glottal stop).

- If the first syllable of the word begins with a vowel, it sounds just the way it is spelled (even if it ends with H or glottal stop).

The Henry orthography has a way of warning the reader that a syllable is pronounced differently than it is spelled: for syllables ending in H, the vowel is underlined; for syllables ending with glottal stop ʔ, the glottal stop is either deleted or moved leftwards when spelling words. Cayuga speakers tend to delete the glottal stop ʔ, and linguists tend to move it instead, but these aren't hard and fast rules.

The pronunciation changes described in the following section are collectively known to linguists as Laryngeal Metathesis. A more technical description of Laryngeal Metathesis can be found in this article:

> Foster, Michael. 1982. Alternating weak and strong syllables in Cayuga words. *International Journal of American Linguistics* 48, 1:59-72.

Examples (and other exceptions) are provided in §7.3 - §7.7.

7.3 *Why do syllables sometimes sound different from the way they are spelled?*

Sometimes syllables such as DǪH or DÉH can sound just like a [t] (an example where DÉH sounds like a [t] is shown in 15): the spelling is quite different from the pronunciation! The reason why the spelling is so different from the pronunciation lies in the meaning:

15. Spelling and meaning

    D<u>e</u>hęnáǫhaʔ.   'They are racing (males only).'

    Degęnáǫhaʔ.   'They are racers (animals).'

Pairs of words like *dęhęnáǫhaʔ* and *degęnáǫhaʔ* in (15) are <u>related</u> in the sense that they have very similar meanings. The Henry orthography, like other writing systems, obeys the following rule of thumb:

16. Words (or parts of words) that are nearly identical in meaning have very similar spellings.

One advantage of the rule of thumb in (16) is that it makes it easier to see the parts of the word. To illustrate, compare examples (17) and (18).[8] The words in (17) are spelled in a more meaning-based way, while the words in (18) are spelled more like they are pronounced.

17. Meaning-based spelling (more phonemic)

    de̱-he̱n-**áǫha**ʔ   de-ge̱n-**áǫha**ʔ

18. Sound-based spelling (more phonetic)

    t-e̱n-**áǫha**ʔ   de-ge̱n-**áǫha**ʔ

Notice that it's fairly easy to figure out the parts of the word in (17) from the spelling, but it's not so obvious in (18). In (17), the *de-* and *-aǫha*ʔ parts together mean 'are racing'; the *he̱n-* part means 'they (males only)' and the *ge̱n-* part means 'they' (animals). In (18), it's harder to see the part of the word that means 'they' (males only).

There are advantages to both ways of spelling. Reg Henry designed the spelling system so that it reflected the meaning more than the pronunciation.

More details on the pronunciation of syllables with an H or with a glottal stop ʔ are provided in the following sections.

7.4 Syllables ending with H

To get an idea about what kinds of pronunciation changes can affect syllables ending with H, here are some examples of whispered and regular syllables.

19. Whispered and regular syllables, compared

whispered		sounds like	regular	
ehyá**dǫh**kwaʔ	'pencil'	ehyátkwaʔ	Ehyá:**dǫh**.	'She writes.'
Dehe̱náǫhaʔ.	'They race (males only).'	Te̱náǫhaʔ	Dege̱náǫhaʔ.	'They are racers (animals).'
Gǫhswahe̱hs.	'I hate you.'	**Kh**swahe̱hs	Gǫnóhweʔs.	'I like you.'
Sahsgá:ne:s	'You long for something'	Sgá:ne:s	**Hah**sgá:ne:s	'You long for something'

After you have compared the whispered and regular syllables, you will notice that in the whispered syllables:

- Whispered syllables can sound just like single a consonant (as in *de̱he̱náǫhaʔ* or *ehyádǫhkwaʔ*). For example, the syllables DE̱ and DǪH can sound just like a [t].

- Regular G can sound like K when it's whispered (as in *gǫhswahe̱hs*).

---

[8] The terms <u>phonemic</u> and <u>phonetic</u> have been added for those of you who have a linguistics background.

- Regular D can sound like T when it's whispered (as in *ehyádǫhkwaʔ*).

- The H disappears as a separate sound in whispered syllables (as in *ehyádǫhkwaʔ*).

- Particularly at the beginning of the word, it can be hard to even hear a whispered syllable (as in *s̲a̲hsgá:ne:s*).

You can see that whispered syllables often sound very different from the way they are spelled. Some particularly difficult cases are described in the next section.

7.5 Two vowels with an H in between

The pronunciation of two vowels with an H in between is quite different from the spelling, particularly when the first vowel is whispered. In fact, two vowels with an H in between can often sound more like a single vowel than two.

The words in the following examples were chosen to help you focus in on the pronunciation of vowels with an H in between. If you are using the on-line version of this manual, you can listen to these words.

The words in (20) illustrate the pronunciation of whispered I̲H and ÉH. The words in the first column in (20) have a whispered syllable followed by a regular one (in bold). In contrast, the words in last the column in (20) have two regular syllables in bold. The words in the middle column are the same as the words in the first column, except that the words in the middle column are spelled more like they are pronounced. Notice that whispered I̲H and ÉH can sound like a whispered Y (as in *niyokdéhú:ʔuh*).[9]

20. Comparison of whispered I̲H, ÉH and regular IH, EH

a whispered syllable plus H plus a regular syllable		sounds like	for comparision: a regular syllable plus H plus another regular syllable	
Gi̲**hé:**yǫhs.	'I am dying.'	**Ky**é:yǫhs	E̲**gíhe:**ʔ.	'I will die.'
Gadí̲**hsiha:**ʔ.	'They are congregated.'	Gadí̲hs**hha:**ʔ	Ha**dihá:**wiʔs.*[10]	'They carry along.'
Agadri̲**hó**ʔda:t.	'I worked.'	Agatrioʔda:t	E̲gao̲**dríhoʔ**da:t.	'They are going to work (females or mixed).'

---

[9] You can also hear a whispered Y sound after the F in 'fjord', after the C in 'cure', or after the P in 'pure'; however, the Y sound isn't spelled out in 'cure' and 'pure'.

[10] For the words marked with an asterisk, the accent placement is an exception to the rules described in §8.

a whispered syllable plus H plus a regular syllable		sounds like	for comparision: a regular syllable plus H plus another regular syllable	
Nihú:ʔuh.	'He is small.'	Nhyú:ʔuh	nigihú:ʔuh	'a small stream'
Agénihę́ʔ	'I stopped, quit.'	Agę́nhyę:ʔ	sęní:hę:	'quit'
Honadrihǫ́:dǫʔ.	'they are agents (males only).'	Honatriǫ́:dǫʔ	Nihǫwáihǫ:t.	'He has appointed him.'
dehenagya:dá:dǫhs	'a circus'	tenagya:dá:dǫhs		
Ękhnégeha ʔ.	'I will drink it.'	Ęknékyaʔ	Snegéhah.	'Drink it.'
hadihǫwaʔgehó:nǫʔ	'sailors, etc.'	hadihǫwaʔkyó:nǫʔ	hahędagehó:nǫʔ	'farmer'
niyokdehú:ʔuh	'small root'	niyoktyú:ʔuh		
Ęgádeheh.	'I will be embarrassed.'	Ęgátyeh	Gadéhęhs.	'I am embarrassed, ashamed.'
ęhsátgehǫ:ʔ	'you will sell'	ęhsátkyǫ:ʔ	Hatgéhǫhaʔ.	'He is an auctioneer.'

The words in (21) illustrate the pronunciation of whispered ĘH. The main thing to notice here is that the whispered syllables can just sound like a single consonant (as in *deyagwihsragęhé:yǫ:* and *howę́hgęhę:ʔ*). Also note that J can sound like a CH [tʃ] (as in *sadejęhí:yohs*), G like a [k] (as in *howę́hgęhę:ʔ*), and D like [t] (as in *degahsdęhodá:gyeʔ*).

21. Comparison of whispered ĘH and regular ĘH

a whispered syllable plus H plus a regular syllable		sounds like	for comparison: a regular syllable plus H plus another regular syllable	
Sadejęhí:yohs.	'Make a good fire.'	Sadechęí:yohs	Wadéhi:ʔ.	'It is stacked.'
Deyagwihsragęhé:yǫ:.	'She is sighing.'	Deyagwihsrakhé:yǫ:	Agyaʔdagęhé:yǫ:.	'I am physically weak, slow.'
degahsdęhodá:gyeʔ	'mountain range; the Rockies'	degahstęodá:gyeʔ	gahsdę́ho:t	'a mountain'

a whispered syllable plus H plus a regular syllable		sounds like	for comparison: a regular syllable plus H plus another regular syllable	
Howęhgęhę:ʔ.	'It used to be his.'	Howęhkę:ʔ	Agawęgęhę:ʔ.	'It used to be mine.'
Ęhsajęhohsgwáę:ʔ.	'You will whisper.'	Ęhsachęhohsgwáę:ʔ	sajęhohsgwáęʔ	'whisper'

The words in (22) illustrate the pronunciation of whispered Qн and Oн. Notice that whispered Oн and Qн can sound like a whispered W (as in *dwaknigohí:yo:*).[11] One interesting point to note is that GQHAʔ in words such as *gʔanígohaʔ* sound like [kwã̃]; the [ã] sound is the same nasal vowel as in the French word *an* 'year'.

You'll also notice that, as before, D sounds like [t], etc., and two syllables sound like one (as in *ęhohdogaʔdohǫ́:gyeʔ*).

22. Comparison of whispered Oн, Qн and regular OH, QH

a whispered syllable plus H plus a regular syllable		sounds like	for comparision: a regular syllable plus H plus another regular syllable	
Ędwádrohe:k.	'We all will gather together (yous and I).'	Ędwátrwe:k	Ęhsróhe:k.	'You will gather.'
Asáhjohaiʔ.	'You did wash your hands.'	Asáhchwaiʔ	Sahjóhai:.	'You wash your hands.'
Ahshagohó:wiʔ.	'He told her.'	Ahshakó:wiʔ		
johonáʔda:t	'one potato'	chonáʔda:t		
Dwaknigohí:yo:.	'I am satisfied, peaceful.'	Dwaknikwí:yo:	Desaʔnigohí:yo:.	'You are satisfied.'
Ahágohe:k.	'He punched it.'	Ahákwe:k, Ahákwę:k	Segóhe:s.	'You hit it all the time.'
gʔanígohaʔ	'the mind'	gʔaníkwaⁿʔ	ogwaʔnigóhaʔ	'our mind'

---

[11] You can also hear a whispered [w] sound after the S in 'swish', after the T in 'twenty', or after the Q in 'queen'; however, the [w] sound is spelled as a U in 'queen'.

a whispered syllable plus H plus a regular syllable	sounds like	for comparison: a regular syllable plus H plus another regular syllable
Sę'nig**ǫhó**'drǫh. 'You are a worrier.'	Sę'ni**kó**'drǫh	Ęhsę'nig**ǫhó**'drǫ:. 'You will worry, despair; you will be desperate.'
Dwaknig**ǫhę́**'ǫh	Dwakni**kwę́**'ǫh	
Ęhohdoga'd**ǫhǫ́**:gye'	Ęhohdoga'**tǫ́**:gye'	G**ǫ**hdogad**ǫ́hǫ**gye'

Finally, the words in (23) illustrate the pronunciation of whispered AH. The main points to notice are that, as before, GR sounds like [kr] (as in gr*a*hé:t), etc., and two syllables can sound like one (as in dehsáhy*a*hiht).

23.   Comparison of whispered AH and regular AH

a whispered syllable plus H plus a regular syllable	sounds like	for comparision: a regular syllable plus H plus another regular syllable
Dehsáhy**a**hiht. 'Cut up the fruit.'	Dehsáh**yai**ht	**ahí**:' 'I thought, intended'
gr**a**hé:t 'a tree'	kr**ae**:t	
agen**a**háotra' 'my hat'	age**nhá**otra'	a**nahá**otra' 'a hat'

By now, you've probably noticed several endings that are spelled the same, but which sound quite different. Here are the most common ones:

24.   Comparison of pronunciation and spelling of two endings

hadihǫwa'**gehó:nǫ'**	'sailors, etc.'	hahęda**gehó:nǫ'**	'farmer'
Ęhohdoga'**dǫhǫ́:gye'**.	'He will be growing along.'	Gǫhdoga**dǫ́hǫgye'**.	'She is growing something.'
Howę́hg**ęhę:'**.	'It used to be his.'	Agawę**géhę:'**.	'It used to be mine.'

The examples in (24) also illustrate the principle (in example 16) that words (or parts of words) should be spelled similarly if they have similar meanings. The words *hadihǫwa'gehó:nǫ'* and *hahędagehó:nǫ'* both have the same ending (which means something like 'people of the' or 'people who live in a certain place...'); the ending sounds quite different in these words, though, because the first syllable of the ending is whispered in *hadihǫwaʔgęhó:nǫʔ* but not in *hahędagehó:nǫʔ*. The words *ęhohdogaʔdǫhǫ́:gyeʔ* and *gohdogadǫ́hǫgyeʔ* share two endings *-dǫh-ǫgyeʔ*, which collectively mean 'go along doing something'. The words *howę́hgęhę:ʔ* and *agawęgę́hę:ʔ* share the ending *-gęhę:ʔ*, which means 'formerly' or 'used to be'.

7.6 Disappearing or hard-to-hear glottal stops

The words in the following examples were chosen to help you focus in on the pronunciation of syllables ending with a glottal stop ʔ. You should listen to the following examples, especially to the bolded syllables. You can also listen to slowed-down versions of each syllable by clicking on the left-hand column of the following table. In the slowed-down versions, it is often easier to hear the <u>disappearing</u> glottal stop.

25.   Disappearing versus non-disappearing glottal stops

slowed-down versions	disappearing		non-disappearing	
gʔa vs. hoʔ	**gʔ**adréhdaʔ	'car, vehicle'	**hoʔ**dréhdaʔ	'his car, vehicle'
sʔa vs. saʔ	S**ʔ**anígǫha:t.	'You are smart.'	De**saʔ**nigǫ́ha:t.	'You are stupid.'
sgʔa vs. joʔ, oʔ	**sgʔ**anhǫ́hsat, **joʔ**nhǫ́hsa:t	'one egg'	**oʔ**nhǫ́hsaʔ	'eggs'
dʔe vs. deʔ	Ęhsa**dʔ**enyę́:dęʔ.	'You will try.'	Sa**deʔ**nyę́:dęh.	'Sample it, try it.'

Once you have compared the two types of syllables, you will notice that in the syllables with a disappearing glottal stop you can sometimes hear a trace of the glottal stop:

- Sometimes the consonant before the glottal stop has a 'popped' release sound.
- Sometimes the vowel after the glottal stop sounds 'swallowed'.

You can see that syllables with a disappearing glottal stop often sound very different from the way they are spelled. More examples are described in the next section.

7.7 Two vowels with a glottal stop in between

The pronunciation of two vowels with a glottal stop ʔ in between can be quite different from the spelling; in particular, the first vowel can sound <u>swallowed</u>. In fact, two vowels with a glottal stop ʔ in between can sound more like a single vowel than two.

The words in the following examples were chosen to help you to focus in on the pronunciation of vowels with a glottal stop ʔ in between.

26. Comparison of syllables with a disappearing glottal stop and syllables with a non-disappearing glottal stop

	syllable with a disappearing glottal stop, followed by a regular syllable		syllable with a non-disappearing glottal stop, followed by a regular syllable	
i̲ʔé	deyotji̲ʔéhta:	'a stampede'		
ʔéa, éʔa	Ageg̲ʔéaji:h.	'I have dark hair.'	Hogéʔaji:h.	'He has dark hair.'
éʔǫ, éʔǫ	Sayę́d̲ęʔǫh.	'You are really good at something.'	Ęsayedę́ʔǫhǫ:k.	'You will be really good at it.'
aʔá, áʔa	ga̲ʔáhdraʔ	'a basket'	agáʔahdraʔ	'my basket'

After listening to the sounds, you will notice that:

- It can be hard to hear the syllable with the disappearing glottal stop (as in *gaʔáhdraʔ*).

- Consonants in the syllable containing the disappearing glottal stop can sound different from the spelling: G can sound like [k] (as in *ageg̲ʔéaji:h*), and D can sound like [t] (as in *sayędę́ʔǫh*).

Recall from section §7.2 that disappearing glottal stops are most likely to be heard in odd-numbered syllables ending with a glottal stop. However, this is not a hard and fast rule: sometimes there is no difference between the pronunciation of odd-numbered and even-numbered syllables ending with a glottal stop. For example, the pronunciation of the syllable RĘʔ in *hodidrę́ʔí:ga:ʔ* and *odrę́ʔí:ga:ʔ* is identical, even though the syllable RĘʔ is odd-numbered in the case of *hodidrę́ʔí:ga:ʔ*, and even-numbered in the case of *odrę́ʔí:ga:ʔ*. Here are some more examples:

27. No disappearing glottal stops, even in odd-numbered syllables

ę́ʔí:	hodidrę́ʔí:gaʔ	'painted turtles'	odrę́ʔí:ga:ʔ	'painted turtle'
ę́ʔę, ę́ʔę:	Ęhsetsgę́ʔędahgoʔ.	'You will remove seeds.'	otsgę́ʔę:ʔ	'peach pit'
ę́ʔǫ	gyohnegę́ʔǫh*	'falling water'	heyohnegę́ʔǫh	'falling water'
ǫʔę́, ǫ́ʔę	Hotgǫhstǫʔę́htaʔ.	'He is shaving.'	Ahotgǫhstǫ́ʔęht.	'He shaved.'
ǫʔǫ, ǫ́ʔǫ	hadihnyǫʔǫhsrá:tęhs	'ironworkers, iron climbers'	gahnyǫ́ʔǫhsraʔ	'iron, steel'

So far, we've looked at Cayuga consonant and vowel pronunciation. Now we'll discuss which vowel gets the accent marker ´ and the lengthener.

8 Accent and length

Most words have an accented vowel — a vowel which is pronounced with higher PITCH.[12] (The 'C' and 'D' notes on a musical scale are examples of what pitch is; the difference between 'C' and 'D' is a difference in pitch, and 'D' has a higher pitch than 'C'.)

The pronunciation marker or diacritic for an accented vowel is the ACUTE ACCENT MARK ´, also sometimes called a "stress point".

This section describes where to put the accent mark, or where accent occurs in words. The description only applies to situations where the speaker is making a fairly neutral statement — the speaker isn't asking a question, isn't too emotional, isn't emphasizing the word, etc. You can find more information about non-neutral statements in section §8.5.

Here are some rules of thumb about accent placement (examples are provided later).

28. Rules of thumb for accent placement

a. Words which are pronounced alone or in isolation have a non-final accent: accent does not fall on the final syllable;

b. Words at the end of a phrase also have a non-final accent;

c. Words which are not at the end of a phrase have a final accent: accent is on the final syllable of the word.

NON-FINAL ACCENT means an accent that falls on the second-last vowel, the third-last vowel, or even on the fourth vowel from the end of the word. Some examples are provided in (29), and the rules for non-final accent placement are described in detail in §8.1.

29. Examples of non-final accent placement

a. Accent falls on the vowel that is second from the end

   Hahá:wiʔ.   'He is carrying it.'
   Hodá:węʔ.   'He has swum.'
   Hahé:haʔ.   'He sets it.'

b. Accent falls on the vowel that is third from the end

   ohnéganohs   'water'
   dewáhǫhde:s   'deer'

c. Accent falls on the vowel that is fourth from the end

   ganagáedahkwaʔ   'a whistle'
   Sayaʔdodrǫhgwáǫnihsgǫ:.   'You are always shivering.'

FINAL ACCENT means that accent is on the last vowel of the word. Examples (30) and (31) illustrate the difference between final and non-final accent. In example (30), the accent is on the final vowel of *aga:tǫ:déʔ* because this word is not at the end of the phrase.

---

[12] Some shorter words have no accented vowel; these words are described later.

30. Final accent placement

   Aga:tǫ:déʔ tsǫ:, tęʔ ni:ʔ degé:gę:ʔ.   'I just heard it, I didn't see it.'

In contrast, example (31) shows that the same word has a non-final accent (*aga:tǫ́:deʔ*) when it <u>is</u> at the end of a phrase.

31. Non-final accent for words that are at the end of a phrase

   Negitsǫ́: **aga:tǫ́:deʔ.**   'I just heard it.'

There are a few complications: for one, some words can have a final accent, but can't have a non-final accent. Some examples are shown in (32): instead of having a non-final accent (an accent on the second-to-last vowel), these words can be pronounced without an accent.

32. Accentless words

   ganyo:ʔ   'wild animal'
   ahsęh   'three'

However, the same words can have a final accent under certain conditions. For example, while the word *ahsęh* in (32) is accentless when it is pronounced alone, the same word has a final accent when it is *not* at the end of a phrase, as shown in (33). (Here, the phrase has just two words in it.)

33. ahsę́h niwáhshę: 'thirty'

Another complication for the description of accent placement is PARTICLES. (Particles are small words with only one vowel.) Normally, particles can be accented when they are pronounced in isolation, as shown in (34).

34. Examples of particles, accented when pronounced in isolation

   tę́ʔ   'not'
   ní:ʔ 'I, me'

In contrast, groups of particles in a phrase tend to share one accent — that is, only one of the particles in a particle group has the accent. (For this reason, some Cayuga speakers sometimes spell particle groups as if they were one word, which is kind of like English speakers spelling *cannot* as one word).

To illustrate, the particle groups in (35), which have been taken out of their sentence contexts, contain three particles each. The particle *tsǫ́:* is accented in (35.a) while the same particle *tsǫ:* is unaccented in (35.b). Basically, the particle group in (35.a) is accented as if it were a single word with final accent. In contrast, the particle group in (35.b) is accented just like a word with non-final accent: the only difference is that the particle groups in (35) contain several words (particles) each.

35. Accent in particle groups

a.   Negitsǫ́:...   'It's just that...' (non-phrase-final particle group; consists of *neʔ giʔ tsǫ:*)
b.   Gyęʔnétsǫ:... 'Just that...' (phrase-final particle group; consists of *gyęʔ neʔ tsǫ:*)

So, to summarize, there are basically two types of accent: final and non-final. The rule for final accent replacement is easy:

36. Rule for final accent placement: accent the final vowel of words that are *not* at the end of a phrase.

In contrast, the rules for *non*-final accent placement are fairly complicated, since either the second-last, third-last, or fourth-last vowel can be accented. The rules are described in the following section.

8.1 Non-final accent placement

In this section, we'll see not only where the accent mark goes, but also where the vowel lengthener goes: accented vowels and vowels preceding the accented one are sometimes long, and there are rules to describe this.

First of all, it's important to consider the second-to-last vowel: most of the time, that vowel is accented, but not always. To find out if it is or not, we need to ask a few questions such as: is the second-to-last vowel even-numbered or odd-numbered? To find this out, we need to count from the beginning of the word: for example, the second, fourth, sixth, etc., vowel from the beginning of the word is even-numbered.

Now, if the second-to-last vowel is even-numbered, it is accented. It's that simple!

The rules for the lengthener are a bit more complicated, though. An even-numbered, second-to-last vowel will also have a lengthener, but only if it is followed by a consonant... as long as the consonant is not H or glottal stop ʔ. This is beginning to sound complicated, so let's use a decision-tree to figure out where to put the accent marker and the lengthener. (Sorry it's so small.)

37. Decision-tree for deciding where to put the accent mark and lengthener

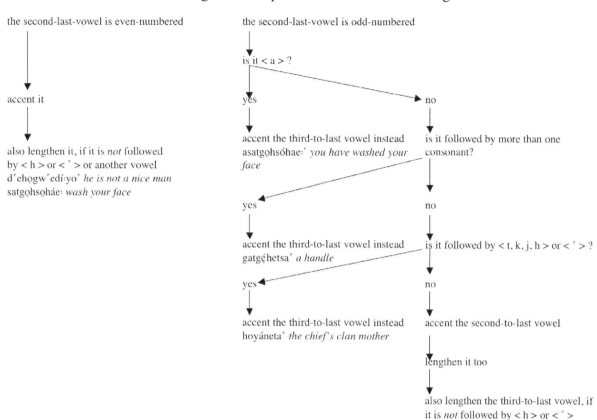

The rules in example (37) work for most words, but there are several exceptions, which are described in the following sections.

8.2 *Words without an accent*

What happens if there is no third-to-last vowel to accent? In this case, the word can be pronounced without an accent. Here are some examples and explanation.

38. Accentless words

a. degrǫʔ   'eight'

   The first vowel is second-to-last and odd-numbered. It is followed by a consonant cluster, GR and so the third-to last vowel should be accented. However, there is no third-to-last vowel, so this word can be pronounced without an accent.

b. agiʔ   'I said'

   The first vowel is second-to-last and odd-numbered. However, it is also the vowel A and so the third-to-last vowel should be accented instead. Since there is no third-to-last vowel, this word can be pronounced without an accent.

8.3 The vowel-to-be-accented is immediately preceded by another vowel

Here's a small addition to the rules in (37): if the vowel-to-be-accented is immediately preceded by another vowel, then the accent shifts to that vowel. "Immediately preceded" means that there is no consonant between the accented vowel and the vowel right before it. An example is provided in (39).

39. If the vowel that is normally accented according to the rules in (37) is immediately preceded by another vowel, then the accent can shift to the preceding vowel.

    ganagáeda̲hkwaʔ   'a whistle'

    The second-to-last, odd-numbered vowel E would normally be accented, but since it is immediately preceded by another vowel, A in this case, the A can be accented instead.

8.4 Just plain exceptions

There are always exceptions to accent placement! Some common exceptions are listed in example (40).

40. Exceptions

a. Vowels <u>before</u> the endings -kʔah and -sʔah are always accented and long (even when odd-numbered).

    ganǫhsá:kʔah   'beside the house'
    onǫhsatgí:sʔah   'an ugly house'

b. The first vowel of the ending -shǫ́:ʔǫh / -sǫ́:ʔǫh or -shǫ́:ʔah / -sǫ́:ʔah is always accented and long, even when odd-numbered.

    (o)gwęni̲hshǫ́:ʔǫh   'change (money)'

c. The vowels in some words are always accented and long, regardless of whether they are odd- or even-numbered, even if they are followed by H or ʔ.

    knó:haʔ   'my mother'
    Hahé:haʔ.   'He sets it.'

d. The vowel A can sometimes be accented and lengthened even when it is odd-numbered, as long as it is followed by only one consonant; this is particularly true if A is the first vowel of a two-vowel word.

    Gá:yęʔ.   'It is lying there.'
    Sá:weh.   'It is yours.'

8.5 Non-neutral statements

The rules (and exceptions) described earlier only apply to the way Cayuga speakers talk when they are making neutral statements. If speakers are emphasizing something, or asking a question, for example, things can change.

One type of exception has to do with emphasized words. As shown in (41), people often say *do:gáʔ* with final accent, even when the word is by itself. (This is an exception to the rule in

28.a.) Similarly, they might accent *í:ʔ* in the phrase *Do: í:ʔ*. In both cases, it seems that words that are emphasized can have a final accent.

41.   Non-neutral statements (emphasis)

a.   Do:gáʔ.   'I don't know.'
b.   Do: í:ʔ.   'Let me (do it).'

Another type of accent pattern can happen with questions. As shown in (42), "[in questions] the tone [or pitch] of voice is perfectly level, not falling at the end the way it does in statements. *This ... is often the only difference between a statement and a question*" (Mithun and Henry 1984:27; emphasis added). Based on this description, we can say that words at the end of a question might not have any accent at all. (In contrast, recall from 28.b that such words would normally have a non-final accent.)

42.   Level pitch in questions (Mithun and Henry 1984:35; orthography modified)

a.   Gaę nhǫ́: disahdęgyǫ:?   'Where do you come from?'
b.   Dęʔ hoʔdę́ʔ sya:sǫh?   'What is your name?'
c.   Dęʔ hoʔdę́ʔ ęhsnegéhaʔ?   'What will you drink?'

8.6 For further reference

If you know another Ǫgwehǫ́:weh language such as Mohawk, you will notice that Cayuga accent placement is more complicated than in Mohawk, where often the second-to-last vowel is accented. This is one of the major differences between Mohawk and Cayuga. Another major difference is Cayuga's whispered syllables and the syllables with disappearing glottal stops (see §7): glottal stops can disappear in Mohawk, but not in the same way as in Cayuga. If you want to learn more about the differences between Mohawk, Cayuga, Seneca, Oneida accent, etc., the following book is an excellent source:

Anonymous. 1988. *Cayuga Thematic Dictionary: A List of Commonly Used Words in the Cayuga Language, Using the Henry Orthography*. Brant: Woodland Publishing, The Woodland Cultural Centre.

Michelson, K. 1988. *A comparative study of Lake-Iroquoian accent*. Studies in Natural Language and Linguistic Theory. Dordrecht: Kluwer Academic Publishers.

3

SGĘ:NQ'

Wadewayę́stanih

Practice the conversation until everyone can take either part.

Wadewayę́stanih

<u>Translating</u>
(or rather, not translating)

     Because Cayuga is so different from English, it is often difficult to translate a word in one language into a perfect equivalent in the other. A word in any language usually has a wide range of meanings, and arouses certain feelings in a speaker. Sometimes it takes a whole sentence in English to translate a single Cayuga word, and sometimes vice versa. Consider just one of the words in the conversation.

Węhnihsrí:yo:.   'It is a nice day.'   or   'The day is nice.'   or   'Nice day.'

Learning to speak a new language involves learning new ways of thinking. This is a pretty exciting process. To learn to think in Cayuga, it is best to learn to associate Cayuga words and phrases with objects and the situations in which speakers use them, instead of their English translations. A word-by-word translation of the conversation above does not make very good sense in English.

Sgę́:nǫʔ.	'Peace.'
Ęhę́ʔ, né:ʔ giʔ á:yę:ʔ.	'Yes, that is just it seems.'
Węhnihsri:yó: wáʔne:ʔ.	'Nice day now.'
Ęhę́ʔ, węhnihsrí:yo:.	'Yes, nice day.'

To a Cayuga speaker, it has an effect more like this:

Hello, how are you?
Not bad, I guess.
Nice day today.
Yes, it certainly is.

The language lessons in this book have been arranged to avoid as much direct translation as possible, so that as you learn Cayuga, you can learn to associate the language with objects, images, and situations, rather than English words. To speak a language well, you must think in that language. The more you practice speaking, alone and with others, the more the words and phrases will take on meanings of their own, not just translations, the more sense they will make, and the better a Cayuga speaker you will become.

<u>Stressful Situations</u>

     You may have noticed that when words are combined into phrases, several things happen. One change involves stress. Stress moves to the end of a Cayuga word when another word immediately follows.

Węhnihsrí:yo:.	'Nice day.'
Węhnihsri:yó: wáʔneʔ.	'Nice day today.'

Wadewayę́stanih

More Weather Expressions

The words below are all Cayuga verbs. Notice that each begins with *o-*. This *o-*, and the *w-* of *wę̱hnihsrí:yo:* mean 'it'.

Otó:weʔ.	'It is cold.'
Oné:nǫʔ.	'It is warm/hot.'
Oʔgróǫ:.	'It looks like snow.'
Osdáǫ:.	'It looks like rain.'

Practice the conversation, substituting one of these words for *wę̱hnihsrí:yo:*. Keep practicing with others in the class until you have used each of the weather verbs.

Particles

Cayuga has a lot of very short words called PARTICLES. Often these particles do not have good English equivalents, and are difficult to translate, but you will notice that good speakers use them often. Sometimes their meaning is clear, like *wʔne:ʔ* 'now', 'today'. Other times it is much more subtle, and adds a tone of modesty, politeness, doubt, or certainty. Sometimes it identifies the source of the information, like 'I guess' or 'I heard'. (Imagine trying to describe to a foreigner what 'just' means in English, from the sentences 'She just left', 'She just loves it', 'She just doesn't know', 'She just took one look', and 'She is quite just'.) Often particles combine into phrases with their own special idiomatic meanings. Speakers tend to pronounce such phrases like a single word, in one breath.

A:yę́:ʔtsǫ:.   'It does seem that way.'   a:yę:ʔ 'it seems'; tsǫ: 'just'

A good way to learn to use particles is to learn phrases and sentences which contain them, like:

A:yę:ʔtsǫ́: wę̱hnihsrí:yo:.   'It seems like a nice day.'

then practice substituting another verb for the main one there:

A:yę:ʔtsǫ́: otó:weʔ.

Before you know it, you will have a feeling for where the particles belong and what they add to the meaning.

Wadewayę́stanih

Vocabulary

węhnihsrí:yo:.	'the day is nice.', 'it is a nice day.'
otó:weʔ.	'it is cold.'
oné:nǫʔ.	'it is warm.', 'it is hot.'
oʔgróǫ:.	'it looks like snow.'
osdáǫ:.	'it looks like rain.'
sgę́:nǫʔ.	'hello.'
ęhęʔ	'yes'
waʔne:ʔ	'now', 'today'
á:yę:ʔ	'it seems'
tsǫ:	'just', 'only'
giʔ	'just', 'as a matter of fact'
ne:ʔ giʔ á:yę:ʔ or ne:ʔ gʔiá:yę:ʔ.	'it seems.', 'I guess so.'
a:yę́:ʔ tsǫ: or a:yę́:ʔtsǫ:.	'it does seem that way.'

Each chapter in this book will be followed by a summary of the new vocabulary encountered in the chapter, like the list above. It is important to know the vocabulary well before moving on to the next chapter, since each new section builds on material from early ones.

4

ĘYOSDÁQDIʔ

Wadewayę́stanih

ĘYOSDAQDI'

Wadewayęstanih

Questions and Answers

Listen to the speaker's tone of voice in the questions in this conversation.

Gaę nǫdahse:ʔ?	'Where did you come from?'
Gaę haʔseʔ?	'Where are you going?'

Notice that the tone of voice is perfectly level, not falling at the end the way it does in statements. This happens in all questions, and is often the only difference between a statement and a question. Practice asking the questions above until you can imitate that level tone of voice.

Next notice the order of the words in the answers.

Ganadagǫ́:	haʔgeʔ.	'I am going to town.'
into-town	I-am-going	

In Cayuga, the most important information is usually put first in the sentence. The questioner already knows that you are going or coming from somewhere. The new, important information is <u>where</u>.

Two particles, *diʔ* and *giʔ*, are often used to tie conversations together. Speakers will often slip *diʔ* into questions right after the first word of the question, to show that the question relates to what went on before somehow. It could be translate roughly 'so', or 'then' in this case.

Gaę haʔseʔ?	'Where are you going?'
Gaę diʔ haʔseʔ?	'So where are you going?'

Speakers often slip *giʔ* into answers, right after the first word, to show that they are answering, that is, supplying the information because they were asked, and that the statement relates to the question. It could be translated very roughly 'well', or 'since you ask', or 'as a matter of fact'.

Ganadagǫ́: giʔ haʔgeʔ.	'Well, as a matter of fact, I'm going to town.'

More Locations

When Cayuga speakers refer to a location in town, they say *ganádagǫ:* 'in town' (*-gǫ:* = 'in'). Here are some other locations you can substitute for this in the conversation. They use *-geh* or *-hneh* for 'at'/'to'.

Wadewayę́stanih

ganyadá:ʔgeh	'to/at the lake'
gihęʔgowáhneh	'to/at the river'
kehsó:tgeh	'to/at my grandmother's'
hehsó:tgeh	'to/at my grandfather's'
hadéjʔęsgeh	'to/at the doctor's'

You can make up good Cayuga words for more locations on your own. To talk about someone's house, simply add *-geh* or *-hneh* to their name. Add *-geh* if the last <u>sound</u> (not letter, sound) is a consonant, and *-hneh* if the last <u>sound</u> is a vowel (A, E, I, O, U).

Petegeh	(last sound, [t]) 'at Pete's'
Ruthgeh	'at Ruth's'
Reggiehneh	'at Reggie's'
Bessiehneh	'at Bessie's'

A Bit More Weather

When Cayuga speakers say 'it will rain', they actually say, literally, 'it will throw drops' (*ę-* 'will', *yo-* 'it', *-sta-* 'drop', *-ǫti* 'throw'). To change the rain to snow, you can simply substitute the drops for snow, *-ʔgr-*.

Ęyoʔgrǫ́:diʔ.	'It will snow.'

Practice

Practice the conversation until you can take either part perfectly. Then try it several times, substituting difference locations for *ganádagǫ:* and *ęyoʔgrǫ́:diʔ* for *ęyosdáǫdiʔ*.

New Vocabulary

ohjíʔgreʔ.	'it is cloudy'	gaę...?	'where...?'
eyosdáǫdiʔ.	'it will rain'	stǫ́:hǫh	'a little'
eyoʔgrǫ́:diʔ.	'it will snow'	diʔ	'so'
		giʔ	'as a matter of fact'
haʔgeʔ.	'I am going there'	gʔishę́hwaʔ	'maybe', 'perhaps'
nǫdá:ge:ʔ.	'I came from there'		
nǫdáhse:ʔ.	'you came from there'		
ganádagǫ:	'in town'	kehsó:tgeh	'to/at my grandmother's'
ganyadá:ʔgeh	'to/at the lake'	hehsó:tgeh	'to/at my grandfather's'
gihęʔgowáhneh	'to/at the river'	hadéjʔęsgeh	'to/at the doctor's'

5

DĘ^ʔ HOʔDĘʔ SYA:SQII?

Wadewayę́stanih

44

Wadewayę́stanih

Wadewayę́stanih

Ko:ká kó:lah.

Ja:dáhk hétgęh.

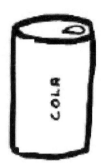
Ohnegagá'ǫh.

Wadewayęstanih

DĘʔ HOʔDĘʔ SYA:SǪH?

Wadewayę́stanih

Wadewayęstanih

More About Combining Words

In earlier conversations, you saw that stress in Cayuga shifts to the last syllable of the word when another word follows.

Tahnawá:deʔ	'Tonawanda'
Tahnawa:déʔ dwagáhdęgyǫ:.	'I come from Tonawanda.'
Tahnawa:déʔ nidwa:ge:noʔ.	'I come from Tonawanda.'

This is also another difference between words in the middle of a sentence and words alone or at the end. If no other word follows, speakers add H to words ending in a single, short vowel.

Ohnegagaʔǫh ęknégeha ʔ.	'I'll drink pop.'
ohnegagáʔǫh	'pop'

Nosy or Interested?
(More about questions)

As before, the speakers' voices remain level in tone in all questions, instead of falling at the end.

Sada:tęhs gęh?	'Are you thirsty?'
Gaę nhǫ́: disahdęgyǫ:?	'Where do you come from?'
Dęʔ hoʔdęʔ sya:sǫh?	'What is your name?'
Dęʔ hoʔdęʔ ęhsnegehaʔ?	'What will you drink?'

Practice imitating the level tone of voice that speakers use for these questions until it is perfect.

There are two basic types of questions in Cayuga. Questions can ask for a simple yes or no, or they can ask for further information. The first type is below.

Shaʔda:tęhs gęh?	'Are you thirsty?'

As you can see, an appropriate answer would be some kind of *yes* or *no*, not something like *Coca Cola*. Yes-no questions are very easy to ask in Cayuga. Compare the pair below.

Shaʔdá:tęhs.	'You are thirsty.'
Shaʔda:tęhs gęh?	'Are you thirsty?'

To ask a yes-no question, simply put *gęh* after the first word of the sentence.

Wadewayę́stanih

Practice making questions from words you already know.

Ohjíʔgreʔ.	'It is cloudy.'	Is it cloudy?
Ęyosdáǫdiʔ.	'It will rain.'	Will it rain?
Ęyoʔgrǫ:diʔ.	'It will snow.'	Will it snow?
Węhnihsrí:yo:.	'It is a nice day.'	Is it a nice day?
Otó:weʔ.	'It is cold.'	Is it cold?
Oné:nǫʔ.	'It is warm.'	Is it warm?
Oʔgróǫ:.	'It looks like snow.'	Does it look like snow?
Osdáǫ:.	'It looks like rain.'	Does it look like rain?

The level tone of voice is so important in asking questions that the *gęh* is sometimes not even added.

Ęyoʔgrǫ:diʔ?   'Will it snow?'

Practice asking all of the questions you asked above leaving off the *gęh*, simply showing that you are asking by the tone of voice.

Some useful answers to yes-no questions might be:

Ęhęʔ.	'Yes.'
Tęʔ.	'No.'
Ęhęʔ, gʔishéhwaʔ.	'Yes, maybe.'
Stǫ́:hǫh.	'A little.'

Speakers often repeat the statement after answering *ęhęʔ*.

Ohjíʔgreʔ gęh?	'Is it cloudy?'
Ęhęʔ, ohjíʔgreʔ.	'Yes, it is.'

Wadewayęstanih

ohnéganohs

ohyá:gri?

ká:fih,
osahe?dá:gri?

odi:

onǫ?gwa?

ohné:ga?

Wadewayę́stanih

Wadewayę́stanih

Another question word used to ask for more information is:

Dę? ho?dę?...?	'What…?'

It is used in two questions in this conversation.

Dę? ho?dę? sya:sǫh?	'What is your name?'
Dę? ho?dę? ęhsnegeha??	'What will you drink?'

The conversation contains the name of one beverage, *ohnegagá?ǫh* 'pop'. Here are some more you should learn, in case anyone asks what you would like. You can substitute any of them for *ohnegagá?ǫ* in the answer:

Ohnegaga?ǫ́ ęknégeha?.	'I'll drink pop.'
ohnéganohs	'water'
onǫ́?gwa?	'milk'
ohyá:gri?	'fruit juice'
odi:	'tea'
káfih, osahe?dá:gri?	'coffee'
ohné:ga?	'liquid' or 'liquor'

(A fancier word for 'liquor' is *dega?nigǫhadé:nyǫhs*, literally, 'it changes the mind'.)

Practice

Ask each person in the room whether he or she is thirsty. Ask each one who says yes what he or she will drink. Reply to each person who asks that you are thirsty, then say what you would like to drink.

Sha?da:tęhs gęh?	Ęhę?, a:yę:? ka?da:tęhs.
Dę? ho?dę? ęhsnegeha??	_____ ęknegeha?.

Notice again that the most important word of the answer, the beverage, comes first.

Wadewayę́stanih

(H)S-...K-/G-
(You and I)

If you compare some of the verbs in this conversation, you can see that a part of the world itself tells who is being talked about.

Gyá:sǫh	'I am called'
Syá:sǫh	'You are called'
Ka?dá:tęhs.	'I am thirsty.' (literally, 'My throat is dry.')
Sha?dá:tęhs.	'You are thirsty.' (literally, 'Your throat is dry.')
Ęknégeha?	'I will drink'
Ęhsnégeha?	'You will drink'

The *k-* or *g-* ('I') refers to the speaker, while the *(h)s-* ('you') refers to the hearer. Watch for this different in the conversation to come.

(N)I:'...(N)I:S

Myrtle told Sam,

Myrtle gya:sǫh.

While Sam said,

Sam ní:? gyá:sǫh.

The particle *ni:?* is optional, and usually shows a contrast of some kind. It can be translated something like 'as for me', and is used when the speaker differs somehow from others.

Sam ní:? gyá:sǫh.	'As for me, my name is Sam (unlike you, Myrtle).'
Ohswe:gę́? ní:? dwagáhdęgyǫ:.	'I, myself, come from Six Nations (in contrast to you, Myrtle, who come from Tonawanda).'

The emphatic particle *í:s* 'as for you' is used in its full form when Myrtle asks Pete where he comes from.

Nę? ne? í:s?	'Well, how about <u>you</u> (I just told you where I am from)?'

Practice

Mingle around the room, asking each person his or her name, with:

Dę? ho?dę́? sya:sǫh?

Wadewayęstanih

Tell anyone who asks what your own name is.

_____ gyá:sǫh.

Once they have asked you yours, and you have replied, ask theirs, using the contrastive particle *i:s*.

Nę' ne' i:s?

A good reply to this question would be:

_____ ní:' gya:sǫh.

New Vocabulary

gyá:sǫh	'my name is…'	Tahnawá:de'	'Tonawanda'
syá:sǫh	'your name is…'	Ohswé:gę'	'Six Nations'
dwagáhdęgyǫ:	'I come from…'	G'ada:grásgęhę:'	'Cattaragus'
disáhdęgyǫ:	'you come from …'	Gyonǫhsadé:gęh	'Cornplanter Reservation'
ka'dá:tęhs	'I am thirsty'	Ganádase:	'Newtown'
sha'dá:tęhs	'you are thirsty'	Ganrahdahé'geh	'Green Bay'
ęknégeha'	'I will drink'	Ohí:yo'	'Allegany'
ęhsnégeha'	'you will drink'	Gyohnéganu:	'Coldspring'
fesa'dráihęh	'hurry up'	Dasgáow'ęgeh	'Tuscarora area'
		Onǫd'ageh	'Onondaga area'
ohnéganohs	'water'	Ohnyáhęh	'Oneida area'
onǫ'gwa'	'milk'	Tayędané:gę'	'Deseronto'
ohyá:gri'	'fruit juice'	Gwésahsneh	'Ahkwesasne'
odi:	'tea'	Gahnáw'ageh	'Caughnawaga'
ka:fih, osahe'da:gri'	'coffee'	Gahnawiyó'geh	'Oklahoma'
		Gahenagǫ:	'Hamilton'
ohné:ga'	'liquid' or 'liquor'	Gyagwé:tro'	'Cayuga (town)'
		Gayógahneh	'Cayuga, Ontario'
ní:'	'as for me', 'myself'	Tganádahe:'	'Brantford'
ní:s	'as for you', 'yourself'	Tganádaę'	'Caledonia'
gęh	question marker	Tganęnogáhe:'	'Haggersville'
tę'	'no' or 'not'	Degyotnǫhsá:kdǫ:	'St. Catherine's'
dę' hó'dę'?	'what?'	Táǫdo'	'Toronto'
gaę nhǫ:?	'where?'	Kyodró:wę:	'Buffalo'
		Gwastón'ǫgeh	'United States'
nę' né' i:s?	'how about you?'	Tganǫhgw'atro'	'Sour Spring'
tgahnáwęhta'	'Niagara Falls'	Gyehahsędáhkwa'	'Ohsweken (village)'

6

SQ: HNE:ʔ NʔAHT TO:GYĘH?

Wadewayę́stanih

(Mercy eyá:sǫh.) (Bessie eyá:sǫh.)

Wadewayę́stanih

OGÁʔǪH

Wadewayęstanih

SQ: HNE:ʔ NʔAHT TO:GYĘH?

Wadewayę́stanih

Wadewayę́stanih

HA- ... E-
(He-ing and She-ing it)

You may recall from the last conversation, that verbs contain parts which identify who is being discussed.

gyá:sǫh	'I am called' or 'my name is'	(*k*- 'I')
syá:sǫh	'you are called' or 'your name is'	(*s*- 'you')

In this conversation, there are some new verbs based on the same stem *-yasǫ* 'be called'.

eyá:sǫh	'she is called'
hayá:sǫh	'he is called'

Notice that the beginning of these words matches the beginning of some other pairs.

eksá:ʔah	'girl'
haksá:ʔah	'boy'
egę́hjih	'old lady'
hagę́hjih	'old man'

The *e-* shows that you are talking about a female, the *ha-* that you are talking about a male.

OGÁʔǪH
(How to compliment the cook)

Myrtle obviously likes her pop, and she says so:

Ogaʔǫ́h   nę:gyę́h   ohnegáʔǫh.
it-is-delicious this   delicious-liquid
'This pop is delicious.'

(Notice how H appears at the end of the last word. Also, you can see the literal meaning of *ohnegáʔǫh*. *o-* 'it' *hneg-* 'liquid' *-gaʔǫ* 'delicious').

You can substitute the name of any other drink or food for *ohnegáʔǫh* and create a good Cayuga sentence.

Ogaʔǫ́h nę:gyę́h onǫ́ʔgwaʔ.	'This milk is delicious.'
Ogaʔǫ́h nę:gyę́h ohnéganohs.	'This water is delicious.'

Again, *ogáʔǫ* appears first in the sentence because it is the most important, new information. We can already see what the speaker is drinking.

Wadewayęstanih

Wadewayę́stanih

SǪ:ʔ
(Who?)

This conversation contains a new question word: *sǫ:* 'who?'. Practice asking others in the class to identify someone in the room, someone visible through the window, or someone in a picture, by saying:

| Sǫ: hne:ʔ nʔaht to:gyę́h? | 'Who is that?' |

When someone asks you to identify a person, reply with the name, saying:

| _____ eyá:sǫh | (for a female) |

or

| _____ hayá:sǫh | (for a male) |

Notice that as usual, the most important information, the name, comes first.

Now, be more specific in your questions. Include the type of person you mean: *eksá:ʔah, haksá:ʔah, agǫ́:gweh, hǫgweh, egę́hjih, hagę́hjih*; for example:

| Sǫ: hne:ʔ nʔaht to:gyę́ agǫ:gweh? | 'Who is that woman?' |

ǪGWEHǪ:WE GEH?
(Real person?)

In Cayuga, Native people are known as *ǫgwehǫ́:weh* or 'real people'. Someone might ask you:

| Ǫgwehǫ́:weh geh? | 'Are you Indian?' |

You could answer this question either:

| Ęhęʔ, ǫgwehǫ́:weh. | 'Yes, I am Indian.' |

Or

| Tęʔ. | 'No.' |

Sometimes, people will add 'you' and 'I' to this.

| Sǫgwehǫ:weh gęh? | 'Are you Indian?' |
| Ęhęʔ, gǫgwehǫ́:weh. | 'Yes, I am Indian.' |

OGWEHOWEHNEHA:ʔ
(Indian language and customs)

Soon, people will begin to ask you about your progress in learning the Cayuga language, if they have not started already. Since anything is easy for a native speaker, they may use overwhelmingly long words, like:

Sawayenheʔohǫ:gyéʔ gęh,	a:satwę:nǫ:dáhk	ǫgwehǫwéhneha:ʔ?
are-you-learning	to-speak	Indian-language

or:

Sʔanigǫhaędáʔs gę ǫgwehǫwehneha:ʔ?
do-you-understand Indian-language

Sahǫkaʔ gę ǫgwehǫwehneha:ʔ?
do-you-hear (speak) Indian-language

You could be pretty fancy yourself in your answer:

Ęhę́ʔ,	agewayęnheʔohǫgyéʔ	a:gatwę:nǫ:dáhk	ǫgwehǫwéhneha:ʔ.
Yes	I-am-learning	to-speak	Indian

or:

Ęhę́ʔ, akʔnigǫháędaʔs.
'Yes, I understand (but probably do not speak).'

Ęhę́ʔ, gahǫkaʔ.
'Yes, I speak.'

You could be a bit more modest, with:

Stǫ́:hoh.
'A little bit.'

or, if you lose your nerve entirely, you can mumble:

Tęʔ tó ne:ʔ.
'Not really.'

Some speakers always use the full form, *ǫgwehǫwéhneha:ʔ* for the Cayuga language, while others sometimes shorten it to *ǫgwehǫ́:weh*.

Wadewayę́stanih

New Vocabulary

eksá:ʔah	'girl', 'child'
haksá:ʔah	'boy'
wgę́hjih	'old lady'
hagę́hjih	'old man'
agǫ́:gweh	'woman'
hǫgweh	'man'
ǫgwehǫ́:weh	'Indian'
ǫgwehǫwéhneha:ʔ	'Indian language', 'Indian ways', 'Indian things'
nę́:dah	'here, take this'
nę́:gyęh	'this'
tó:gyęh	'that'
sǫ:	'who?'
Waʔheh	'just now'
Ne:ʔ giʔ …	'That is…'
ó:nęh	'already', 'at this time'
nę́ne:ʔ	'you know', 'mind you'
tęʔ tó ne:ʔ	'not really'
oihwí:yoʔ	'it is certain'
eyá:sǫh	'she is called'
hayá:sǫh	'he is called'
gyagóhdęgyǫ:	'she comes from there'
tohdę́:gyǫ:	'he comes from there'
gahǫkaʔ	'I speak a language'
sahǫkaʔ	'you speak a language'
ǫhǫ́:kaʔ	'she speaks a language'
hahǫ́:kaʔ	'he speaks a language'
tę́ʔ dʔeǫhǫkaʔ	'she does not speak that language'
tę́ʔ dʔeháhǫkaʔ	'he does not speak that language'
tę́ʔ dʔegáhǫkaʔ	'I do not speak that language'
akʔnigǫháędaʔs	'I understand'
sʔanigǫháędaʔs	'you understand'
hoʔnigǫháędaʔs	'he understands'
gʔonigǫháędaʔs	'she understands'
tę́ʔ dʔeakʔnigǫháędaʔs	'I do not understand'

Wadewayęstanih

a:satwę:nǫ́:dahk	'you could talk'
a:gatwę:nǫ́:dahk	'I could talk'
swęní:yo:	'you speak well' (literally, 'Your words are good.')
snegéhah	'drink it'
ogáʔǫh.	'It is delicious'
gasheyędéi	'you know them'
sǫ: hne:ʔ nʔaht?	'who is that?'

7

OHSHÉ:DA?

7 já:dahk		4 géi
6 hyéi?	5 hwihs	3 ahsẹh
2 dekni:		6 hyéi?
	9 gy<u>o</u>hdǫ:	
8 degrǫ?		1 sga:t
	6 hyéi?	
5 hwihs		7 já:dahk
	9 gy<u>o</u>hdǫ:	
8 degrǫ?		2 dekni:
	3 ahsẹh	
10 w<u>a</u>hshẹ:		3 ahsẹh
	4 géi	
9 gy<u>o</u>hdǫ:		7 já:dahk
	5 hwihs	
1 sga:t		10 w<u>a</u>hshẹ:
	2 dekni:	
4 géi		

Wadewayęstanih

Do: ni:yǫ:?

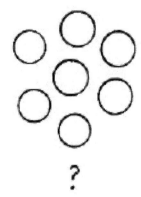
?

?

?

?

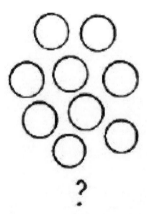
?

Wadewayęstanih

Ohshé:da⁷

1. sga:t	11. sga:t sgahe⁷	21. dewahshę́: sga:t
2. dekni:	12. dekni: sgahe⁷	22. dewahshę́: dekni:
3. ahsęh	13. ahsę́ sgahe⁷	23. dewahshę́: ahsęh
4. géi	14. géi sgahe⁷	24. dewahshę́: géi
5. hwíhs	15. hwíhs sgahe⁷	25. dewahshę́: hwihs
6. hyéi⁷	16. hyéi⁷ sgahe⁷	26. dewahshę́: hyéi⁷
7. já:dahk	17. ja:dáhk sgahe⁷	27. dewahshę́: já:dahk
8. degrǫ⁷	18. degrǫ⁷ sgahe⁷	28. dewahshę́: degrǫ⁷
9. gyohdǫ:	19. gyohdǫ: sgahe⁷	29. dewahshę́: gyohdǫ:
10. wahshę:	20. dewáhshę:	30. ahsę́ niwáhshę:

31. ahsę́ niwáhshę: sga:t
32. ahsę́ niwáhshę: dekni:
33. ahsę́ niwáhshę: ahsęh
34. ahsę́ niwáhshę: géi
35. ahsę́ niwáhshę: hwihs
36. ahsę́ niwáhshę: hyéi⁷
37. ahsę́ niwáhshę: já:dahk
38. ahsę́ niwáhshę: degrǫ⁷
39. ahsę́ niwáhshę: gyohdǫ:
40. géi niwáhshę:

41. géi niwáhshę: sga:t
42. géi niwáhshę: dekni:
43. géi niwáhshę: ahsęh
44. géi niwáhshę: géi
45. géi niwáhshę: hwihs
46. géi niwáhshę: hyéi⁷
47. géi niwáhshę: já:dahk
48. géi niwáhshę: degrǫ⁷
49. géi niwáhshę: gyohdǫ:
50. hwíhs niwáhshę:

51. hwíhs niwáhshę: sga:t
52. hwíhs niwáhshę: dekni:
53. hwíhs niwáhshę: ahsęh
54. hwíhs niwáhshę: géi
55. hwíhs niwáhshę: hwihs
56. hwíhs niwáhshę: hyéi⁷
57. hwíhs niwáhshę: já:dahk
58. hwíhs niwáhshę: degrǫ⁷
59. hwíhs niwáhshę: gyohdǫ:
60. hyéi⁷ niwáhshę:

61. hyéi⁷ niwáhshę: sga:t
62. hyéi⁷ niwáhshę: dekni:
63. hyéi⁷ niwáhshę: ahsęh
64. hyéi⁷ niwáhshę: géi
65. hyéi⁷ niwáhshę: hwihs
66. hyéi⁷ niwáhshę: hyéi⁷
67. hyéi⁷ niwáhshę: já:dahk
68. hyéi⁷ niwáhshę: degrǫ⁷
69. hyéi⁷ niwáhshę: gyohdǫ:
70. ja:dáhk niwáhshę:

71. já:dahk niwáhshę: sga:t
72. já:dahk niwáhshę: dekni:
73. já:dahk niwáhshę: ahsęh
74. já:dahk niwáhshę: géi
75. já:dahk niwáhshę: hwihs
76. já:dahk niwáhshę: hyéi⁷
77. já:dahk niwáhshę: já:dahk
78. já:dahk niwáhshę: degrǫ⁷
79. já:dahk niwáhshę: gyohdǫ:
80. degrǫ́⁷ niwáhshę:

81. degrǫ́⁷ niwáhshę: sga:t
82. degrǫ́⁷ niwáhshę: dekni:
83. degrǫ́⁷ niwáhshę: ahsęh
84. degrǫ́⁷ niwáhshę: géi
85. degrǫ́⁷ niwáhshę: hwihs
86. degrǫ́⁷ niwáhshę: hyéi⁷
87. degrǫ́⁷ niwáhshę: já:dahk
88. degrǫ́⁷ niwáhshę: degrǫ⁷
89. degrǫ́⁷ niwáhshę: gyohdǫ:
90. gyohdǫ: niwáhshę:

Wadewayę́stanih

100. sga:t dewę́ʔnyawʔe:
200. dekni: dewę́ʔnyawʔe:
300. ahsę́ nʔadewʔęnyá:wʔe:
400. géi nʔadewʔęnyá:wʔe:
500. hwihs nʔadewʔęnyá:wʔe:

600. hyéiʔ nʔadewʔęnyá:wʔe:
700. já:dahk nʔadewʔęnyá:wʔe:
800. degróʔ nʔadewʔęnyá:wʔe:
900. gyohdǫ́: nʔadewʔęnyá:wʔe:
1000. nʔadewʔęnyá:wʔe:

345. ahsę́ nʔadewʔęnyá:wʔe: géi niwahshę́: hwihs

The System

If you look at the numbers for awhile, you will see that you do not really need to memorize one hundred thousand different phrases in order to count to one hundred thousand. Once you know the numbers from one through ten, you need only a few more words to count that high, once you see how the system works.

sgaheʔ	'teen' (literally, 'one is set on it')
dewáhshę:	'twenty' (literally, 'two tens')
niwáhshę:	'-ty' (or thirty and above, literally, 'so many tens')
dewę́ʔnyawʔe:	'hundred'
nʔadewʔęnyá:wʔe:	'hundreds' (for three or more)

For higher numbers, you simply count hundreds, then tens, then ones.

ja:dáhk	nʔadewʔęnya:wʔé:	degróʔ	niwahshę́:	hyéiʔ	
7	hundreds	8	tens	6	= 786

For practice, read off these numbers aloud in good Cayuga.

3	14	30	64	100
7	20	33	77	101
8	25	46	83	111
9	29	52	99	268
1000	1289	3642	8210	4023

Wadewayęstanih

Form a circle. Let one member write a number on the board or on a piece of paper to show to the group. The first person to read the number in correct Cayuga wins a point. Let the next person in the circle then write a number. Continue around the circle in this way until some player wins fifteen points.

Wadewayęstanih

DO: NISOHSRIYA'GǪH?
(How many winters have you crossed?)

When Cayuga speakers ask about a person's age, they actually refer to the number of winters crossed. (*-ohsr-* = 'winter' and *-iya'k* = 'cross') If you care to answer such a question, you can simply state a number first, then add the word *niwagohsríy'agǫh* 'so many winters have I crossed'.

Do: nisohsriya'gǫh? / Do: nidihsé:nǫ'?
'How old are you?'

Ahsę́ niwahshę́: gyohdǫ́: niwagohsríy'agǫh.
'I am thirty nine years old.'

To ask about women's and girls' ages, you can use the word *niyagaohsriya'gǫh* 'so many winters has she crossed'. To ask about the ages of men and boys, you can use the word *nihaohsríy'agǫh* 'so many winters has he crossed'. As with all questions, the tone of voice stays level, instead of dropping at the end.

Do: niyagaohsríya'gǫh? / Do: niyagoné:nǫ'?
'How old is she?'

Degrǫ́' niyagaohsríya'gǫh. / Degrǫ́': niyagoné:nǫ'.
'She is eight years old.'

Do: nihaohsríy'agǫh? / Do: nitoné:nǫ'?
'How old is he?'

Hwihs sgahe' nihaohsríy'agǫh. / Hwihs sgahe' nitoné:nǫ'.
'He is fifteen.'

Wadewayę́stanih

New Vocabulary

sga:t	'one'
dekni:	'two'
ahsęh	'three'
géi	'four'
Hwíhs	'five'
hyéiʔ	'six'
já:dahk	'seven'
degrǫʔ	'eight'
gyohdǫ:	'nine'
wahshę:	'ten'
dewáhshę:	'twenty'
niwáhshę:	'-ty', 'tens' (for thirty or more)
sgahe?	'-teen'
dewęʔnyawʔe:	'hundred'
nʔadewʔęnyá:wʔe:	'hundreds'
do:?	'how many?'
do: ni:yǫ:?	'how many of them?'
niwagohsríyʔagǫh	'so many winters I have crossed', 'I am __ years old'
nisohsriyáʔgǫh, nidihsé:nǫʔ	'you are __ years old'
niyagaohsriyáʔgǫh, niyagoné:nǫʔ	'she is __ years old'
nihaohsríyʔagǫh, nitoné:nǫʔ	'he is __ years old'

8
EKSAʔGÓ:WAH

Wadewayę́stanih

agǫ́:gweh

gá:gǫgweh

eksá:ʔah

haksá:ʔah

gaeksʔashǫ́:ʔǫh

83

Wadewayę́stanih

eksaʔdí:yo:

haksaʔdí:yo:

eksaʔd<u>a</u>hetgę̨ʔ

haksaʔd<u>a</u>hetgę̨ʔ

gaeksʔadí:yo:

hadiksʔadí:yo:

gaeksʔadáhetgę̨ʔ

hadiksʔadáhetgę̨ʔ

Wadewayę́stanih

GÁEGĘHJIH

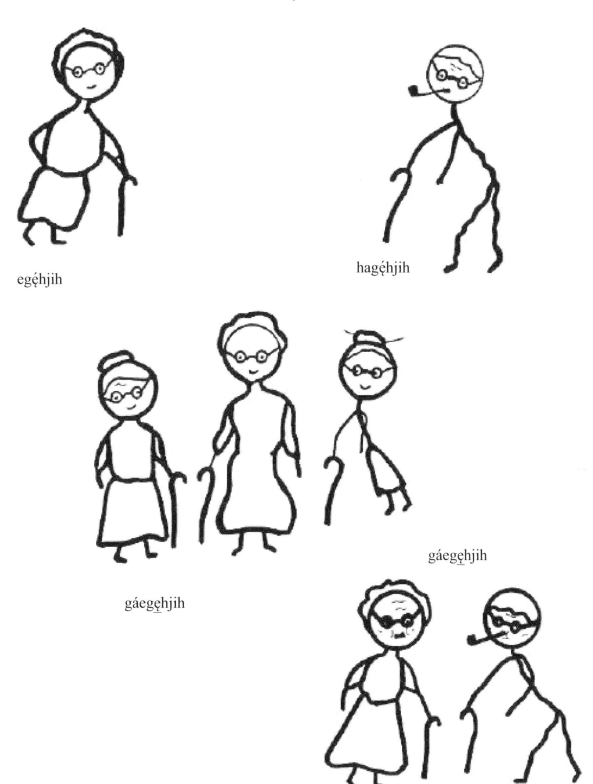

egę́hjih

hagę́hjih

gáegę̱hjih

gáegę̱hjih

Wadewayę́stanih

Wadewayę́stanih

SANYA:GǪ GĘH?

Wadewayęstanih

EKSAʔGÓ:WAH

Wadewayęstanih

AK-/AG-/GO-/HO-
(About Me/Her/Him)

In earlier conversations, you saw that you could tell who was being talked about by the beginning of words.

Gyá:sǫh…	'I am called…'
Eya:sǫh…	'She is called…'
Haya:sǫh…	'He is called…'

The parts that tell who, the *k-* or *g-* 'I', the *e-* 'she', and the *ha-* 'he', are pronouns.

Some words use a different set of pronouns for 'I', 'she', and 'he'. A number of them are in this conversation.

Aknǫhgę́:t.	'I have light hair.'
Gonǫhgę́:t.	'She has light hair.'
Honǫhgę́:t.	'He has light hair.'
Agegeʔá:ji:.	'I have dark hair.'
Gogéʔaji:.	'She has dark hair.'
Hogéʔaji:.	'He has dark hair.'
Agénhraʔtę̣ʔ.	'I have gray hair.'
Gonhraʔtę̣ʔ.	'She has gray hair.'
Honhraʔtę̣ʔ.	'He has gray hair.'
Age:nyá:gǫh.	'I am married.'
Gonyá:gǫh.	'She is married.'
Honyá:gǫh.	'He is married.'

Notice how close the forms are for 'he' and 'she' with this set of pronouns. After the first syllable, they are exactly the same. Try changing the words below from 'she' to 'he'.

Gogé:gaʔs.	'She likes the taste.'	He?
Godehsrǫnísʔǫh.	'She is ready.'	He?
Gonǫ́hdǫʔ.	'She knows.'	He?

Now try changing these from 'he' to 'she'.

Hogwáihse:.	'He has finished cooking.'	She?
Hode:kǫ́:ni:.	'He has eaten.'	She?
Hokgę́hǫh.	'He is up.' or 'He has gotten up.'	She?

You will hear these pronouns constantly in spoken Cayuga. If you listen closely, you can already get an idea who is being discussed, even if you cannot tell yet what they have done.

Wadewayę́stanih

GAE-
(About those women)

Compare these words:

Eyá:sǫh…	'She is called…'
Gaeyá:sǫh…	'They are called (female or mixed group)…'
Eksaʔgó:wah.	'She is pretty.'
Gaeksʔagó:wah.	'They are pretty.'
Egę́hjih.	'She is old.' or 'an old lady'
Gáegęhjih.	'They are old.', 'old ladies' or 'old people'

You can see that the *ga-* at the beginning of a word shows that more than one person is involved. While *e-* means 'she', *gae-* means 'they', referring to two or more women or girls, or a mixed group. (A different form is used for a group of men.)

There are several more words in this conversation with the plural *ga-*. See how many you can identify.

New Vocabulary

eksaʔgó:wah	'she is pretty'
gaeksʔagó:wah	'they are pretty'
gaeksʔashǫ́:ǫh	'children'
sǫgweʔdí:yo:	'you are a nice person'
ga:gǫgweʔdí:yo:	'they are nice people (females or mixed)'
gá:gǫgweh	'women'
gaeyá:sǫh	'they are called (females or mixed)'
agwęʔdrǫʔ	'we all live (they and I)'
tgáeʔdrǫʔ	'they live there (females or mixed)'
snagreʔ	'you reside, live'
dagáęʔ	'they are coming (females or mixed)'
gá:gǫnheʔ	'they live (females or mixed)'
gaǫdatáwahksǫʔ	'their children (females or mixed)'
ddegaǫdęhnǫ́:de:ʔ	'they two are sisters'
degáekęh	'they are twins (females or mixed)'
gáegęhjih	'they are old (females or mixed)'
degaejáǫ	'both of them (females or mixed)'

Wadewayéstanih

aknǫhgę́:t	'I have fair hair'
honǫhgę́:t	'he has fair hair'
gonǫhgę́:t	'she has fair hair'
ageg'eá:ji:	'I have dark hair'
hogé'aji:	'he has dark hair'
gogé'aji:	'she has dark hair'
agénhra'tę'	'I have gray hair'
honhrá'tę'	'he has gray hair'
gonhrá'tę'	'she has gray hair'
tę' d'eagége'o:t	'I have no hair'
tę' d'ehog'eo:t	'he has no hair'
age:nyá:gǫh	'I am married'
sanyá:gǫh	'you are married'
gonyá:gǫh	'she is married'
honyá:gǫh	'he is married'
tę́' d'eagenyá:gǫh	'I am not married'
tę́' d'eagonyá:gǫh	'she is not married'
tę́' d'eho:nyá:gǫh	'he is not married'
tę́' d'esgahǫ́:dǫ'	'you didn't ask me'
tę́' d'eaknǫhwé'ǫ:'	'I didn't like it'
da:sgadagyę̨de'	'you should introduce me'
ǫg'nigǫhsá:dǫ'k	'I got lonesome'
do: niyagonohsriya'gǫh?	'How old are they?'
dahoyagę'ǫhǫ́:gye'	'he is coming out'
ho:'	'her husband', 'his wife'
joháhadih	'across the road'
tganǫ́hso:t	'house' (literally, 'house standing there' -nǫhs- 'house')
deyagyanǫhsané:gę:	'my neighbor' (literally, 'our two houses are side by side')
swęnǫhsanékahǫ'	'your neighbors' (literally, 'all your houses are side by side')
odǫkgá:de'	'it is fun, enjoyable'
he'nó:shahs	'I envy him'
hni'	'and' or 'also'

Wadewayę́stanih

shęh	'how'
shę n(i)yó:weh	'how much'
sih	'over there'
ne:ʔ	'it is so', 'it is that'
né:ʔ tsǫ:	'but' (literally, 'it is only')
né:ʔ diʔ gęh?	'is that it/them?'
ǫ́:weh	'really'
ǫh	'I guess'
trehs	'because'

9

DO: NIYOHWIHSDAʔE:?

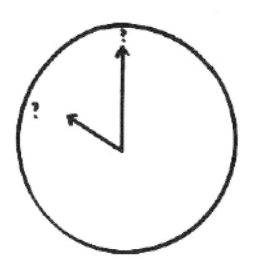

Wadewayę́stanih

DO: NIYOHWIHSDA'E:?

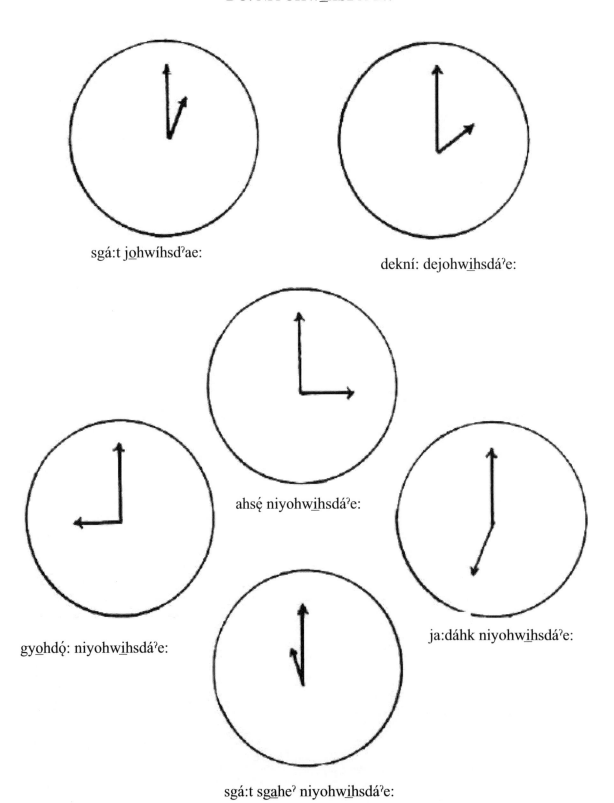

sgá:t johwíhsd'ae:

dekní: dejohwihsdá'e:

ahsę́ niyohwihsdá'e:

gyohdǫ́: niyohwihsdá'e:

ja:dáhk niyohwihsdá'e:

sgá:t sgahe' niyohwihsdá'e:

100

Wadewayę́stanih

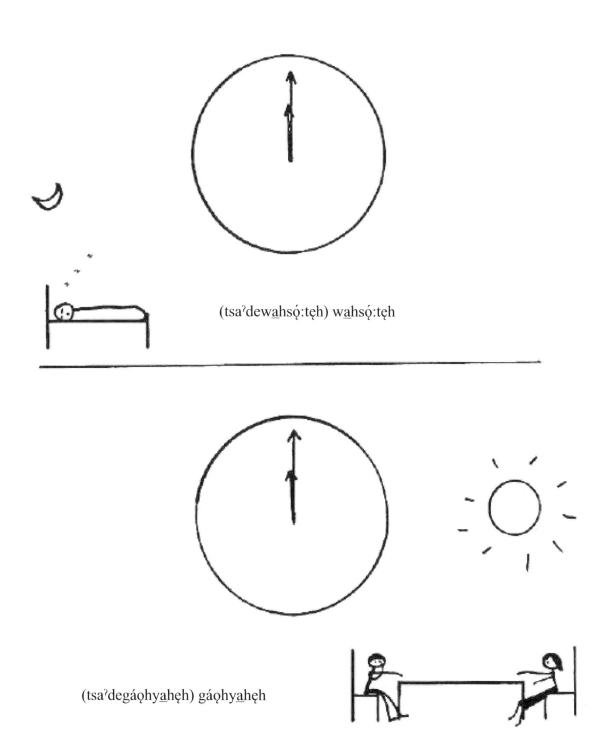

(tsaʔdewahsǫ́:tęh) wahsǫ́:tęh

(tsaʔdegáǫhyahęh) gáǫhyahęh

Wadewayę́stanih

DO: NIYOHWIHSDAʔE:?

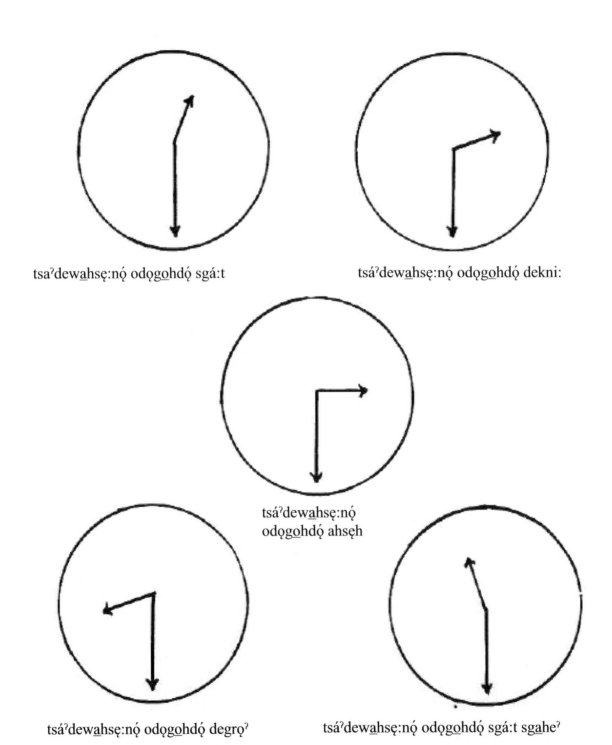

tsaʔdewahsę:nǫ́ odǫgohdǫ́ sgá:t

tsáʔdewahsę:nǫ́ odǫgohdǫ́ dekni:

tsáʔdewahsę:nǫ́ odǫgohdǫ́ ahsęh

tsáʔdewahsę:nǫ́ odǫgohdǫ́ degrǫʔ

tsáʔdewahsę:nǫ́ odǫgohdǫ́ sgá:t sgaheʔ

Wadewayę́stanih

DO: NIYOHWIHSDAʔE:?

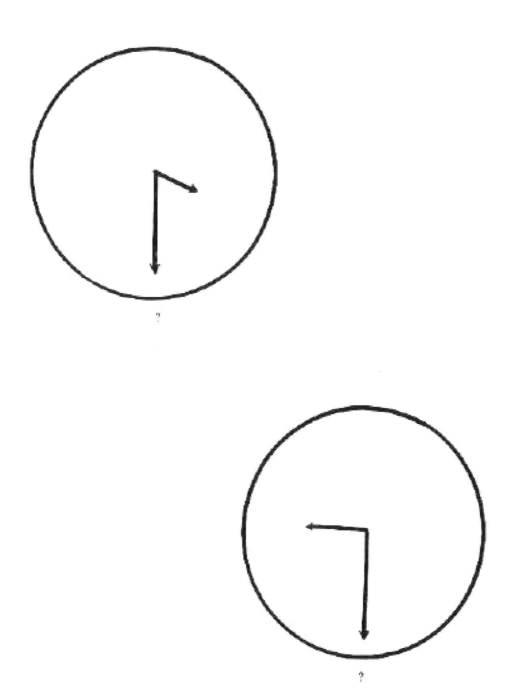

Wadewayę́stanih

DO: NIYOHWIHSDAʔE:?

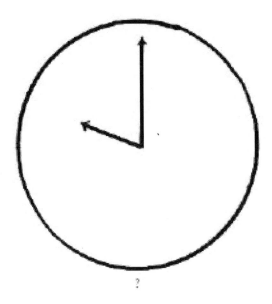
?

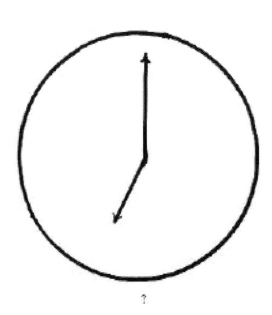
?

Wadewayęstanih

DO: NIYOHWIHSDAʔE:?

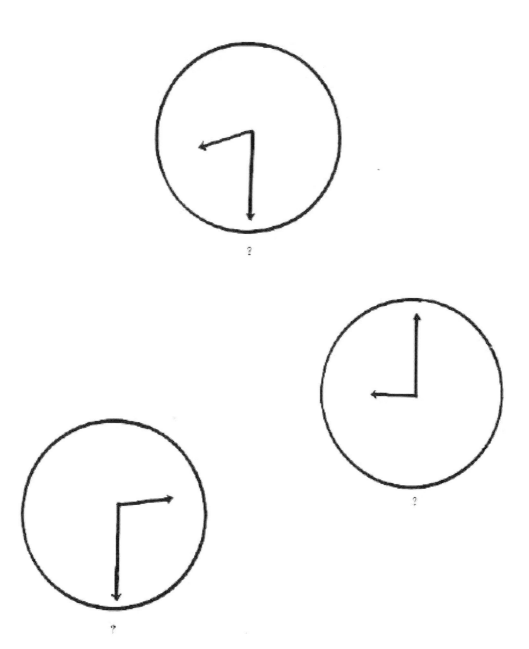

105

Wadewayę́stanih

DO: NIYOHWIHSDAʔE:?

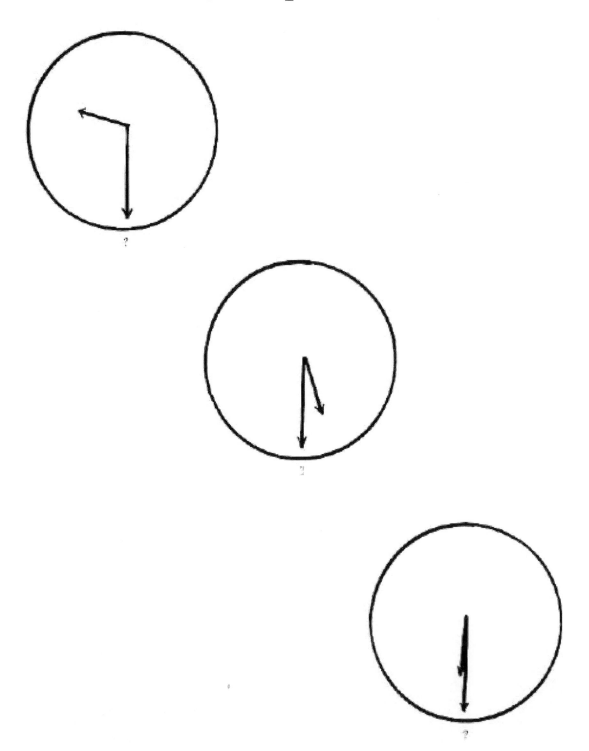

106

Wadewayę́stanih

DO: NIYOHWIHSDAʔE:?

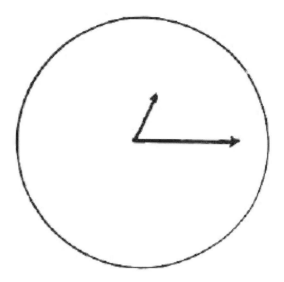

hwíhs sgahe' odǫgohdǫ́ sgá:t

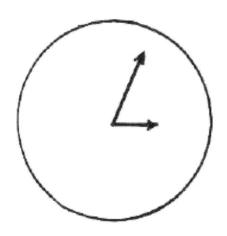

hwíhs odǫgohdǫ́ ahsęh

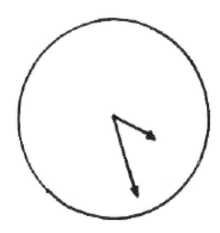

dewahshę: hwíhs odǫgohdǫ́ géi

Wadewayę́stanih

DO: NIYOHWIHSDAʔE:?

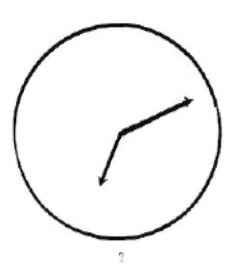

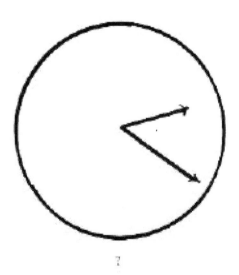

Wadewayę́stanih

DO: NIYOHWIHSDAʔE:?

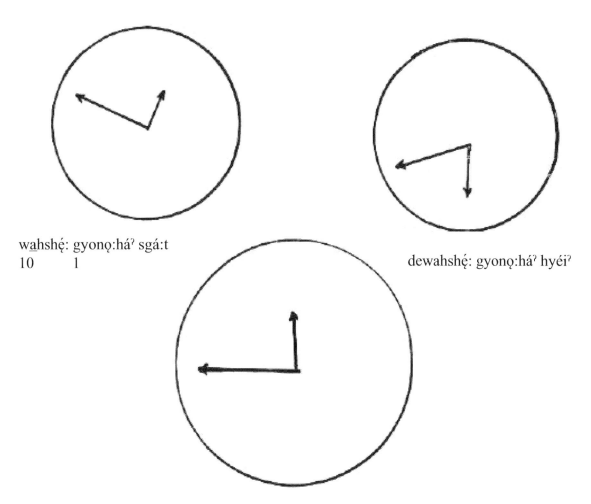

wahshę́: gyonǫ:háʔ sgá:t
10   1

dewahshę́: gyonǫ:háʔ hyéiʔ

hwíhs sgahéʔ gyonǫ:háʔ dekhní: sgaheʔ

Wadewayę́stanih

DO: NIYOHWIHSDAʔE:?

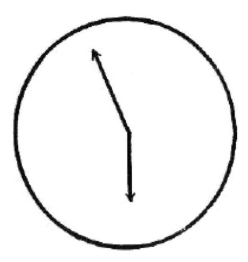

hwíhs gyonǫ:háʔ hyéiʔ

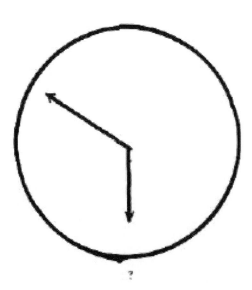

Wadewayęstanih

DO: NIYOHWIHSDAʔE:?

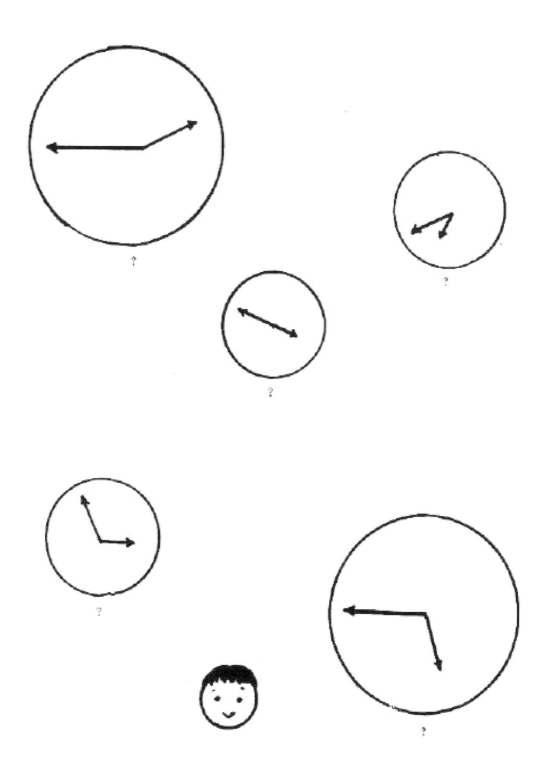

Wadewayę́stanih

DO: NIYOHWIHSDAʔE:?

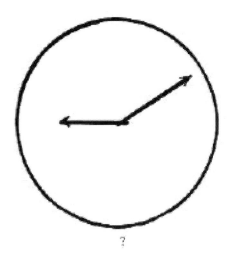
?

?

?

Wadewayę́stanih

DO: NIYOHWIHSDAʔE:?

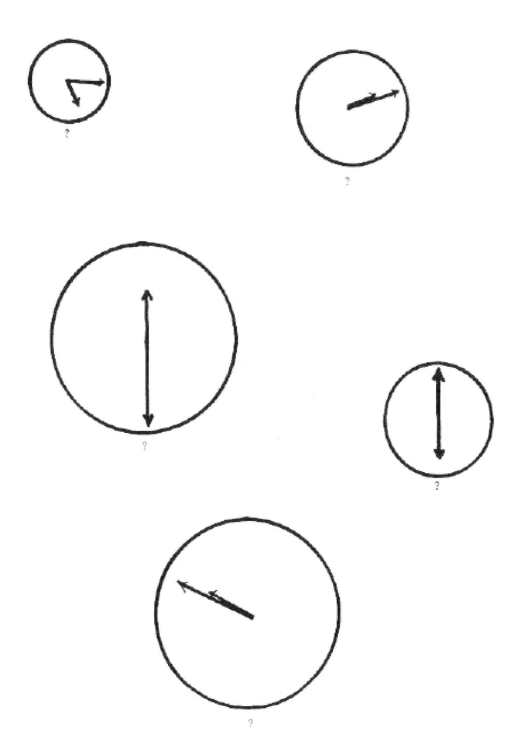

Wadewayęstanih

Wadewayę́stanih

Wadewayę́stanih

Wadewayę́stanih

DO: NIYOHWIHSDAʔE. . .?
(What time. . .?)

You can use this question to ask about people's habits, if you are interested. As with all questions, your voice should stay level in pitch.

Dó: niyohw<u>i</u>hsdaʔé: satgęhęhs?
'What time do you get up?'

Dó: niyohw<u>i</u>hsdaʔé: sade:kǫ:nihs?
'What time do you eat?'

Dó: niyohw<u>i</u>hsdaʔé: s<u>a</u>hdę:gyeʔs?
'What time do you leave?'

The -*s* on the ends of these words show that the activity you are asking about is a habit. To answer such a question, you can simply state the appropriate time (the most important information), then repeat the habitual activity, changing the first *s*- 'you' to *g*- or *k*- 'I'.

Hyéiʔ niyohw<u>i</u>hsdaʔé: gatgęhęhs.
'I get up at six o'clock.'

Hwíhs sg<u>a</u>heʔ od<u>ǫgo</u>hdǫ́ degrǫ́ʔ niyohw<u>i</u>hsdaʔé: gade:kǫ́:nihs.
'I eat at a quarter past eight.'

Dewahsę́: hwíhs gyonǫhá ʔ gy<u>o</u>hdǫ́: niyohw<u>i</u>hsdaʔé: g<u>a</u>hdę:gyeʔs.
'I leave at twenty-five to nine.'

Practice asking each person in the room about their morning habits, using the verbs above. Answer each question which comes your way as precisely as possible.

Wadewayę́stanih

New Vocabulary

do: niyohwihsdaʔe:?	'what time is it?'
sgá:t johwíhsdʔae, sgá:t ohwíhsdʔae	'one o'clock'
dekní: dejohwihsdaʔe:, dekní: deyohswihsdáʔe:	'two o'clock'
ahsę́ niyohswihsdáʔe:	'three o'clock'
géi niyohswihsdáʔe:	'four o'clock'
tsaʔdewahsǫ́:tęh	'midnight'
tsaʔdegaǫ́hyahęh, gáǫhyahęh	'noon'
odǫ́gohdǫh	'past', 'after'
gyonǫ́:haʔ	'till', 'before', 'of' (for time)
gatgę́hęhs	'I get up' (habitually)
satgę́hęhs	'you get up' (habitually)
gade:kǫ́:nihs	'I eat'
sade:kǫ́:nihs	'you eat'
gahdę́:gyeʔs	'I leave'
sahdę́:gyeʔs	'you leave'
tsaʔdewahsę́:nǫh	'half'

10

GYʔADÁʔGEH

Wadewayę́stanih

GYʔADÁʔGEH

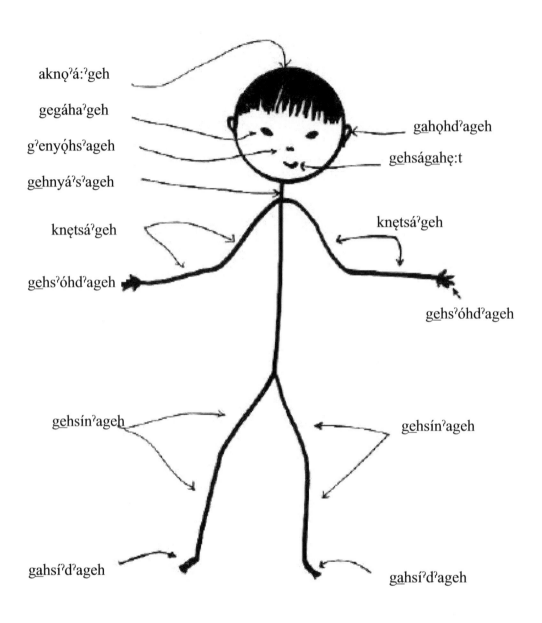

Wadewayę́stanih

GEGǪHS'AGEH

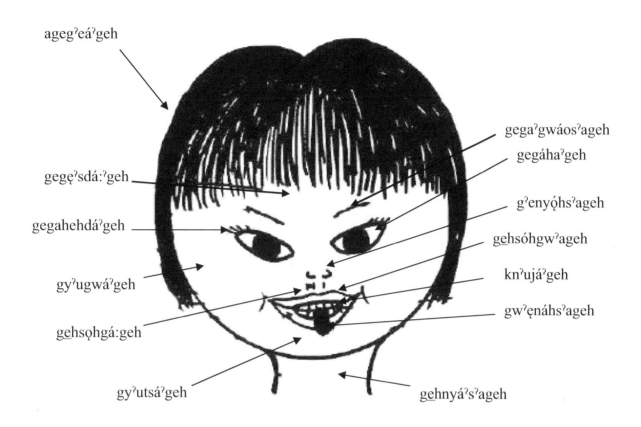

Wadewayę́stanih

GEGǪHS'AGEH

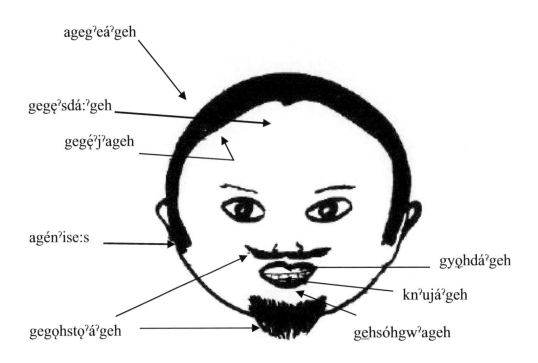

Wadewayęstanih

GEHSʔÓHDʔAGEH

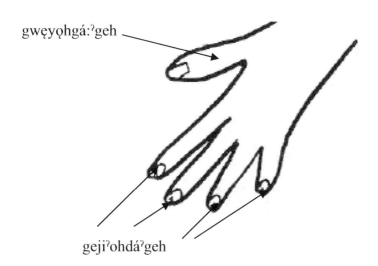

GAHSÍʔDʔAGEH

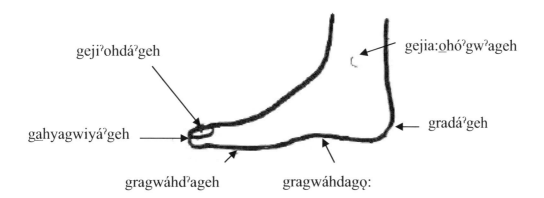

Wadewayęstanih

GYʔADÁʔGEH

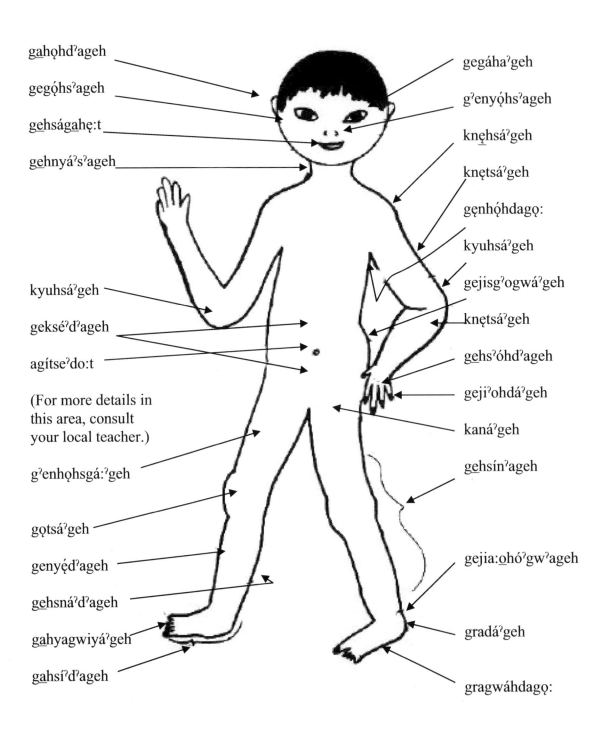

gahǫhdʔageh
gegǫ́hsʔageh
gehságahę:t
gehnyáʔsʔageh

kyuhsáʔgeh
geksé'dʔageh
agítseʔdo:t

(For more details in this area, consult your local teacher.)

gʔenhǫhsgá:ʔgeh

gǫtsáʔgeh
genyę́dʔageh
gehsnáʔdʔageh
gahyagwiyáʔgeh
gahsíʔdʔageh

gegáhaʔgeh
gʔenyǫ́hsʔageh
knęhsáʔgeh
knętsáʔgeh
gęnhǫ́hdagǫ:
kyuhsáʔgeh
gejisgʔogwáʔgeh
knętsáʔgeh
gehsʔóhdʔageh
gejiʔohdáʔgeh
kanáʔgeh
gehsínʔageh

gejia:ohóʔgwʔageh

gradáʔgeh

gragwáhdagǫ:

126

Wadewayę́stanih

Wadewayę́stanih

Wadewayę́stanih

GYʔADAʔGEH / SYʔADAʔGEH
(My Body / Your Body)

When Cayuga speakers talk about parts of the body, they generally specify who the parts belong to. You can see from the illustrations that *g-* or *k-* is used for 'my' body part, and *s-* for 'your' body part.

gahǫhdʔageh	'on my ear'
sahǫhdʔageh	'on your ear'

For any body part on the chart, you can simply substitute *s-* 'your' for *g-* or *k-* 'my' and create a good Cayuga word. This *g-* or *k-* is the same pronoun as the *g-* in *gyá:sǫh* 'I am called', and the *s-* is the same as the *s-* in *syá:sǫh* 'you are called'.

You may have noticed that the body parts on the charts generally end in *-geh*. This part means 'on' or 'at', as you may recall from earlier conversations (*ganyadá:ʔgeh* 'at the lake'). When speakers talk about a body part which has an outside surface, they generally add this *-geh* to the word.

Cayuga speakers do not generally specify how many of a body part they are talking about. The same word means one or many.

gǫtsáʔgeh	'on my knee' or 'on my knees'
gahyagwiyáʔgeh	'on my toe' or 'on my toes'

In some cases, the number is obvious.

gʔenyǫ́hsʔageh	'on my nose'
gitséʔdo:t	'my navel'

A very few body parts use the *ak-/age-/ag-* forms for 'my'.

agegʔeáʔgeh	'on my hair'
aknoʔá:ʔgeh	'on my head'
agénʔise:s	'my sideburns'

These body parts use *sa-* for 'you'.

sagéʔaʔgeh	'on your hair'
sanoʔá:ʔgeh	'on your head'
saníʔse:s	'your sideburns'

Wadewayę́stanih

Wadewayę́stanih

SW(A)-
(Yous)

When Cayuga speakers talk to three or more people, they change the pronoun *s(e)-* 'you' to *sw(a)-* 'yous'. Compare these words.

gah̠ǫhdʔageh	'on my ear' or 'on my ears'
sah̠ǫhdʔageh	'on your ear (to one person)' or 'on your ears'
swah̠ǫhdʔageh	'on your ears (to three or more people)'
gegǫ́hsʔageh	'on my face'
segǫ́hsʔageh	'on your face (to one person)'
swagǫ́hsʔageh	'on your faces (to three or more people)'
gekséʔdʔageh	'on my belly'
sekséʔdʔageh	'on your belly (to one person)'
swakséʔdʔageh	'on your bellies (to three or more people)'
geh̠sínʔageh	'on my leg' or 'on my legs'
seh̠sínʔageh	'on your leg' or 'on your legs (to one person)'
swah̠sínʔageh	'on your legs (to three or more people)'

The change from 'you' to 'yous' sometimes shifts the stress, glottal stops, and whispered vowels.

gyʔadáʔgeh	'on my body'
syʔadáʔgeh	'on your body (to one person)'
swayáʔdʔageh	'on your bodies (to three or more people)'
gʔahsáʔgeh	'on my chest'
sʔahsáʔgeh	'on your chest (to one person)'
swaʔáhsʔageh	'on your chests (to three or more people)'
gwęyǫhgá:ʔgeh	'on my thumb'
swęyǫhgá:ʔgeh	'on your thumb' or 'on your thumbs (to one person)'
swawęyǫhgá:ʔgeh	'on your thumbs (to three or more people)'
kyuhsáʔgeh	'on my elbow'
syuhsáʔgeh	'on your thumb' or 'on your thumbs (to one person)'
swah̠yúhsʔageh	'on your elbows (to three or more people)'

It is easy to tell how many people are being spoken to by simply listening to the beginning of the word for *s-* or *sw-*. You can find the exact forms for all of the body parts with *sw(a)-* 'yous' under New Vocabulary, on the next page.

Wadewayęstanih

New Vocabulary

For three or more people

gyʔadáʔgeh	'on my body'	swayáʔdʔageh	'on your bodies'
agegʔeáʔgeh	'on my hair'	swagéʔaʔgeh	'on your hair'
aknǫʔá:ʔgeh	'on my head'	swanǫʔá:ʔgeh	'on your heads'
gegǫ́hsʔageh	'on my face'	swagǫ́hsʔageh	'on your faces'
gegę̨ʔsdá:ʔgeh	'on my forehead'	swagę̨ʔsdá:ʔgeh	'on your foreheads'
gegę́ʔjʔageh	'on my hairline'	swagę́ʔjʔageh	'on your hairlines'
gegaʔgwáosʔageh	'on my eyebrow'	swagaʔgwáosʔageh	'on your eyebrows'
gegahehdáʔgeh	'on my eyelashes'	swagahehdáʔgeh	'on your eyelashes'
gegáhaʔgeh	'on my eye'	swagáhaʔgeh	'on your eyes'
gahǫhdʔageh	'on my ear'	swahǫhdʔageh	'on your ears'
gʔenyǫ́hsʔageh	'on my nose'	swʔanyǫ́hsʔageh	'on your noses'
gehsǫhgá:ʔgeh	'on my upper lip'	swahsǫhgá:ʔgeh	'on your upper lips'
gehsóhgwʔageh	'on my lip'	swahsóhgwʔageh	'on your lips'
gehságahę:d	'my mouth'	swahságahę:t	'your mouths'
knʔujáʔgeh	'on my teeth'	swanúʔjʔageh	'on your teeth'
gyǫhdáʔgeh	'on my gum'	swayǫ́hdʔageh	'on your gums'
gwʔęnáhsʔageh	'on my tongue'	swawęʔnahsáʔgeh	'on your tongues'
gyʔugwá:ʔgeh	'on my cheek'	swayuʔgwá:ʔgeh	'on your cheeks'
gyʔutsáʔgeh	'on my chin'	swayúʔtsaʔgeh	'on your chins'
gehnyáʔsʔageh	'on my neck'	swahnyáʔsʔageh	'on your necks'
geséhdagǫ:	'at my nape'	swaséhdagǫ:	'on the napes of your necks'
knęhsáʔgeh	'on my shoulder'	swanę́hsʔageh	'on your shoulders'
knętsáʔgeh	'on my arm'	swanę́tsaʔgeh	'on your arms'
kyuhsáʔgeh	'on my elbow'	swahyúhsʔageh	'on your elbows'
gehsʔóhdʔageh	'on my hand'	swahsʔóhdʔageh	'on your hands'
gwęnyǫhgá:ʔgeh	'on my thumb'	swawęnyǫhgá:ʔgeh	'on your thumbs'
gejíʔohdáʔgeh	'on my nail'	swajíʔohdáʔgeh	'on your nails'
gehswéʔnʔageh	'on my upper back'	swahswéʔnʔageh	'on your upper backs'
gehsǫhneh	'on my lower back'	swahsǫ́hneh	'on your lower backs'
gʔahsáʔgeh	'on my chest'	swʔáhsʔageh	'on your chests'
knʔǫgwaʔgeh	'on my breast'	swanǫ́ʔgwʔageh	'on your breasts'
knǫnhéʔdrʔageh	'on my nipple'	swanǫnheʔdráʔgeh	'on your nipples'

Wadewayęstanih

		For three or more people	
gehdegá:ʔgeh	'on my rib'	swahdegá:ʔgeh	'on your ribs'
gyʔagá:ʔgeh	'on my waist'	swayaʔgá:ʔgeh	'on your waists'
gekséʔdʔageh	'on my belly'	swakséʔdʔageh	'on your bellies'
agítseʔdo:t	'my navel'	swętséʔdo:t	'your navels'
gejísgʔogwáʔgeh	'on my hip'	swajísgʔogwáʔgeh	'on your hips'
kanáʔgeh	'on my groin'	swahánʔageh	'on your groins'
knaʔtsáʔgeh	'on my buttock'	swahnáʔtsaʔgeh	'on your buttocks'
gehsínʔageh	'on my leg'	swahsínʔageh	'on your legs'
gʔensǫhsgá:ʔgeh	'on my thigh'	swʔansǫhsgá:ʔgeh	'on your thighs'
gǫtsáʔgeh	'on my knee'	jǫtsáʔgeh	'on your knees'
gehsnaʔdʔageh	'on my calf'	swahsnaʔdʔageh	'on your calves'
genyę́dʔageh	'on my shin'	swanyę́dʔageh	'on your shins'
gejía:ohóʔgwʔageh	'on my ankle'	swajía:ohóʔgwʔageh	'on your ankles'
gahsíʔdʔageh	'on my foot'	swahsíʔdʔageh	'on your feet'
gahyagwiyáʔgeh	'on my toe'	swahyagwiyáʔgeh	'on your toes'
gragwáhdʔageh	'on the ball of my foot'	swa:gwahdáʔgeh	'on the balls of your feet'
gragwáhdagǫ:	'on my sole'	swa:gwahdá:gǫ:	'on the soles of your feet'
gradáʔgeh	'on my heel'	swá:dʔageh	'on your heels'
gegǫhsdǫʔáʔgeh	'on my whiskers', 'on my moustache'	hagǫhsdǫʔáʔgeh	'on his whiskers', 'on his moustache'
agénʔise:s	'I have long sideburns'	honíʔse:s	'he has long sideburns'

11

SATGẸH

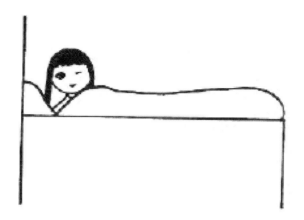

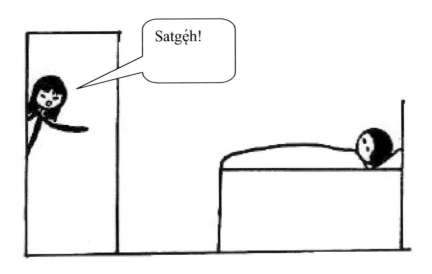

Wadewayęstanih

Wadewayęstanih

agyaʔdawíʔtraʔ

agyaʔdawíʔtraʔ

anaháotraʔ

anaháotraʔ

anaháotraʔ

agyaʔdawíʔtraʔ

Wadewayę́stanih

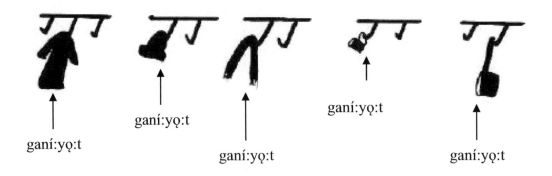

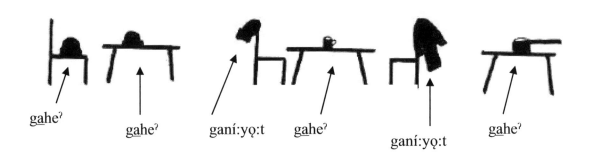

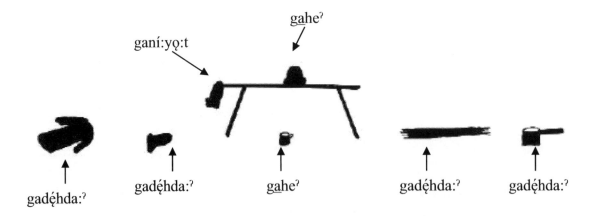

gá:yęˀ

Wadewayę́stanih

Wadewayéstanih

SATGĘH

Wadewayę́stanih

Wadewayęstanih

Wadewayéstanih

DESAʔDRAIHEH
(How to Order People Around)

Earlier conversations contained a few commands.

Snegéhah.	'Drink it.'
Satgę́ʔse:.	'Have a look.' or 'Watch.'

This conversation has several more:

Satgęh.	'Get up.'
Satgohsoháe.	'Wash your face.'
Sade:kǫ́:nih.	'Eat.'

You may have noticed that all of these commands begin with *s-*. This is the s- which means 'you'. Unlike English, Cayuga commands always specify who the order is addressed to. *Snegéhah* actually means, 'You drink it!'.

Some commands begin with another syllable, such as *de-,* but the *s-* 'you' comes right afterward:

Desaʔdráihęh.	'Hurry up.'

Two other commands you might find useful are:

Sagyę́:.	'Sit down.'
Desdáʔ.	'Stand up.'

Wadewayęstanih

TĘ' D'E-
(How to Be Negative)

Several words in this conversation begin with *tę' d'e-*.

Tę' d'eagatgẹ́họh.	'I haven't gotten up.'
Tę' d'eagẹnǫ́hdǫ'.	'I don't know.'
Tę' d'eagekwę́d'aọh.	'I haven't finished eating.'
Tę' d'eagatgọhsọháe'.	'I haven't washed my face.'

If you compare them to the words below, you can discover the meaning of the *tę' d'e-*.

Agatgẹhọh.	'I have gotten up.'
Agẹ́nọhdọ'.	'I know.'
Agekwẹdá'ọh.	'I have finished eating.'
Agatgọhsoháe'.	'I have washed my face.'

In fact, you already know some negative words from earlier conversations.

Age:nyá:gọh.	'I am married.'
Tę' d'eagenyá:gọh.	'I am not married.'
Ag'nigọháęda's.	'I understand.'
Tę' d'eag'nigọháęda's.	'I don't understand.'

Although both parts, *tę'* and *d'e-* are necessary to make a statement negative, another short word or two can go between the parts.

Tę' ahsǫ́ d'eagekwę́d'aọ.	'I haven't finished eating yet.'
Tę' ahsǫ́ d'eagatgọhsọháe'.	'I haven't washed my face yet.'

Listen for the *tę' d'e-* in any Cayuga conversations you can eavesdrop on. It is very common, of course.* Speakers often swallow the *e-*, especially in normal, rapid speech, so that you might hear something more like:

Tę' d'agẹnǫ́hdǫ' for Tę' d'eagẹnǫ́hdǫ'	'I don't know.'

*(A Note for Only Those Who Are Especially Interested)

Adding the *d'e-* sometimes shifts the stress, glottal stops, and whispered vowels in words. If you look through this book, you will notice that all whispered vowels have two things in common. They always come before H, and they are always odd-numbered (first, third, fifth, seventh, etc.) counting from the beginning of the word.

agatgọhsóhae' (third whispered)   tę' d'eagatgọhsọháe' (fifth whispered)
1 2 3   4 56   1 2 3   4 5 67

Wadewayęstanih

Adding *d'e-* shifts the syllable count, so different vowels are odd-numbered, and whisperable. With practice, you will probably find yourself whispering odd-numbered vowels before H automatically, without even realizing it.

GĘH?
(Huh?)

Listen to a speaker pronounce the two words below very carefully, paying special attention to the endings:

Satgǫhsoháe.	'Wash your face.' (command)
Satgǫhsoháeʔ.	'You have washed your face.' (statement)

Just the glottal stop at the end of this word changes the command to a statement!

Practice changing the commands below into statements. (Simply add a glottal stop or catch at the end.)

Satnuʔjoháe.	'Brush your teeth.'
Sadahǫhdóhae.	'Wash your ears.'
Sahjóhae.	'Wash your hands.'
Sę:sʔidóhae.	'Wash your feet.'

Now, change each statement to a question. To do this, simply add the question marker *gęh* after the statement. Keep your voice level in pitch.

Satgǫhsohae gęh?	'Have you washed your face?'

ĘHĘʔ
(Yes)

Here are some answers to the questions you just asked:

Ęhęʔ, agatgǫhsóhaeʔ.	'Yes, I have washed my face.'
Ęhęʔ, agatnʔujóhaeʔ.	'Yes, I have brushed my teeth.'
Ęhęʔ, agadahǫhdoháeʔ.	'Yes, I have washed my ears.'
Ęhęʔ, agęhsiʔdoháeʔ.	'Yes, I have washed my feet.'

TÉʔ
(No)

Sometimes you may not want to answer 'yes'. To answer 'no', add *téʔ dʔe-* before the answer. Here are the negative answers to the questions you asked.

Satgohsohaeʔ gęh?	'Have you washed your face?'
Tę́ʔ, tę́ʔ dʔeagatgohsoháeʔ.	'No, I have not washed my face.'
Satnuʔjohaeʔ gęh?	'Have you brushed your teeth?'
Tę́ʔ, tę́ʔ dʔeagatnuʔjoháeʔ.	'No, I have not brushed my teeth.'
Sadahǫhdohaeʔ gęh?	'Have you washed your ears?'
Tę́ʔ, tę́ʔ dʔeagadahǫhdóhaeʔ.	'No, I have not washed my ears."
Sę:sʔidohaeʔ gęh?	'Have you washed your feet?'
Tę́ʔ, tę́ʔ dʔeagę:sʔidóhaeʔ.	'No, I have not washed my feet.'

New Vocabulary

anaháotraʔ	'hat'
sanaháotraʔ	'your hat'
agyaʔdawíʔtraʔ	'coat'
sagyaʔdawíʔtraʔ	'your coat'
Satgę́h!	'Get up!'
Satgohsoháe!	'Wash your face!'
Sagyę:!	'Sit down!'
Desaʔdráihęh!	'Hurry up!'
Desdáʔ!	'Stand up!'
gokwáihse:	'she has finished cooking the food'
ęgyahdę́:diʔ.	'you and I will leave'
gyahdę́:dih	'let's both leave'
Sade:kǫ́:nih!	'Eat!'
nigá:yęʔ	'it is laying (somewhere)'
tganí:yǫ:t	'it is hanging there'
agátgęhǫh	'I have gotten up'
tę́ʔ dʔeagatgę́hǫh	'I haven't gotten up'
agę́nǫhdǫʔ	'I know'
tę́ʔ dʔeagęnǫ́hdǫʔ	'I don't know'
agekwędáʔǫh	'I have finished eating'
tę́ʔ dʔeagekwę́dʔaǫh	'I haven't finished eating'

satgohsoháeʔ	'you have washed your face'
agatgohsóhaeʔ	'I have washed my face'
tę́ʔ dʔeagatgohsoháeʔ	'I haven't washed my face'
Sadnuʔjoháe!	'Brush your teeth!'
satnuʔjoháeʔ	'you have brushed your teeth'
sgatnʔujóhaeʔ	'I have brushed my teeth'
tę́ʔ dʔeagatnuʔjoháeʔ	'I haven't brushed my teeth'
Sadahohdóhae!	'Wash your ears!'
sadahohdóhaeʔ	'you have washed your ears'
agadahohdoháeʔ	'I have washed my ears'
tę́ʔ dʔeagadahohdóhaeʔ	'I haven't washed my ears'
Sę:sʔidóhae!	'Wash your feet!'
sę:sʔidóhaeʔ	'you have washed your feet'
agęhsiʔdoháeʔ	'I have washed my feet'
tę́ʔ dʔeagę:sʔidóhae'	'I have not washed my feet'
haoʔ	'let's go', 'come on'
ha:oʔ	'OK', 'all right'
diʔ	'then'
ó:nęh	'now', 'then', 'already', 'when'
o:nę́ tó:hah	'almost'
tę́ʔ ahsǫh	'not yet'
waʔjítsǫ:	'pretty soon'
waʔjíhya:	'wait a minute'
haoʔ dʔenyoh	'OK, fine'
gʔisęh	'maybe'
sigwá:dih	'over there'
gʔató:hah	'somewhere'
gwé:	'well'
do:	'how'

12

GYODEHNÍ:NQH

Wadewayę́stanih

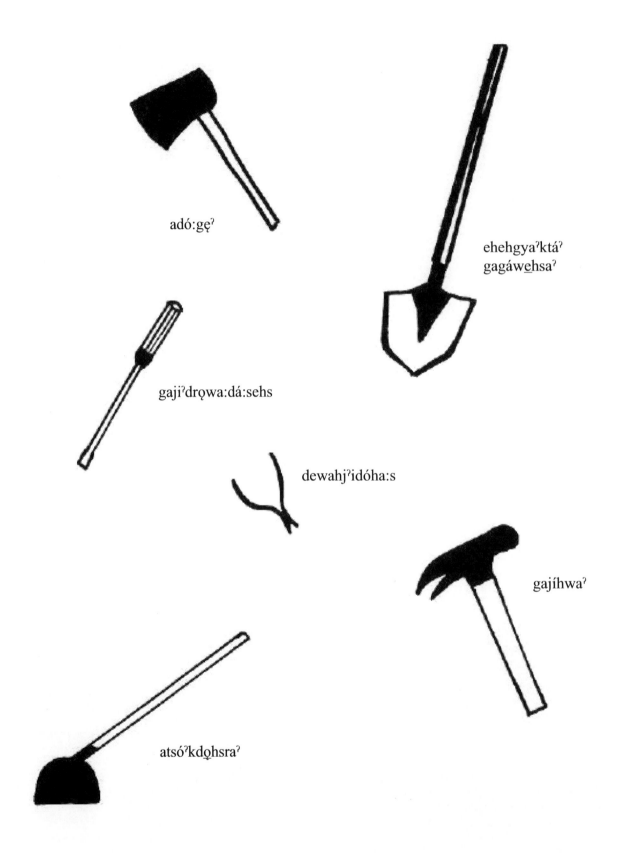

Wadewayęstanih

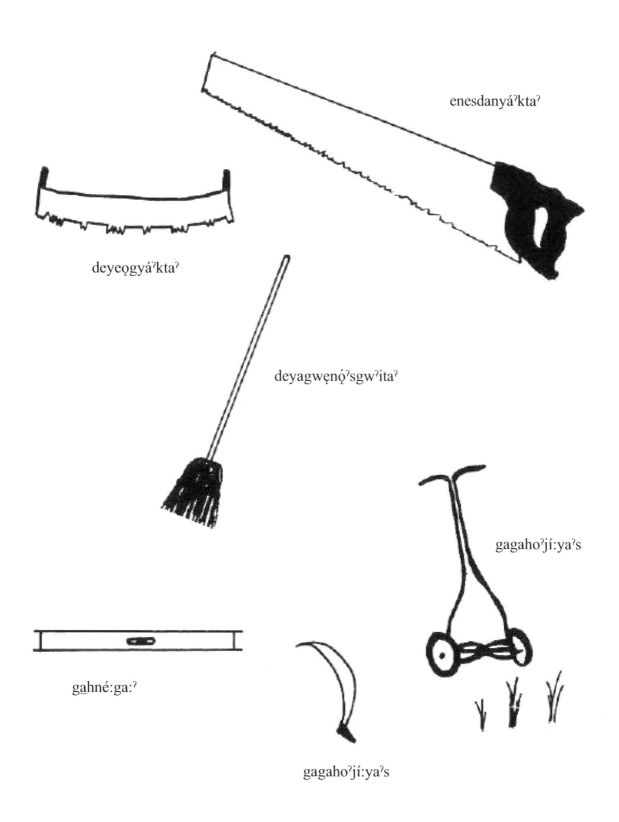

enesdanyá'kta'

deyeǫgyá'kta'

deyagwęnǫ'sgw'ita'

gagaho'jí:ya's

gahné:ga:'

gagaho'jí:ya's

Wadewayę́stanih

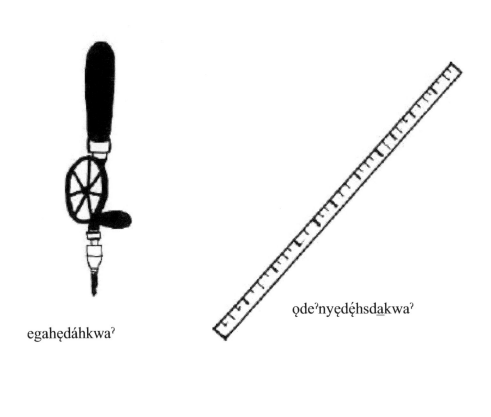

egahędáhkwaʔ

ǫdeʔnyędę́hsdakwaʔ

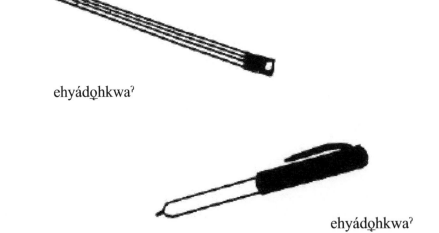

ehyádǫhkwaʔ

ehyádǫhkwaʔ

Wadewayę́stanih

gajíhwaʔ

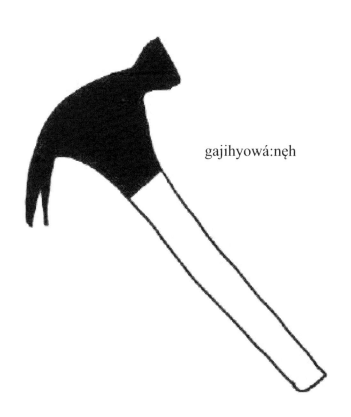

gajihyowá:nęh

nigajihyú:ʔuh

Wadewayę́stanih

DĘ' HO'DĘ' SIHSA:S?

Wadewayę́stanih

ganǫ́:ʔ

wagyé:sęh

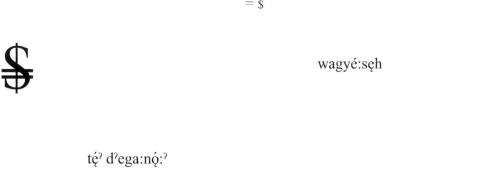

tę́ʔ dʔega:nǫ́:ʔ

Wadewayę́stanih

DO: NIGA:NQ:ˀ?

sga̲hwihsdá:t niga:nǫ:ˀ

ahsę́ nigahw i̲hsda:gé: niga:nǫ:ˀ

degahw i̲hsda:gé: niga:nǫ:ˀ

géi nigahw i̲hsda:gé: niga:nǫ:ˀ

hwíhs nigahw i̲hsda:gé: niga:nǫ:ˀ

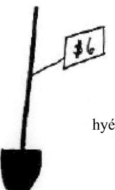
hyéi nigahw i̲hsda:gé: niga:nǫ:ˀ

Wadewayęstanih

GYQDĘHNÍ:NQH

Wadewayę́stanih

Wadewayę́stanih

Wadewayę́stanih

GWĘNIHSǪ́:ˀǪH

 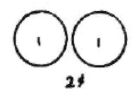 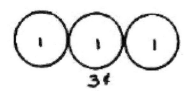

sgá:t gwęnihs   dekní: gwęnihs   ahsę́ gwęnihs
(or, sgagwę́nˀida:t)

wahsę́: gwęnihs

hwíhs gwęnihs

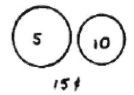 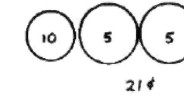

hwíhs sgahe ˀ gwęnihs

dewahsę́: sgá:t gwęnihs

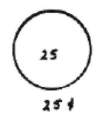

syǫ́ˀtrage: (or, degahsiyǫ́ˀtrage:)

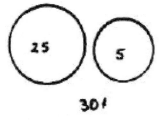 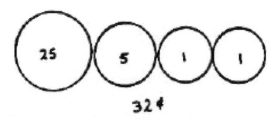

ahsę́ niyogwęníˀdahsę́:   ahsę́ niyogwęníˀdahsę́: dekní:

Wadewayę́stanih

syǫ́'trage: (degahsiyǫ́'trage:)

géi nigahsiyǫ́'trage:

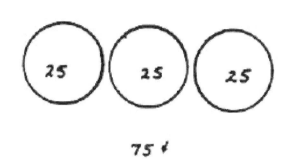

hyéi nigahsiyǫ́'trage:

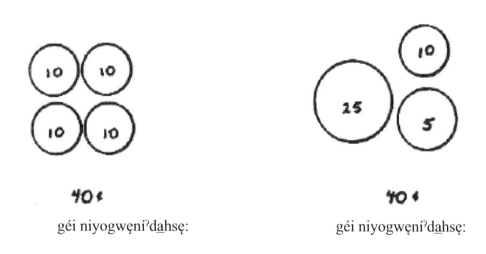

géi niyogwęní'dahsę: géi niyogwęní'dahsę:

Wadewayęstanih

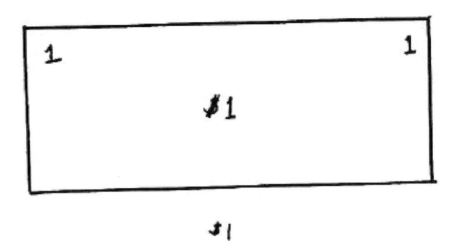

sgahwíhsda:t

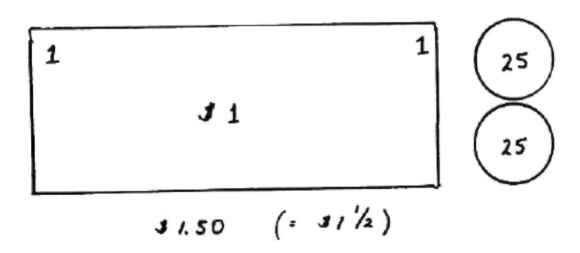

sgahwihsdá:t tsaʔdeswahsę́:nǫh

Wadewayęstanih

DO: NIGA:NQ:ʔ?

géi niyogwęniʔdahsę: hwíhs

ahsę́ nigahwihsdá:ge:

hwíhs sgahe? nigahwihsdá:ge:

sgá:t dewę?nyaw?é: nigahwihsdá:ge:

sgá:t dewę?nyaw?é: degrǫ́? niwahsę́: nigahwihsdá:ge:

dekní: dewę?nyaw?é: nigahwihsdá:ge:

dekní: dewę?nyaw?é: wahsę́: nigahwihsdá:ge:

géi nʔadewʔęnyawʔé: dekní: sgahe? nigahwihsda:gé: hwíhs sgahe? gwęnihs

Wadewayę́stanih

ehyádǫhkwaʔ

Ehyádǫhaʔ.

Kyadǫ́haʔ.

Gadeʔnyędę́hęʔ.

Ǫdeʔnyędę́hsdahkwaʔ

Ǫdeʔnyędę́hęʔ.

Wadewayęstanih

Wadewayę́stanih

-HKWAʔ/-HTAʔ/-ʔTAʔ
(Uses)

You may have noticed that several of the words for tools end the same way:

ehyádǫhkwaʔ	'pencil' or 'pen'
ǫdeʔnyędę́hsdahkwaʔ	'ruler', 'measuring cup' or 'measuring instrument'
egahędáhkwaʔ	'drill'
enesdanyáʔktaʔ	'saw (board cutter)'
deyeǫgyáʔktaʔ	'crosscut saw (log cutter)'
enǫhsǫnyáʔtaʔ	'house building tool'
deyagwęnóʔsgwʔitaʔ	'broom'

If you compare these words with some others, you can see what the endings mean.

ehyádǫhaʔ	'she writes' or 'one writes'
ǫdeʔnyędę́hęʔ	'she measures' or 'one measures'
enésdanyaʔs	'she cuts boards' or 'one cuts boards'
deyéǫgyaʔs	'she cuts logs' or 'one cuts logs'
enǫhsǫ́:nihs	'she builds houses' or 'one builds houses'
deyagwęnóʔsgwiʔs	'she sweeps' or 'one sweeps'

The endings *-hkwaʔ/-htaʔ/-ʔtaʔ* mean 'with it', so the literal meaning of 'pen', for example, is 'one writes with it', and for 'ruler', 'one measures with it'. Cayuga names for tools very often describe exactly what the tool is used for.

Wadewayęstanih

HEYÓHE:, AQHĘ:ˀĘH, ...
(More and Most)

While Sam is buying the tools, the salesman talks about price, size, and quality. These are good terms to know.

Wagyé:sęh.	'It is cheap.'
Neˀ wagyé:sęh	'The cheap one'
Ganǫ́:ˀ.	'It is expensive.'
Neˀ ganǫ́:ˀ	'The expensive one'
Gowá:nęh.	'It is big.'
Neˀ gowá:nęh	'The big one'
Gajihyowá:nęh.	'The hammer is big.'
Neˀ gajihyowá:nęh	'The big hammer'
Oyá:nreˀ.	'It is good.'
Neˀ oyá:nreˀ	'The good one'
Neˀ oyá:nreˀs	'The good ones'
Ohyuˀtí:yeht.	'It is sharp.'
Neˀ ohyuˀtí:yeht	'The sharp one'

The salesman can emphasize these features by adding *gwahs* 'very'.

Neˀ wagyé:sęh	'The cheap one'
Neˀ gwahs wagyé:sęh	'The very cheap one'
Neˀ gajihyowá:nęh	'The big hammer'
Neˀ gwahs gajihyowá:nęh	'The very big hammer'

If the salesman wants to compare the quality of two things, he can use the word *heyóhe:* 'more' or '-er'. The particle *né:ˀ* can be used to mean 'it is', or 'this one is'.

Wagyé:sęh.	'It is cheap.'
Né:ˀ heyohé: wagyé:sę	'It is cheaper'
Ganǫ́:ˀ.	'It is expensive.'
Né:ˀ heyohé: ganǫ́:ˀ	'It is more expensive'

How would you say these in Cayuga?

It is bigger.
It is better.   It is sharper.

Wadewayę́stanih

The salesman can emphasize the difference in quality or size with the phrase *gwahs heyohe:* 'much more', 'much ... -er'.

Né:ʔ heyohé: wagyé:sęh	'It is cheaper'
Né:ʔ gwáhs heyohé: wagyé:sęh	'It is much cheaper'
Né:ʔ heyohé: ganǫ́:ʔ	'It is more expensive'
Né:ʔ gwáhs heyohé: ganǫ́:ʔ	'It is much more expensive'

How would you say these in Cayuga?

It is much bigger.
It is much better.
It is much sharper.

If there is a whole group of objects, instead of just one or two, the salesman can compare one to the others in the group. To do this, he uses *aǫhę:ʔęh* 'most' or *gyaǫhę:ʔęh* 'most of all'. The word following this *gyaǫhę:ʔęh*, that is, the description, begins with *t-* or *d-*.

Wagyé:sęh	'The cheap one'
Neʔ gyaǫhę:ʔę́ dwagyé:sęh	'The cheapest one of all'
Neʔ ganǫ́:ʔ	'The expensive one'
Neʔ gyaǫhę:ʔę́ tganǫ́:ʔ	'The most expensive one of all'

As you can see, the additional sound on the next word is *t-* or *d-*. Before O, *gy-* is added.

Neʔ oyá:nreʔ	'The good one'
Neʔ gyaǫhę:ʔę́ gyoyá:nreʔ	'The best one of all'

Can you imagine how to say these in Cayuga?

The biggest one of all
The biggest hammer of all
The sharpest one of all

-AH
(Sort of)

You may have noticed that the salesman tells Sam that a hammer is fairly cheap. Compare 'cheap' and 'fairly cheap'.

Wagyé:sęh.	'It is cheap.'
Wagye:sę́:hah.	'It is fairly cheap.'
Wagyésęʔǫh.	'It got cheap (on sale).'

Now compare these.

Oyá:nreʔ.	'It is good.'
Oya:nréːʔah.	'It is pretty good.'
Gowá:nęh.	'It is big.'
Gowa:nę:hah.	'It is fairly big.'

To soften such a statement a bit, and add the meaning 'a little', 'sort of', 'fairly', 'pretty', etc., speakers can add -*ah* onto the end of a description. Notice that the next to the last syllable is long and loud. (: and ʔ).

If you know how to say 'it is old', would you know how to say, 'it is sort of old'?

Ogá:yǫh.	'It is old.'
Tiyógayǫh, oga:yó:hah.	'It is sort of old.'
Gajihyowá:nęh.	'The hammer is big.'
Gajihyowa:nę:hah.	'The hammer is sort of big.'

Listen for this little -*ah* at the end of words in any Cayuga you hear around you and in the conversations to come.

NEW VOCABULARY

gajíhwaʔ	'hammer'
gajihyowá:nęh	'big hammer'
nigajihyú:ʔuh	'small hammer'
do: nigajihwa:nǫ:ʔ?	'how expensive is the hammer?'
knesdá:nyaʔs	'I am cutting boards'
enésdanyaʔs	'she is cutting boards'
enesdanyáʔktaʔ	'saw'
deyeǫgyaʔktaʔ	'crosscut saw' (literally, 'one cuts logs with it')
gahenʔatrí:yo:	'good cutter'
oyá:nreʔ	'it is good'
oyá:nreʔs	'good ones'
gwáhs gyaǫhę́:ʔę tgahenʔatrí:yo:	'the best cutter/blade'
gyaǫhę́:ʔę tganǫ́:ʔ	'most expensive'
ganǫ́:ʔ	'it is expensive'
ehehgyaʔktaʔ gagáwehsaʔ	'shovel' (literally, 'one cuts dirt with it, one paddles with it', 'dirt-cutting paddle')
gagahoʔjí:yaʔs	'lawnmower', 'scythe' (literally, 'it cuts grass')
degę́nʔosgwihs, degęnʔohsgwihǫh	'I am sweeping'
deyagonóʔsgwihs	'she is sweeping'
deyagonóʔsgwʔitaʔ	'broom' (literally, 'one sweeps with it')
egahędáhkwaʔ	'drill' (literally, 'one makes holes with it')
gahné:ga:ʔ	'level' (literally, 'it has liquid in it')
gadeʔnyędę́hę́ʔ	'I am measuring it', 'I am trying/testing it'
ǫdeʔnyędę́hęʔ	'she is measuring it'
ǫdę́ʔnyędę́hsdahkwaʔ	'ruler', 'measuring instrument'
kyadǫ́haʔ	'I am writing'
ehyádǫhaʔ	'she is writing'
ehyádǫhkwaʔ	'pen', 'pencil' (literally, 'one writes with it')
sá:dǫh	'you say'
gá:dǫh	'I say'
gihsa:s	'I am looking for it'
sihsa:s	'you are looking for it'
hihsa:s	'he is looking for it'
áihsa:s	'she is looking for it'

Wadewayę́stanih

adó:gę̨ʔ	'axe'
gajiʔdrǫwa:dá:sehs	'screwdriver'
dewahjʔidóha:s	'pliers' (literally, 'it pinches')
atsóʔkdǫhsraʔ	'hoe' (= *atsóʔkdǫhfraʔ*)
swá:yę̨ʔ	'you have'
ǫgwá:yę̨ʔ	'we all have'
adwákyuʔkdę̨ʔ	'it got dull'
ohyuʔtí:yeht	'it is sharp'
dewagadǫhwęjó:nih	'I need/want it'
desadǫhwę:jó:nih	'you need/want it'
tę́ʔ dʔeóyanreʔ	'it is not good'
heyóhe:	'more'
gwáhs heyohé: gajihyowá:nęh	'bigger hammer'
dó: niga:nǫ:ʔʔ	'how expensive is it?'
sę niganǫ́:nyǫʔ	'how expensive they are'
wagyé:sęh	'it is cheap'
wagye:sę́:hah	'it is fairly cheap'
degyahdiháhnǫʔ	'there is a variety', 'they are different'
sgahwíhsda:t	'one dollar'
degahwihsdá:ge:	'two dollars'
ahsę́ nigahwihsdá:ge:	'three dollars'
gwęnihs	'pennies'
niyogwęníʔdahsę:	'tens of cents'
syǫ́ʔtrage: or degahsiyǫ́ʔtrage:	'quarter', 'two bits' ('shillings')
nigahsiyǫ́ʔtrage:	'bits' (=12½ ¢)
géi nigahsiyǫ́ʔtrage:	50¢
hyeiʔ nigahsiyǫ́ʔtrage:	75¢
tsaʔdeswahsę́:nǫh	'half'
hegwé:gǫh	'everything there', 'total'
gyǫdęhní:nǫh	'store' (literally, 'one sells things there')
tgahǫʔ	'it sits there'
tgahǫnyǫʔ	'several things sitting there'
gahe:ʔ	'it sits on it'
hegáhe:ʔ	'it sits over there'
wagyesęhsǫ́:ʔǫh	'cheap ones'
ohsnó:weʔ	'it is fast', 'quickly'

13

GATGWĘʔDAʔ

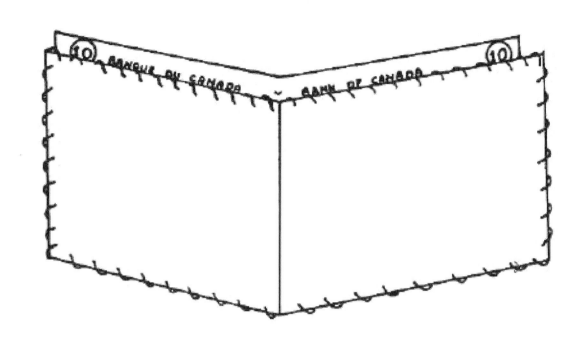

Wadewayę́stanih

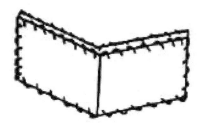

gatgwę́ʔdaʔ

gatgwę́ʔdaʔ

gatgwę́ʔdaʔ

Wadewayę́stanih

Wadewayęstanih

Wadewayę́stanih

Honǫhǫkdá:nih. Hodaʔgrahgwá:nih.

Gonǫhokdá:nih.

Gonǫhǫkdá:nih. Gotowinyǫ́ʔse:.

Honǫhǫkdá:nih. Hotowinyǫ́ʔse:.

Wadewayęstanih

GATGWĘʔDAʔ

THĘˀ DˀĘ-
(Not Again)

This conversation has some more negative questions and statements. You can recognize them, of course, by the *tęˀ dˀe-*.

Tęˀ dˀegé:gę:.	'I haven't seen it.'
Tęˀ dˀesé:gę:.	'You haven't seen it.'
Tęˀ dˀeagęnǫ́hdǫˀ.	'I don't know.'
Tęˀ dˀehęˀs.	'He is not around.'

Pete and Sam have also sprinkled some more particles between the two parts of the negative.

Tęˀ gˀató dˀegé:gę:.	'I haven't seen it anywhere.'
Tęˀ giˀ gwáhs a:yę́:ˀ dˀeagęnǫ́hdǫˀ.	'I don't really seem to know.'

AG-/AK-/GO-/HO-
(I/she/he again)

This lesson has some more examples of the second set of pronouns. Notice again how easy it is to switch from 'he' to 'she' with these.

Aknǫhǫkdá:nih.	'I am sick.'
Gonǫhǫkdá:nih.	'She is sick.'
Honǫhǫkdá:nih.	'He is sick.'
Agadˀagráhgwanih.	'I have the measles.'
Godaˀgrahgwá:nih.	'She has the measles.'
Hodaˀgrahgwá:nih.	'He has the measles.'
Agatowínyˀǫse:.	'I have a cold.'
Gotowinyǫ́ˀse:.	'She has a cold.'
Hotowinyǫ́ˀse:.	'He has a cold.'

-SǪˀ
(-s)

Although most words for objects do not specify whether there is just one or many, there is a way that Cayuga speakers can talk about an assortment of some kind. They add *-sǫˀ* to the end of the word.

agétgwˀęda?	'my suitcase, etc.'	satgwę́ˀdaˀ	'your suitcase, etc'
agetgwˀędáˀsǫˀ	'my baggage'	satgwę́ˀdˀasǫˀ	'your baggage'

ǪGAHDǪ:ʔ
(I Have Lost It)

Practice complaining. Tell each person in the group that you have lost your wallet, purse, or baggage.

Ne:ʔ gęh tóne:ʔ ǫgahdǫ́:ʔ tone:ʔ neʔ agétgwʔędaʔ.

Ask whether they have seen it.

Tę́ʔ gęh ní:s gʔató dʔe:se:gę:?

If someone complains to you, ask them what it looked like.

Dę́ʔ diʔ hoʔdę́ʔ ni:yóht neʔ satgwęʔdaʔ?

Some answers to this could be:

oya:nréʔ hóʔdęʔ	'a good one'	oya:nré:ʔa hóʔdęʔ	'a fairly good one'
otgi:sʔá hóʔdęʔ	'an ugly one'	gowá:nęh	'it is big.'
ganehwáʔ hóʔdęʔ	'a leather one'	gowa:nę́:hah	'it is fairly big.'
á:se:ʔ hóʔdęʔ	'a new one'	a:sé:ʔah	'it is fairly new.'
ogá:yǫ hóʔdęʔ	'an old one'	oga:yǫ́:hah	'a fairly old one'

If these conversations leave you with a desire to be able to discuss color, move right on to the next section.

NEW VOCABULARY

gatgwę́ʔdaʔ	'wallet', 'purse', 'suitcase'
agétgwʔędaʔ	'my wallet', 'my purse', 'my suitcase'
agetgwʔędáʔsǫʔ	'my baggage'
satgwę́ʔdaʔ	'your wallet', 'your purse', 'your suitcase'
satgwę́ʔdʔasǫʔ	'your baggage'
ǫgáhdǫ:ʔ	'I have lost it'
ǫgetgwʔędáhdǫ:ʔ	'I have lost my wallet' (etc.)
desáhdǫ:ʔ	(where) 'you have lost it'
dǫgáhdǫ:ʔ	(where) 'I have lost it'
tę́ʔ dʔegé:gę:	'I haven't seen it'
tę́ʔ dʔesé:gę:	'you haven't seen it'
iheʔs	'he is around'
tę́ʔ dʔeheʔs	'he is not around'
ęga:shé:gęʔ	'you will see them'
ęgashehó:wiʔ	'you will tell them'
dejadęhnǫ́:de:ʔ.	'you two are siblings', 'your brother', 'your sister'
gaęgwaʔ nhǫ́:	'somewhere'
sǫgá:ʔah	'anyone'
aknǫhǫkdá:nih	'I am sick'
gonǫhokdá:nih	'she is sick'
honǫhokdá:nih	'he is sick'
agadʔagráhgwanih	'I have the measles'
godaʔgrahgwá:nih	'she has the measles'
hodaʔgrahgwá:nih	'he has the measles'
agatowíny ʔǫse:, agatuwínyʔǫse:	'I have a cold'
gotowinyǫ́ʔse:, gotuwinyǫ́ʔse:	'she has a cold'
hotowinyǫ́ʔse:, hotuwinyǫ́ʔse:	'he has a cold'
otgí:sʔah	'it is ugly', 'it is sort of dirty'
ganéhwaʔ	'leather', 'hide'
á:se:ʔ	'it is new'
ogá:yǫh	'it is old'
hóʔdęʔ	'kind', 'type'
dęʔ hóʔdęʔ ni:yóht?	'what is it like?'
gyę́:gwaʔ	'if', 'perhaps'

14

OHSQHGWA'

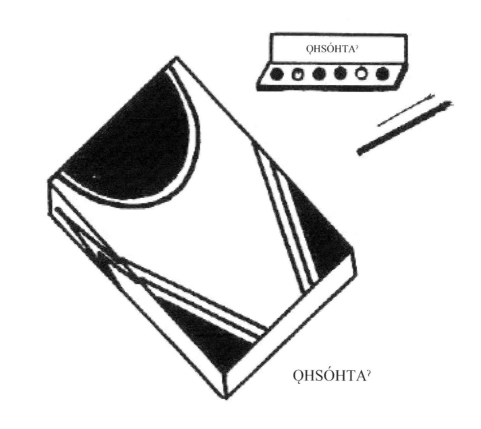

QHSÓHTA'

QHSÓHTA'

DĘ:ˀ HOˀDĘˀ NIYOHSOHGOˀDĘ:?

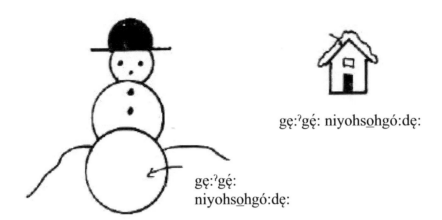

gę:ˀgę́: niyohsohgó:dę:

gę:ˀgę́:
niyohsohgó:dę:

gę:ˀgę́:
niyohsohgó:dę:

gę:ˀgę́:
niyohsohgó:dę:

gę:ˀgę́:
niyohsohgó:dę:

Wadewayęstanih

ǫhy'áę' niyohsohgó:dę: ǫhy'áę' niyohsohgó:dę:

ǫhy'áę' niyohsohgó:dę:

ǫhy'áę' niyohsohgó:dę:

ǫhy'áę' niyohsohgó:dę:

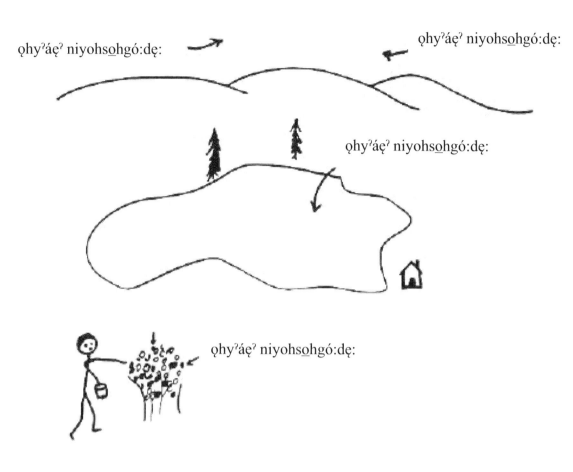

DĘ' HO'DĘ' NIYOHSOHGO'DĘ:?

Wadewayę́stanih

onrahdʔáéʔ niyohsohgó:dę:

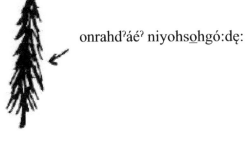

onrahdʔáéʔ niyohsohgó:dę:

onrahdʔáéʔ
niyohsohgó:dę:

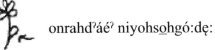

onrahdʔáéʔ niyohsohgó:dę:

DĘʔ HOʔDĘʔ NIYOHSOHGOʔDĘ:?

Wadewayę́stanih

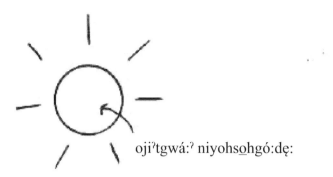
oji'tgwá:' niyohsohgó:dę:

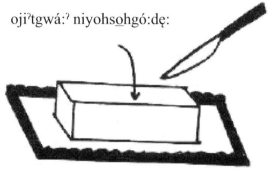
oji'tgwá:' niyohsohgó:dę:

oji'tgwá:' niyohsohgó:dę:

oji'tgwá:'
niyohsohgó:dę:

oji'tgwá:'
niyohsohgó:dę:

DĘ' HO'DĘ' NIYOHSOHGO'DĘ:?

Wadewayę́stanih

DĘ? HO?DĘ? NIYOHSOHGO?DĘ:?

Wadewayę́stanih

DĘ' HO'DĘ' NIYOHSOHGO'DĘ:?

Wadewayę́stanih

DĘʔ HOʔDĘʔ NIYOHSOHGOʔDĘ:?

Wadewayęstanih

 swę'd'áę' niyohsohgó:dę:

swę'd'áę' niyohsohgó:dę:

swę'd'áę' niyohsohgó:dę:

 swę'd'áę' niyohsohgó:dę:

DĘ' HO'DĘ' NIYOHSOHGO'DĘ:?

Wadewayęstanih

AKNÍ:NǪʔ
(I Bought It!)

Now you can finally talk about colour. This time, go around the room, telling each person that you have bought something, such as a wallet or purse, baggage, a coat, a hat, a pencil or pen, a ruler, tools, etc.

Gatgwęʔdáʔ
Agyaʔdawiʔtráʔ akní:nǫʔ.
Ehyadǫhkwaʔ
etc.

(Put the object first, since this is new and the most important information.)

Each time someone announces a new purchase to you, ask them about it. One question you can now ask is what colour it is.

Dęʔ hoʔdęʔ niyohsohgoʔdę: neʔ   satgwęʔdaʔ?
                                       sagyaʔdawiʔtraʔ?
                                       ehyadǫhkwaʔ?
                                       etc.

Answer all questions that come your way. Be sure to include the colour word with all answers about colour.

Swęʔdʔáeʔ niyohsgóʔdę:. etc.

New Vocabulary

dęʔ hoʔdęʔ niyohsohgoʔdę:?	'what colour is it?'
ohsóhgwaʔ	'colour', 'paint'
gę:ʔgé: niyohsohgoʔdę:	'white coloured'
ǫhyʔáeʔ niyohsohgoʔdę:	'blue coloured'
(o)nrahdʔáęʔ niyohsohgoʔdę:	'green coloured'
(o)jiʔtgwa:ʔ niyohsohgoʔdę:	'yellow coloured'
deyodʔagęhyʔagǫ́h niyohsohgoʔdę:	'gray coloured'
tgwęhjʔiáʔ niyohsohgoʔdę:	'red coloured'
hehsʔáęʔ niyohsohgoʔdę:	'brown coloured'
swęʔdʔáeʔ niyohsohgoʔdę:	'black coloured'
ohsóhdaʔ	'crayon', 'paintbrush', etc. literally, 'one colours/paints with it'

15

AHGWĘ:NYAʔ

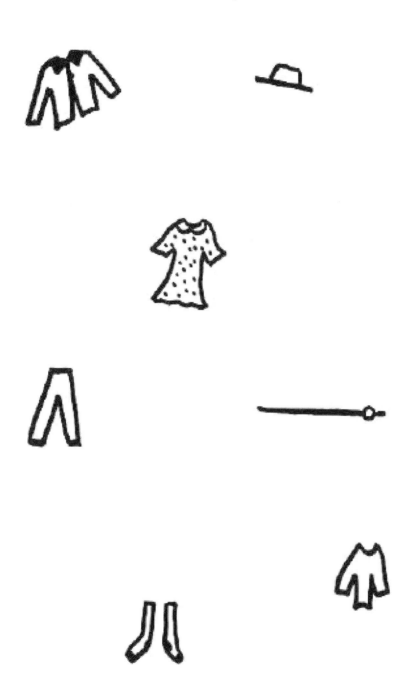

Wadewayę́stanih

anaháotra^ʔ

anaháotra^ʔ

anaháotra^ʔ

agya^ʔdawí^ʔtra^ʔ

agya^ʔdawí^ʔtra^ʔ

agya^ʔdawí^ʔtra^ʔ

Wadewayęstanih

adéhswaʔ

adéhswaʔ

adéhswaʔ

Wadewayę́stanih

ę'nyó:tra'

gatgwę́'da'

g'aká:'

ahdáhgwa'

agya'dawí'tra'

ę'nyó:tra'

Wadewayęstanih

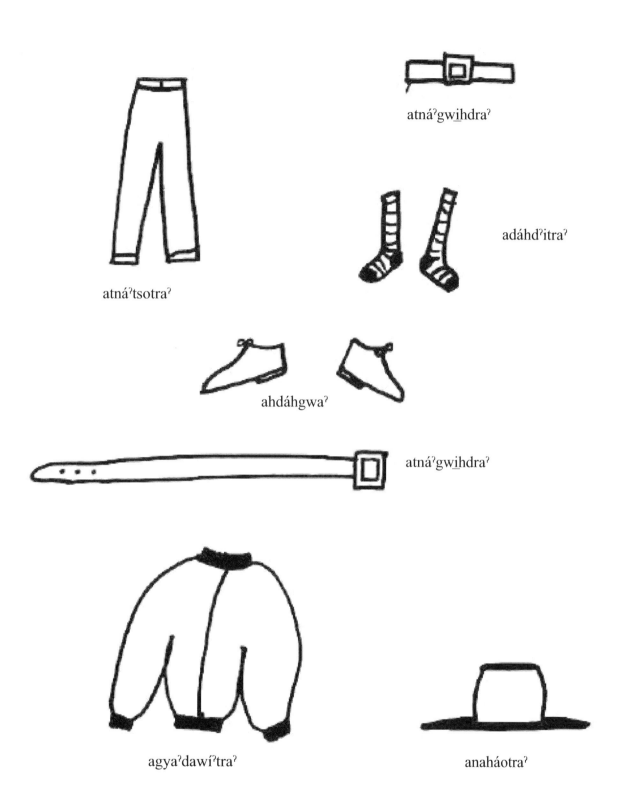

Wadewayę́stanih

Wadewayę́stanih

205

Wadewayéstanih

Wadewayę́stanih

SA:WĘH AGA:WĘH HNI'
(Yours and mine)

You can see how to tell who owns what by comparing the words below.

sá:węh	'yours' or 'you have it'
sgá:węh	'mine' or 'I have it'
agya'dawí'tra'	'coat', 'dress' or 'shirt'
sagya'dawí'tra'	'your coat', 'your dress' or 'your shirt'
agagy'adáw'itra'	'my coat', 'my dress' or 'my shirt'
anaháotra'	'hat'
sanaháotra'	'your hat'
agenaháotra'	'my hat'
gatgwę́'da'	'purse', 'wallet' or 'suitcase'
satgwę́'da'	'your purse', 'your wallet' or 'your suitcase'
agétgw'éda'	'my purse', 'my wallet' or 'my suitcase'
atná'tsotra'	'pants'
satná'tsotra'	'your pants'
agatná'tsó:tra'	'my pants'
atná'gwihdra'	'belt'
satná'gwihdra'	'your belt'
agatn'agwíhdra'	'my belt'
adáhd'itra'	'socks'
sadáhd'itra'	'your socks'
agadahdí'tra'	'my socks'
ahdáhgwa'	'shoes'
sahdáhgwa'	'your shoes'
agáhdahgwa'	'my shoes'
ę'nyó:tra'	'gloves' or 'mittens'
s'ęnyó:tra'	'your gloves' or 'your mittens'
agę'nyótra'	'my gloves' or 'my mittens'

The *sa-* or *s-* at the beginning shows that the clothes belong to the hearer, 'you'. The *ak-*, *ag-* or *age-* at the beginning shows that the clothes belong to the speaker. You may have noticed that to a Cayuga speaker, owning objects like clothing is a different matter than 'owning' most attached body parts. You can see this from the form of 'my', which is *ak-*, *ag-* or *age-* for objects, but *g-*, *k-* or *ge-* for most body parts. (Notice again that adding the 'my' adds an extra syllable to the front of the word, so the stress, whispered vowels, and glottal stops change.)

NEW VOCABULARY

sá:węh	'yours', 'you have it'
agá:węh	'mine', 'I have it'
agagyʔadáwʔitraʔ	'my coat', 'my dress', 'my shirt'
agęnaháotraʔ	'my hat'
atnáʔtsotraʔ	'pants'
satnáʔtsotraʔ	'your pants'
agatnaʔtsó:traʔ	'my pants'
atnáʔgwihdraʔ	'belt'
satnáʔgwihdraʔ	'your belt'
agatnʔagwíhdraʔ	'my belt'
adáhdʔitraʔ	'socks'
sadáhdʔitraʔ	'your socks'
agadahdíʔtraʔ	'my socks'
ahdáhgwaʔ	'shoes'
sahdáhgwaʔ	'your shoes'
agáhdahgwaʔ	'my shoes'
ęʔnyó:traʔ	'gloves', 'mittens'
sʔęnyó:traʔ	'your gloves', 'your mittens'
agę́ʔnyotraʔ	'my gloves', 'my mittens'
adéhswaʔ	'blouse', 'middy'
agatrǫníhsʔa:ʔ	'I am ready'

Practice

Now that you know colours and a number of names of objects, you are in a position to be competitive. Begin by reviewing colours. Divide into several teams. The teacher will ask people to find things of certain colours with a question like this.

Sǫ: nʔaht ęye:gwe:níʔ ęye:tsę́iʔ sgahoʔdę́:ʔęh nrahdʔáe niyohsohgoʔdę:?
who ever will-be-able to-find something green coloured
'Who can find something green coloured?'

(Different colours can be substituted for 'green'.) The first person to point to something of the appropriate colour wins a point for his or her team. Continue this until everyone is good at it, perhaps with students taking turns at asking the questions.

Next, be more specific in the question. Mention an object, like this.

Sǫ nʔaht ęye:gwe:níʔ ęye:tsę́iʔ neʔ nrahdʔáęʔ niyohsohgoʔdę: agyaʔdawíʔtraʔ?
who ever will-be-able to-find it green coloured dress/coat/shirt
'Who can find a green coloured dress/coat/shirt?'

16

SATRǪ:NIH!

Wadewayę́stanih

Wadewayę́stanih

-(H)SI / -GO
(Un-)

Look at the differences between these pairs of words.

Sasatnʔatsóweksih.	'Take your pants back off.'
Sasatnʔatsó:we:k.	'Put your pants back on.'
Dǫsasatnaʔgwihdrę́hsih.	'Take your belt back off.'
Dǫsasatnaʔgwíhdrę:.	'Put your belt back on.'
Sasagyʔadáwihsih.	'Take your shirt back off.'
Sasagyʔadá:wiʔt.	'Put your shirt back on.'
Sasanahaowé:ksih.	'Take your hat back off.'
Sasanaháowe:k.	'Put your hat back on.'

As you can see, the *-hsi* at the end of the word reverses the action from putting things on to taking them off. (The H is swallowed between K and S.) This *-hsi* is about like *un-* in English.

Sasatrǫnyáhsih.	'Get undressed again.'
Sasa:trǫ́:nih.	'Get dressed again.'

Another syllable which has the same effect is *-go* 'un-'.

Sasadahdiʔtradáhgoh.	'Take your socks back off.'
Sasadahdiʔtrǫdá:.	'Put your socks back on.'
Senho:dǫ́:goh.	'Open the door.'
Senhó:dǫ:.	'Close the door.' or 'Lock the door.'

(There is no good way to predict which of these, *-hsi* or *-go,* a verb will use. It is just like 'un-' and 'in-' in English. All speakers say 'unusual' and 'indecent', and never 'inusual' or 'undecent', but they could not explain why.)

Could you predict how to say these in Cayuga?

'Close the door again'
'Open the door back up'

S-
(And that's an order)

You can see that Cayuga does not use just one word for 'put on' different kinds of clothes.

Satrǫ:nih.	'Get dressed.'
Satnaʔtsó:we:k.	'Put your pants on.'
Desatnʔagwíhdrę:.	'Put your belt on.'
Sagyáʔdawiʔt.	'Put your shirt/jacket/dress on.'
Sadahdʔitrǫda:.	'Put your socks on.'
Desęhsó:we:k.	'Put your shoes on.'
Sanaháowe:k.	'Put your hat on.'

You can see that they are all commands given to just one person, since they all begin with *s-* or *(de)s-*. Many of them order someone to cover a certain part of their body. *Desęhsó:we:k* actually says something like 'cover your feet'. *Sanaháowe:k* tells you to cover your head. *Sagyáʔsawiʔt* tells you to put your body into a tube.

SA-SA-

Once Lila's poor son is completely undressed again, she tells him to get dressed all over again. There is an easy way to show that this is a repeat performance in Cayuga. If the command began with *sa-*, she simply adds *sa-* 'again'.

Sasa:trǫ́:nih.	'Get dressed again.'

(Compare *satrǫ́:nih* 'get dressed'.)

Sasatnʔatsó:we:k.	'Put your pants back on.'
Sasagyʔadá:wiʔt.	'Put your shirt/jacket/dress back on.'
Sasadahdiʔtrǫdá:.	'Put your socks back on.'
Sasanaháowe:k.	'Put your hat back on.'

(Since adding the extra *sa-* changes the number of syllables in the word, the stress, length, and glottals change a bit.)

If a command began with *de-*, this is changed to *dǫsa-* 'again'.

Dǫsasatnáʔgwihdrę:.	'Put your belt back on.'
Dǫsasę:só:we:k.	'Put your shoes back on.'

NEW VOCABULARY

satrǫ́:nih	'get dressed'
sasa:trǫ́:nih	'get dressed again'
sasatrǫnyáhsih	'get undressed again'
sasatrǫnyáhsiʔ	'you are undressed again'
sagatrǫnyáhsiʔ	'I am undressed again'
satnaʔtsó:we:k	'put your pants on'
sasatnʔatsó:we:k	'put your pants back on'
sasatnaʔtsóweksih	'take your pants back off'
desatnʔagwíhdrę:	'put your belt on'
dǫsasatnáʔgwihdrę:	'put your belt back on'
dǫsasatnáʔgwihdrę́hsih	'take your belt back off'
sagyáʔdawiʔt	'put your shirt/jacket/dress on'
sasagyʔadá:wiʔt	'put your shirt/jacket/dress back on'
sasagyʔadáwihsih	'take your shirt/jacket/dress back off'
sadahdʔitrǫda:	'put your socks on'
sasadahdiʔtrǫdá:	'put your socks back on'
sasadahdiʔtradáhgoh	'take your socks back off'
desęhsó:we:k	'put your shoes on'
dǫsasę:só:we:k	'put your shoes back on'
sasęhsó:tsih	'take your shoes back off'
sanaháowe:k	'put your hat on'
sasanaháowe:k	'put your hat back on'
sasanahaowé:ksih	'take your hat back off'
hękne:ʔ	'we two will go there (you and I)'
gaoʔ shęh nyo:	'before'
ęsatnʔatsó:trę́ʔs	'your pants will fall down'
agáyesaʔ	'it is too bad'
ahgwih ęjisʔanígǫhęh	'don't forget'
sasę́dʔadrah	'go back to sleep'
ęyosdaędʔáǫhǫ:k	'it will have stopped raining'
agasdáędaʔ	'it stopped raining'
ętsyeh	'you will wake up'
sasá:tgęh	'get back up'
tę́ʔ dʔeakwihsdáę́ʔ	'I have no money'
hekne:	'let us two go there'

17

AGYAʔDAWÍʔTRAʔ

Wadewayę́stanih

tréhs gowá:nehs

tréhs niwú:sʔuh

ne:ʔ giʔ tóhjih.

tréhs niwú:sʔuh

tréhs gowá:nehs

ne:ʔ giʔ tóhjih.

Wadewayęstanih

HNÁʔGOHKA:ʔ

Wadewayę́stanih

DO: NIYOHSHE:DĘH?

ahsę́h sgahe² niyoshé:dęh

hwíhs niyoshé:dęh

degrǫ² niyoshé:dęh

hwíhs niwahshę: dekní: niyoshé:dęh

ahsę́h niwahshę́h

géi niwahshę́: niyoshé:dęh

ahsę́h niwahshę́: niyoshé:dęh

wahshę́: niyoshé:dęh

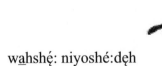

wahshę́: niyoshé:dęh

tsa²deyohshé:dęh

AGYAʔDAWÍʔTRAʔ

Wadewayęstanih

Wadewayę́stanih

HOʔDĘʔ
(a kind)

The saleslady needs to know what kind of dress Lila is after, so she uses the word *hóʔdęʔ* 'kind'.

Neʔ haʔdewęhnihsragehká:ʔ	hóʔdęʔ.
the everyday	kind

'The everyday kind.'

Agyaʔdawiʔtri:yó:	hóʔdęʔ.
good dress	kind

'The good kind.'

This is the same *hóʔdęʔ* that you used when discussing the lost wallet earlier.

Dęʔ hóʔdęʔ ni:yoht?
'What kind is it? (or 'What does it look like?')

Oya:nr<u>e</u>ʔ hóʔdęʔ.   'A good one.'

Otgi:sʔá hóʔdęʔ.   'An ugly one.' or 'A sort of dirty one.'

Listen for this *hoʔdęʔ* in conversations around you and in later conversations in this book. It is very common and useful.

GAĘ NI:GA:ʔ
(Which one?)

As Lila and the saleslady are picking dresses out of a group, they use a new question word:

Gaę ni:ga:?
Which one?

You can use this phrase to make a lot of questions.

Gaę ni:ga:	snǫhweʔs?	'Which one do you like?'
which one	you-like	

Gaę ni:ga:	desadǫhwęjo:nih?	'Which one do you want?'
which one	you-want	

Gaę ni:ga:	ęhsni:nǫh?	'Which one will you buy?
which one	you-will-buy	

One noncommittal answer you might be able to use is:

Gaę gwaʔ giʔ ni:gá: nę́:gyęh.   'Any one of these.'

TREHS
(too)

There is a good Cayuga word for talking about excess.

Trehs   niwú:ʔuh.   (*Niwú:ʔuh.*   'It is small.')
too   so-it-is-small
'It is too small.'

Trehs   gowá:nęh.   (*Gowá:nęh.*   'It is big.')
too   it-is-big
'It is too big.'

Based on these two sentences, could you complain about the excesses below?

It is too fast.	(Ohsnó:weʔ.	'It is fast.')
It is too slow.	(Sgę:nǫ́:ǫh.	'It is slow.')
He is too tall.	(Hahnę́:ye:s.	'He is tall.')
He is too short.	(Nihahnę:yá:kʔah.	'He is short.')
He is too thin.	(Hohsgyǫ́ʔwatę:.	'He is thin.')
He is too fat.	(Hohsę:.	'He is fat.')

When talking about the size of clothing, you will generally want to say that it is too large or too small <u>for</u> someone in particular. In this case, the words change slightly to include the <u>for</u>.

Trehs   niwú:sʔuh.
Too   so-it-is-small-for
'It is too small (for someone).'

Trehs   gowá:nęʔs.
too   it-is-big-for
'It is too big (for someone).'

GYẸ:GWAʔ
(If)

In the store, Lila uses the word *gyẹ:gwaʔ* 'if'. It is handy to be able to state your conditions if someone asks you certain questions. Here is a question with some possible answers.

Questions: Ẹhsní:nǫʔ gẹh?
'Will you buy it?'

Answer: Ẹhẹ́ʔ, giʔ gyẹ́:gwaʔ akwíhsdaẹʔ.
yes in fact if I have money
'Yes, in fact, if I have money.'

Answer: Ẹhẹ́ʔ, giʔ gyẹ́:gwaʔ tẹ́ʔ dʔega:nǫ́:ʔ.
yes in fact if not it is not expensive
'Yes, in fact, if it is not expensive.'

Answer: Ẹhẹ́ʔ, giʔ gyẹ́:gwaʔ hẹwa:gí:dẹʔ.
yes in fact if it will fit
'Yes, in fact, if it will fit.'

Answer: Gyẹ́:gwaʔ hne:hwaʔ.
maybe
'Maybe.'

TSAʔDE-
(When two are the same)

The saleslady uses a number of words which begin with *tsaʔde-*.

Tsaʔde:yoht. 'The two are the same style.'

Tsaʔdeyohse:dẹh. 'The two are the same size (number).'

Tsaʔdegadi:yáǫʔdʔodẹ:. 'The two are the same shape.'

As you can see, this combination *tsaʔ-de-* indicates that two things are the same in some way.

Practice

Divide into small groups. Let each group prepare a skit about a trip to the store and present it to the class. You can discuss the kind and colour of merchandise the customer is looking for, as well as the quality, fit, and price.

NEW VOCABULARY

ihse:	'you want', 'you hope'
í:wi:	'I want', 'I hope'
ahi:ʔ	'I thought'
a:sní:nǫʔ	'you would buy'
a:kní:nǫʔ	'I would buy'
gihsa:s	'I am looking for'
gihsá:kah	'let me go look for it'
ohse:dęh	'number size'
do: niyohse:dęh?	'what number?', 'what size?'
sehstaʔ	'you use', 'you wear'
ęhsehs	'you will use', 'you will wear'
knǫhweʔs	'I like'
snǫhweʔs	'you like'
tęʔ dʔeknǫhweʔs	'I do not like'
haʔdewęhníhsrage:	'everyday'
haʔdeyohsóhgwage:	'all sorts of colours'
ojiʔtgwa:gę́:dʔah	'sort of light yellow'
otgwęhjʔia:gę́:t	'pink'
sadeʔnyę́:dęh	'try it'
heʔsaí:dęʔ	'it fit you'
tęʔ dʔaǫ ha:wagí:dęʔ	'it can't fit me'
hǫʔgí:dęʔ	'it fit me'
haʔga:í:t	'it fit'
tsaʔde:yoht	'the same style'
tsaʔdeyohse:dęh	'the same number (size)'
tsaʔdegadi:yáǫʔdʔodę:	'the same shape'
tsigaihwá:ʔah	'even', 'at least'
degyáhdihęh	'they are different'
sę ní:waʔs	'how big'
wagyesʔageh	'it is easy'
aʔosdagwá:ęh	'it gets/got dirty'
a:wadahsgwʔidrǫ́:niʔ	'it could get wrinkled'
ęgę́:ne:ʔ	'they will match', 'they will go together'

Wadewayę́stanih

tę́ˀ taˀdesadǫhwęjó:nih	'you do not want'
hnáˀgǫhha:ˀ	'underclothes'
ǫ́:weh	'really'
gaęgwaˀ nhǫ́:	'somewhere around'
swá:yę̨ˀ	'yous have'
agyaˀdawiˀtrí:yo:	'a good dress', 'coat', 'shirt'
waˀgyęh	'let me'
ǫgadrˀaswíyohsdę̨ˀ	'I got lucky'
age:tsę́iˀ	'I found it'
haesatrǫniha:k	'you would be dressed'
aesę́:daˀ	'you would sleep'
ó:yaˀ	'other'
tójih	'it is just right', 'exactly'
do: ni:waˀs?	'how big?'
haˀdewę̨hnihsragehka:ˀ	'everyday-ish'
dó:gęhs	'certainly'

18

DO: NIGA:GQ:?

Wadewayęstanih

DO: NIGA:GQ:?

sayá'da:t

jeyá'da:t

degaeyáhse:

degaeyáhse:

dehadiyáhse:

Wadewayęstanih

DO: NIGA:GǪ:?

ahsę nihę́:nǫ:

géi nigá:gǫ:

hwíhs nihę́:nǫ:

hyéiʔ nigá:gǫ:

degrǫ́ʔ nigá:gǫ:

DO: NIGA:GQ:?
(How many people are there?)

As you can see, Cayuga speakers specify the sex of the people they count. To talk about one person, you use these forms:

jeyá?da:t	'one female person'
shayá?da:t	'one male person'

To talk about two people, you use these forms:

degaeyáhse:	'two female people' or 'one female and one male'
dehadiyáhse:	'two male people'

To talk about three or more people, you simply substitute the number you want for the X:

X nigá:gǫ:	'X female people' or 'X people' (females or mixed)
X nihę́:nǫ:	'X male people'

Here are some examples of that:

ahsę nigá:gǫ:	'three people' (females or mixed)
ja:dáhk nihę́:nǫ:	'seven males'

As you can see, if even just one woman is present in a group, the feminine counters are used.

Wadewayęstanih

DO: NIGA:GQ:?

Wadewayęstanih

DO: NIGA:GQ:?

jeya'dá:t eksá:'ah saya'dá:t haksá:'ah

degaeyahsé: gaeksá:'ah dehadiyahsé: hadi:ksá:'ah

hyéi' niga:gǫ́: gaeks'asǫ́:'ǫh

246

Wadewayę́stanih

DO: NIGA:GQ:?

jeya'dá:t egę́hjih

saya'dá:t hagę́hjih

degaeyahsé: gáegęhjih

dehadiyahsé: hadígęhjih

degaeyahsé: gáegęhjih

géi niga:gǫ́: gaegęhjíhsǫ'

ahsę́ niga:gǫ́: gaegęhjíhsǫ'

ahsę́ nihę:nǫ́: hadigęhjíhsǫ'

Wadewayęstanih

DO: NIGA:GQ:?

?

?

?

?

Wadewayęstanih

NEW VOCABULARY

sayá'da:t	'one male person'
jeyá'da:t	'one female person'
dehadiyáhse:	'two male people'
degaeyáhse:	'two people, including at least one female' (either two women or one man and one woman)
X nihé:no:	'X male people' (X = three or more)
X nigá:go:	'X people, including at least one female' (X = three or more)
hadígehjih	'old men'
hadigehjíhsho'	'many old men' (usually three or more)
gáegehjih	'old people' (females or mixed)
gaegehjíhsho'	'many old people' (females or mixed)

19

GAHWAJIYÁ:DE?

Wadewayęstanih

Wadewayę́stanih

Wadewayęstanih

Wadewayę́stanih

Wadewayę́stanih

egówanęh

niya:gú:ʔuh

niga:gú:sʔuh

nihú:ʔuh

hagówanęh

Wadewayęstanih

GAHWAJIYÁ:DEʔ

Wadewayę́stanih

Wadewayę́stanih

Wadewayęstanih

Degaeyahsé: deyagwadęhnǫ:de:ʔ.
Gakehjiʔáshǫʔ.

Ahsęh niga:gǫ́: deyagwadęhnǫdrǫʔ. Gakehjiʔáshǫʔ.

Wadewayę́stanih

Wadewayęstanih

SQ: HNE:ʔ NʔAHT?
(Who is that?)

    Cayuga speakers distinguish older brothers and sisters from younger ones. Here is how you can introduce your brothers and sisters.

Older Sisters:
1) Jeyaʔdá:t   deyagyadęhnǫ́:de:ʔ.   Kehjíʔah.
   one-female   we-two-are-siblings   she-is-my-older-sister
   'This is my older sister.'

2) Degaeyahsé: deyagwadęhnǫ́:de:ʔ.   Gakehjiʔáhsǫʔ.
   two-of-them   we-all-are-siblings   they-are-my-older-siblings
   'These are my two older sisters.' or 'This is my older sister and brother.'

3) Ahsę   niga:gǫ́:   deyagwadęhnǫdrǫʔ.   Gakehjiʔáhsǫʔ.
   three   of-them   we-all-are-siblings   they-are-my-older-siblings
   'These are my three older sisters.' or 'These are my three older sisters and brothers (at least one sister).'

For four or more, simply substitute the appropriate number in place of *ahsęh* 'three'.

5) Hwíhs   niga:gǫ́:   deyagwadęhnǫdrǫʔ.   Gakehjiʔáhsǫʔ.
   five   of-them   we-all-are-siblings   they-are-my-older-siblings
   'These are my five older sisters.' or 'These are my five older brothers and sisters (at least one sister).'

If you have at least one older sister, you should use one of the sentences above. If you are talking about just older brothers, however, you should use the forms below.

Older Brothers
1) Sayaʔdá:t   deyagyadęhnǫ́:de:ʔ.   Hehjíʔah.
   one-male   we-two-are-siblings   he-is-my-older-brother
   'This is my older brother.'

2) Dehadiyahsé: deyagwadęhnǫ́:de:ʔ.   Gakehjiʔáhsǫʔ.
   two-males   we-two-are-siblings   they-are-my-older-siblings
   'These are my two older brothers.'

3) Ahsę   nihę:nǫ́:   deyagwadęhnǫdrǫʔ.   Gakehjiʔáhsǫʔ.
   three   of-males   we-all-are-siblings   they-are-my-older-siblings
   'These are my three older brothers.'

For more brothers, simply substitute the appropriate number for *ahsęh*.

Wadewayęstanih

DESADĘHNǪ:DRǪˀ GĘH?
(Do you have any brothers or sisters?)

If your brothers and sisters are not around, but you would like to talk about them anyway, here is how you can answer this question. Use sentences like those for introducing brothers and sisters, but use the words *degadęhnǫ:de:ˀ* ('I have one or two brothers and/or sisters') or *degadęhnǫ:drǫ:ˀ* ('I have many brothers and/or sisters') in the middle.

Older Sisters
1) Jeyaˀdá:t   deyagyadęhnǫ:de:ˀ.   Kehjíˀah.
   one-female   I-have-sibling   she-is-my-older-sister
   'I have one older sister.'

2) Degaeyahsé: degadęhnǫ:de:ˀ.   Gakehjíˀahsǫˀ.
   two-of-them   I-have-sibling   they-are-my-older-siblings
   'I have two older   or   'I have one older brother and one sister.'
   sisters.'

3) Ahsę   niga:gǫ́:   deyagwadęhnǫ́:drǫˀ.   Gakehjíˀahsǫˀ.
   three   of-them   I-have-siblings   they-are-my-older-siblings
   'I have three older sisters and   or   'I have three older sisters.'
   brothers.'

Again, for more than three, simply substitute the appropriate number for *ahsęh* in the sentence above.

Older Brothers
1) Sayaˀdá:t   degadęhnǫ́:de:ˀ.   Hehjíˀah.
   one-male   I-have-sibling   he-is-my-older brother
   'I have one older brother.'

2) Dehadiyahsé: degadęhnǫ́:de:ˀ.   Gakehjiˀáhsǫˀ.
   two-males   I-have-siblings   they-are-my-older siblings
   'I have two older brothers.'

3) Ahsę   nihę:nǫ́:   degadęhnǫ́:drǫˀ.   Gakehjiˀahsǫˀ.
   three   of-them   I-have-siblings   they-are-my-older-siblings
   'I have three older brothers.'

As before, if you have more than three older brothers, you can say this by substituting the appropriate number for *ahsęh*.

6) Hyéiˀ   nihę:nǫ́:   degadęhnǫ́:drǫˀ.   Gakehjíˀahsǫˀ.
   six   of-males   I-have-siblings   they-are-my-older-siblings
   'I have six older brothers.'

Wadewayę́stanih

Wadewayęstanih

Wadewayę́stanih

Younger sisters:
1) Jeyaʔdá:t   agéʔgʔętsęʔ.
    one-female   my-younger-sibling
    'I have one younger sister.'

2) Degaeyahsé: agéʔgʔętsęʔ.
    two-of-them   my-younger-sibling
    'I have two younger sisters (or one sister and one brother).'

3) Ahsę́   niga:gǫ́:   ageʔgʔętsę́:dǫʔ.
    three   of-them   my-younger-siblings
    'I have three younger sisters (or brothers and sisters).'

For more younger brothers and sisters, simply substitute the appropriate number for *ahsę́* 'three'.

4) Géi   niga:gǫ́:   ageʔgʔętsę́:dǫʔ.
    four   of-them   my-younger-siblings
    'I have four younger brothers and sisters (or sisters).'

Younger brothers:
1) Sayaʔdá:t   agéʔgʔętsęʔ.
    one-male   my-younger-sibling
    'I have one younger brother.'

2) De̱hadiyahsé: agéʔgʔętsęʔ.
    two-males   my-younger-siblings
    'I have two younger brothers.'

3) Ahsę́   ni̱hę:nǫ́:   ageʔgʔętsę́:dǫʔ.
    three   of-male   my-younger-siblings
    'I have three younger brothers.'

For more younger brothers, simply substitute the appropriate number for *ahsę́* 'three'.

7) Ja:dáhk   ni̱hę:nǫ́:   ageʔgʔętsę́:dǫʔ.
    seven   of-males   my-younger-siblings
    'I have seven younger brothers.'

As you can see, talking about one brother or sister, or any set of all brothers, leaves no room for doubt. When discussing two or more sisters, however, the words are the same as for a group of mixed brothers and sisters.

    As you can see, it takes very few new words to talk about brothers and sisters, once you know how to count people.

Deyagyadęhnǫ́:de:ʔ.   'He/she and I are siblings (my brother or sister).'

Wadewayę́stanih

Deyagwadęhnǫ́:de:ʔ.	'They and I are siblings (my brothers or sisters).'
agéʔgʔętsęʔ	'my younger sibling'
ageʔgʔętsę́:dǫʔ	'...siblings'

Né:ʔ nę:gyę́ deyagwadęhnǫ́:de:ʔ, kehjíʔah, heʔgę:ʔę́h hniʔ.

Né:ʔ nę:gyę́ deyagwadęhnǫ́:de:ʔ, hehjíʔah, keʔgę:ʔę́h hniʔ.

Wadewayę́stanih

Wadewayę́stanih

Wadewayęstanih

Here are some other terms for relatives which might prove useful when discussing your family.

kehá:wahk	'my daughter'
hehá:wahk	'my son'
keyá:dreʔ	'my granddaughter'
heyá:dreʔ	'my grandson'
gakeyadreʔsǫ́:ʔǫh	'my grandchildren'
kegę́hjih	'my wife'
hegę́hjih	'my husband'
knohá:ʔah	'my aunt'
knóʔsęh (haknóʔsęh)	'my uncle'
agya:dę́:nǫhk	'my cousin' or 'we two are related (s/he and I)'
ǫgyaʔse:ʔ	'my relative'
agwadęnǫ́hksǫʔ	'my cousins' or 'we all (they and I) are related' or 'my relatives'

To talk about friends, you might want these.

ǫgyá:tsih	'my friend' or 'we two are friends (s/he and I)'
ǫgya:dáoʔ	'my friend' or 'we two are friends (s/he and I)'

The first, *ǫgyá:tsih*, is used for more familiar friends, and can mean 'my girlfriend' or 'my boyfriend'. The second, *ǫgya:dáoʔ*, is used for more formal friendships.

Wadewayę́stanih

S- AND K-/G-
(Just you and I)

You probably recall from earlier conversations that *s-* is often used for 'you' when speaking to one person, and *k-* or *g-* for 'I'.

Syá:sǫh... 'You are called...'
Gyá:sǫh... 'I am called...'

This conversation contains some more pairs like this.

Sá:wiʔ. 'You are carrying it.'
Ká:wiʔ. 'I am carrying it.'

SWA-
(yous)

You may remember from the section on body parts that Cayuga speakers distinguish how many people they are talking to: one, two, or more. Several words in this conversation begin with *swa-*.

swayáʔda:ʔ   'your picture (to three or more people)'

sw<u>a</u>hwa:jí:yaʔ   'your family (to three or more people)'

Swatgáʔdeʔ.   'Yous are numerous.' or 'There are a lot of yous.'

The *swa-* shows that three or more people are included. Can you guess what the word below would mean?

sw<u>a</u>há:wiʔ

PRACTICE

If possible, bring snapshots of your family to class. Using the pictures, tell everyone about your family: how each person is related to you, what his or her name is, and any other information you know how to discuss and care to add, such as age, physical description, or likes and dislikes.

Wadewayę́stanih

NEW VOCABULARY

gahwajiyá:deʔ	'family' (exists)
hayáʔda:ʔ	'his picture'
swayáʔda:ʔ	'your picture' (to two or more people)
agwáyʔada:ʔ	'our picture (theirs and mine)'
swahwa:jí:yaʔ	'your family', 'your relatives'
swahwajiyówanęh	'your family is big' (yous)
dó: niswahwají:yaʔ?	'how big is your family?'
to niyagwahwa:jí:yaʔ	'that is how big our family is'
agwahwajiyowa:nę́:hah	'our family is fairly big (theirs and mine)'
háʔnih	'my father'
hyʔanih	'your father'
knó:haʔ	'my mother'
sanó:haʔ	'your mother'
deyagyadęhnǫ́:de:ʔ	'we two are siblings (s/he and I)', 'my brother', 'my sister'
deyagwadęhnǫdrǫʔ	'we all are siblings (they and I)' 'my brothers and sisters'
gakehjʔiáhsǫʔ	'my older siblings'
kehjíʔah	'my older brother or sister'
hehjíʔah	'my older brother'
kehjíʔah	'my older sister'
agéʔgʔętsęʔ	'I have a younger brother or sister'
keʔgę́:ʔęh	'my younger sister'
heʔgę́:ʔęh	'my younger brother'
seʔgę́:ʔęh	'your younger sister'
heseʔgę́:ʔęh	'your younger brother'
kso:t	'my grandmother or grandfather'
gakéhsotsǫʔ	'my grandparents'
kehso:t	'my grandmother'
hehso:t	'my grandfather'
gwá:dih/gwái	'here'
da…gwá:dih/gwái, dagwái	'over here'
gwé:gǫh	'all'
ó:yaʔ	'other'
hę́ʔhne:ʔ	'also', 'too'

Wadewayę́stanih

dó:	'how'
toh	'there', 'that much'
tó:hah	'almost'
hwędǫ́gwaʔ	'sometime'
swatgáʔdeʔ	'you are many'
ǫgwatgʔadé:ʔah	'there are quite a few of us'
iha:t	'he is standing'
gáet	'they are standing' (females or mixed)
satgę́ʔse:	'have a look', 'watch'
ęgátgʔęse:ʔ	'I will have a look'
sá:wiʔ	'you are carrying it'
ká:wiʔ	'I am carrying it'
ętsá:wiʔ	'you will bring it'
kegę́hjih	'my wife'
hegę́hjih	'my husband'
agwíyaęʔ	'I have a child'
dekní: dewagwiyáęʔ	'I have two children'
X niwagwiyáęʔdǫʔ	'I have X children' (X = three or more)
kehá:wahk	'my daughter'
hehá:wahk	'my son'
keyá:dreʔ	'my granddaughter'
heyá:dreʔ	'my grandson'
gakeyadreʔsǫ́:ʔǫh	'my grandchildren'
knóʔsęh, haknóʔsęh	'my uncle'
knohá:ʔah	'my aunt'
agwadęnǫ́hksǫʔ	'my cousins' (literally, 'we all are related to each other (they and I)')
agya:dę́:nǫhk	'my cousin' (literally, 'we two are related to each other (they and I)')
ǫgyá:jih	'my friend'
ǫgyá:deǫʔ	'my friend'

20

ODWĘNODÁHTAʔ

Wadewayę́stanih

g'adréhda'

Age'dr<u>e</u>hdáę'.

Wadewayęstanih

ODWĘNODÁHTA'

DẸ' HO'DẸ' NIHSAGYEHA'?
(What are you doing?)

This is a question for curious people. When Sam called, Pete wasn't doing much, so he could answer:

A:yẹ:'	gi'	hne:'	tẹ'	gwáhs	sgaho'dẹ'.
it-seems	just	in-fact	not	really	anything

'Oh, nothing much, really, I guess.'

Notice how many particles he uses. The particles are the mark of a good speaker. If he had just said:

Tẹ' sgaho'dẹ'.
not anything
'Nothing.'

Sam may have gotten the message, but the conversation would probably have fallen pretty flat right away. That answer would have been impolite and unnatural. The *a:yẹ:'* 'it seems', and *gwahs* 'really' serve about the same purpose as 'I guess' and 'really' in English. The speaker is not guessing, he is being relaxed and informal. Imagine how you would feel if you called a good friend and said,

'Well, what are you up to these days?'

And your friend said only,

'Nothing.'

In case anyone calls you and asks, in Cayuga, what you yourself are up to, you might want to have some answers ready.

Gagya'doháe gi'.	'As a matter of fact, I am taking a bath.'
Dewagewayẹnha'ǫ gi'.	'As a matter of fact, I am busy.'
Age:kǫ́:ni:.	'I am cooking.'
Gadadrihǫ́nyanih.	'I am reading.'
Gaya'tá' gatgẹ́'seh.	'I am watching a movie.'
Degatnǫhsóhda:s.	'I am cleaning house.'
Geksoháehǫh.	'I am washing dishes.'
Agrího'dẹ'.	'I am working.'
Agid'áǫ hné:' gi'. Ahsgyeht.	'As a matter of fact, I was asleep. You woke me up.'

Wadewayę́stanih

SQ:ʔQH
(How not to worry about being punctual)

Sam did not want to be too precise about the time he planned to pick up Pete, or when dinner would be ready. Instead of saying that it would be six o'clock on the dot:

hyeiʔ 'six'

He added -sǫ́:ʔǫh to the time:

hyeiʔsǫ́:ʔǫh   'sixish' or 'around six'

You can be wishy-washy about any time you want, simply by adding this -sǫ́:ʔǫh to the hour.

degrǫʔsǫ́:ʔǫh 'eightish' or 'around eight o'clock'
jadahksǫ́:ʔǫh 'sevenish' or 'around seven o'clock'

Ę-
(Future, or, promises, promises)

Sam and Pete use a number of words in their telephone conversation which start with ę-. You already know some words which begin with this.

Ęyosdáǫdiʔ.   'It will rain.'
Ęyoʔgrǫ́:diʔ.   'It will snow.'

Ędwadekǫ́:niʔ.   'We all will eat (yous and I).'
Ęyagokwaihséha:k.   'She will have the food cooked.'
Ętsgíhnǫkseʔ.   'You will come to get me.'
Ętgǫ́hnǫkseʔ.   'I will come to get you.'
Ęhsadehsrǫnisʔǫ́hǫ:k. 'You will be ready.'

As you can see, all of the words which begin with ę- talk about something which is going to happen in the future. You will hear a lot of future verbs in conversations around you, if you listen for this sound at the beginning. You will also come across it quite often in the conversations to come.

Practice

Call someone up from the class and talk for a few minutes, all in Cayuga. Ask them how they are, and what they are doing. Be ready with some answers when they ask you the same thing.

NEW VOCABULARY

ahi:ʔ	'I thought'
aodasagyʔoséheʔ	'you would come and visit'
daedwá:do:t	'we all (yous and I) eat here together'
edwadekǫ́:niʔ	'we all (yous and I) will eat'
áodahseʔ	'you should come'
eyagokwaihséha:k	'she will have the food cooked'
etsgíhnokseʔ	'you will come get me'
etgóhnokseʔ	'I will come get you'
esadehsronihsʔǫ́ho:k	'you will be ready'
gagyaʔdoháe	'I am taking a bath'
gatgę́ʔseh	'I am watching'
agídʔaoh	'I am asleep'
ahsgyeht	'you woke me up'
age:kǫ́:ni:	'I am cooking'
dewagewayenháʔoh	'I am busy'
ageʔdrehdáę̨ʔ	'I have a car'
tę́ʔ dʔeagʔedréhdaęʔ	'I don't have a car'
giʔ	'actually', 'in fact'
hne:ʔ	'in fact'
diʔ	'so', 'then'
seʔ	'just'
-sǫ́:ʔoh	'-ish' as in *hyeiʔsǫ́:ʔoh* 'sixish'
dęʔ hoʔdęʔ nihsagyehaʔʔ	'what are you doing?'
tę́ʔ sgahoʔdęʔ	'nothing'
dęʔ hoʔdęʔ ihse:ʔʔ	'what do you want?'
haoʔ dʔenyóh	'OK'
gadadrihǫ́nyanih.	'I am reading'
gayáʔtaʔ	'movie'
degatnohsóhda:s, degatnohsáhsnyeʔ	'I am cleaning house'
geksoháehoh	'I am washing dishes'
gadeʔdrehdóhae	'I am washing my car'
agríhoʔdeʔ	'I am working'

21

SEKSÁHQ:!

Wadewayęstanih

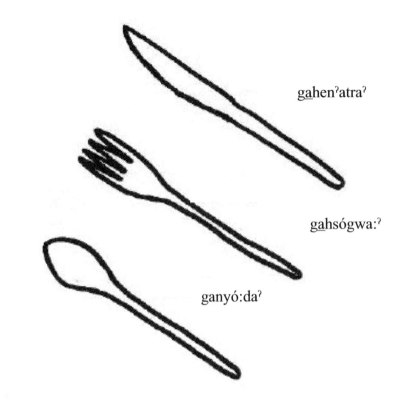

gahen'atra'

gahsógwa:'

ganyó:da'

deyowidrá:teh

ganá'johgwa'

deyọdeksá'drahkwa'

Wadewayęstanih

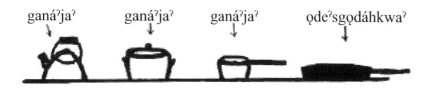
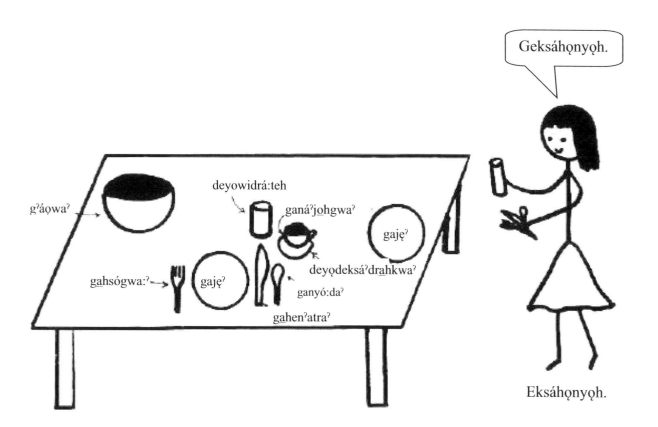

Wadewayę́stanih

GAKWAʔ

degáhswaʔne:t

ohya:jiʔ hoʔdę́ʔ
degáhswaʔne:t

ohyá:jiʔ

ojíkeʔdaʔ

deyóhsait

nawę́ʔdaʔ

onǫ́ʔgwaʔ

owidrá:taʔ

onáʔda:ʔ

onáʔda:ʔ

ohǫ́nʔadaʔ

Wadewayę́stanih

gwá'yǫ'

gwísgwis

sóhǫ:t

gwísgwis

sóhǫ:t

onráhda'

NEW VOCABULARY

seksáhǫ:	'set the table'
geksáhǫnyǫh	'I am setting the table'
eksáhǫnyǫh	'she is setting the table'
haksáhǫnyǫh	'he is setting the table'
gahenʔatraʔ	'knife'
gahsógwa:ʔ	'fork'
ganyó:daʔ	'spoon'
ganáʔjohgwaʔ	'cup'
deyǫdeksáʔdrahkwaʔ	'saucer'
deyowidrá:teh	'glass', 'tumbler'
gajęʔ	'dish'
gʔáǫwaʔ	'bowl', 'butter dish', 'trough'
ganáʔjaʔ	'pot', 'pan', 'kettle', 'pail'
ǫdeʔsgǫdáhkwaʔ	'frying pan'
degáhswaʔne:t	'pie'
ohyá:jiʔ	'blueberry'
ojíkeʔdaʔ	'salt'
deyóhsait	'pepper'
nawę́ʔdaʔ	'sugar'
onǫ́ʔgwaʔ	'milk'
owidrá:taʔ	'butter'
onáʔda:ʔ	'bread'
ohǫ́nʔadaʔ	'potato'
gwáʔyǫʔ	'rabbit'
gwísgwis	'pig'
sóhǫ:t	'turkey'
onráhdaʔ	'leaf'

22

DWADE:KǪ:NIH

Wadewayę́stanih

Wadewayę́stanih

Wadewayęstanih

DWADE:KǪ:NIH

Wadewayęstanih

Wadewayę́stanih

Wadewayę́stanih

Wadewayę́stanih

<u>Dasha:</u>
(How to get what you want)

You may have noticed that Pete is not always very subtle or polite. To ask for things at the table, you can either just name what you want, or ask someone to pass it.

Onaʔdá:ʔ dasha:.	or	Dashá: onáʔda:ʔ.
bread pass-it		pass-it bread
'<u>Please</u> pass the bread.'		'<u>Please</u> pass the bread.'

If you want something else passed, just substitute the word for it in place of *onáʔda:ʔ*.

_____ giʔ gyę́:ʔ hníʔ dasha:.
'*Please* pass the _____, too.'

Some things you might want passed are:

ohnaʔ	'gravy' or 'grease'
ojíkeʔdaʔ	'salt'
deyóhsait	'pepper'
nawę́ʔdaʔ	'sugar'
oʔwáhǫh	'meat'
ohǫ́nʔadaʔ	'potatoes'
ohyá:griʔ	'fruit juice'
onǫ́ʔgwaʔ	'milk'
owidrá:taʔ	'butter'

If you would like to ask for several things as once, you can do it like this:

Dashá:	onaʔdá:ʔ	owidra:táʔ	hniʔ.
pass	bread	butter	too
'<u>Please</u> pass the bread and butter.'			

You can substitute any food items for the words *onáʔda:ʔ* and *owidrá:taʔ* in this sentence.

TREHS/GYÓ:DOʔK
(How to become unpopular in a hurry)

If you would like to complain, a good word to know is *trehs*, 'too' or the phrase *jiʔ do:s*. You can see how it works by comparing the sentences here.

Ojikeʔdá:weht.	'It is salty.'
Tréhs jiʔ do:s ojikeʔdá:weht.	'It is too salty.'
Nawę́ʔdaweht.	'It is sweet.'
Tréhs nawę́ʔdaweht.	'It is too sweet.'
Oʔdáihę:.	'It is hot.'
Tréhs oʔdáihę:.	'It is too hot.'
Onáʔnu:.	'It is cold.'
Tréhs onáʔnu:.	'It is too cold.'

If your complaint runs in the opposite direction, you can use *gyó:doʔk* 'it is lacking'.

ojíkeʔdaʔ	'salt'
Gyo:dóʔk ojíkeʔdaʔ.	'It needs salt.'
nawę́ʔdaʔ	'sugar'
Gyo:dóʔk nawę́ʔdaʔ.	'It needs sugar.'
deyóhsait	'pepper'
Gyo:dóʔk deyóhsait.	'It needs pepper.'

S(A)-… GĘH?   AG- / AGE- / AK-…
(Some questions and answers just between you and me)

    Sam, Pete, and Lila ask a number of questions in this conversation. Notice how the verbs begin differently in the questions and answers. The questions begin with *s-* or *sa-*, while the answers begin with *ak-* or *age-*. The *s-* or *sa-* means 'you', and the *ak-* or *ag-* or *age-* means 'I'.

Sadehsrǫníhs'ǫ gęh?
you-are-ready   ?
'Are you ready?'

Ęhę́', agadehsrǫnihs'ǫh.
yes,   I-am-ready
'Yes, I am ready.'

Sadǫhswe'dá:nih gęh?
you-are-hungry   ?
'Are you hungry?'

Ęhę́', agadǫhswé'danih.
yes,   I-am-hungry
'Yes, I am hungry.'

Sá:ga's gęh   sóhǫ:t?
you-like   ? turkey
'Do you like turkey?'

Ęhę́', agé:ga's.
yes, I-like
'Yes, I like it.'

(The change from 'you' to 'I' often shifts the voiceless vowels and the stress, because it adds another syllable to the front. You may remember that only odd-numbered vowels before H can be whispered.)

    Here are a few more questions and answers you can use.

Sahdá'ǫh gęh?   Saidręhdá:s   gęh?
you-are-full ?   you-are-sleepy ?
'Are you full?'   'Are you sleepy?'

Ęhę́', agáhd'aǫh.   Ęhę́', agidręhdá:s.
'Yes, I am full.'   'Yes, I am sleepy.'

OGÁ'ǪH
(How to compliment the cook)

As you saw in an earlier conversation, you can use the verb *ogá:ǫh* 'it is delicious' with any food or drink.

Oga'ǫh   nę:gyęh   odi:.
it-is-delicious   this   tea
'This tea is delicious.'

Oga'ǫh   nę:gyęh   o'wáhǫh.
it-is-delicious   this   meat
'This meat is delicious.'

In the dinner conversation, Pete incorporates the food right into the verb 'delicious'.

Ona'dá:g'aǫh. 'The pie (or bread) is delicious.'

Here are some more compliments you might like to have in reserve. The last two syllables, -*ga'ǫh* or -*g'aǫh* are the part which means 'delicious'.

O'wahaga'ǫh nę:gyęh.	'This meat is delicious.'
Ohǫn'adag'áǫh nę:gyęh.	'These potatoes are delicious.'
Ohnegagri'traga'ǫh nę:gyęh.	'This soup is delicious.'
O'nhǫhsaga'ǫh nę:gyęh.	'These eggs are delicious.'
Ohyag'áǫh nę:gyęh.	'This fruit is delicious.'
Oditraga'ǫh nę:gyęh.	'This tea is delicious.'

Wadewayę́stanih

Ę̱-
(More about your future)

You may have detected some more future verbs in this conversation, from the *ę-* at the beginning of the word.

Ę̱hsadekǫ́nyahna'.	'You will go and eat.'
Ę́:ge:k.	'I will eat it.'
Ę̱sgahdę́:di'.	'I will leave/go back/go home.'
Ęyónise'.	'It will be a long time.'
Dę̱sgátahahk.	'I will walk back.' or 'I will walk again.'
Hę̱sge:'.	'I will go there again.' or 'I will go back there.'
Dę̱tsé' é:'.	'You will come back again.'
Ha'dę̱gakwáę̱da'.	'The meal will settle.'

Watch for more future verbs in the conversations to come. They are very common and easy to spot.

AHGWIH
(Don't)

To tell someone **not** to do something, you can use the word *ahgwíh* with future verbs (without their glottal stops at the end).

Ahgwíh ę̱hse:k.	'Don't eat it.'	Ahgwíh ę̱hsnégehah.	'Don't drink it.'
Ahgwíh ę̱hsrih.	'Don't spill it.'	Ahgwíh dę̱hsriht.	'Don't break it.'
Ahgwíh ę̱hsá:gyę:.	'Don't sit down.'	Ahgwíh ę̱sę́:da'.	'Don't go to sleep.'
Ahgwíh ę̱hsá'sęht.	'Don't drop it.'	Ahgwíh ę̱hsé:tight.	'Don't get it dirty.'
Ahgwíh tó nę̱hsye:.	'Don't do that.'	Ahgwíh ę̱sáhdǫ't.	'Don't lose it.'
Ahgwíh ę̱hsahdę́:dih.	'Don't go away.'	Ahgwíh ę̱hsídagra'.	'Don't fall.'
Ahgwíh ę̱hsátgahtoh.	'Don't look.'	Ahgwíh ę̱sánǫhya'k.	'Don't get hurt.'
Ahgwíh ę̱sán'akwę̱h.	'Don't get mad.'	Ahgwíh ę̱sahsdáę'.	'Don't cry.'
Ahgwíh n'tó hę̱hse:.	'Don't go there.'	Ahgwíh ę̱hsádatre:.	'Don't cut yourself.'

To make it more emphatic, you can add *gwa'* or *gwa' tsǫ:* 'just'.

Ahgwígwa' ę̱hsá:gyę:!	'Don't you sit down!'
Ahgwígwa' tsǫ: ę̱hseniksé'd'ę̱goh!	'Just don't you get a swelled belly!'

TĘ^ʔ D^ʔE-...
(How to be negative)

This conversation has some more negative verbs, as you can see from the sequence *tę́ʔ dʔe-* ...

Tę́ʔ dʔegágęhjih.   'It is not old.'
  (Compare *Gagę́hjih.* 'It is old'.)

Tę́ʔ dʔeagʔedréhdaę́ʔ. 'I don't have a car.'
  (Compare *Ageʔdrę̱hdáę́ʔ.*   'I have a car'.)

Tę́ʔ ní:ʔ dʔea:gé:gaʔs. 'I don't like it.'
  (Compare *Agé:gaʔs.* 'I like it'.)

Tę́ʔ ní:ʔ dʔege:s. 'I don't eat it.'
  (Compare *Í:ge:s.* 'I eat it'.)

(Recall that the *ní:ʔ* just emphasizes the speaker, in contrast to others, having a translation something like 'as for me, in contrast to you or other people'.)

Here are some more negative verbs you can probably use when people ask the questions on the last page.

Tę́ʔ dʔeagadehsrǫ́ni̱hsʔǫh.   'I am not ready.'
Tę́ʔ dʔeagadǫhsweʔdá:nih.   'I am not hungry.'
Tę́ʔ ní:ʔ dʔea:gé:gaʔs.   'As for me, I don't like the taste of it.'
Tę́ʔ dʔeaga̱hdáʔǫh.   'I am not full.'
Tę́ʔ dʔeagidrę́hda:s.   'I am not sleepy.'

As you listen to a good speaker pronounce these words, notice again that the syllable *dʔea-* tends to be reduced almost to *dʔa-* in normal, fast speech.

TĘ' NI:'... D'EGĘ:
(How to defend your identity)

The negative *tę' d'e-* is used only with verbs. Look at the sentence Pete uses when he refuses the salad.

Tę'   ní:'   gwa'yǫ'   d'egę:.
not   I   rabbit   not-is-it
'I'm no rabbit.'

You can substitute the name of any person or kind of animal or object for *gwa'yǫ'* in this sentence and make another perfectly good Cayuga sentence.

Tę' ní:' gwisgwís d'egę:.
'I'm no pig.'

Tę' ní:' so:wá:s d'egę:.
'I'm no dog.'

Tę' ní:' sohǫ́:t d'egę:.
'I'm no turkey.'

Tę' ní:' Sám d'egę:.
'I'm not Sam.'

Instead of *ni:'* 'I', you could substitute the emphatic *ni:s* 'you'.

Tę' ní:s gwa'yǫ' d'egę:.
'You're no rabbit.'

(It might be a challenge to try to work one of these sentences into a conversation.)

PRACTICE

Let the group divide into pairs. Each pair can then create a skit entirely in Cayuga about a guest coming to dinner, then present it to the class.

NEW VOCABULARY

sadehsrọníhsʔọh	'you are ready'
agadehsrọ́nihsʔọh	'I am ready'
tẹ́ʔ dʔeagadehsrọníhsʔọh	'I am not ready'
sadọhsweʔdá:nih	'you are hungry'
agadọhswéʔdanih	'I am hungry'
tẹ́ʔ dʔeagadọhsweʔdá:nih	'I am not hungry'
sá:gaʔs	'you like the taste'
agé:gaʔs	'I like the taste'
tẹ́ʔ dʔea:gé:gaʔs	'I don't like the taste of it'
sahdáʔọh	'you are full'
agáhdʔaọh	'I am full'
tẹ́ʔ dʔeagahdáʔọh	'I am not full'
saidrẹhdá:s	'you are sleepy'
agidrẹhdá:s	'I am sleepy'
tẹ́ʔ dʔeagidrẹ́hda:s	'I'm not sleepy'
wáʔne:ʔ	'now', 'today'
í:ge:s	'I eat it'
tẹ́ʔ dʔege:s	'I don't eat it'
ẹ́:ge:k	'I will eat it.'
ẹwágahdaʔ	'I will be full.'
ẹhsadekọ́nyahnaʔ	'you will go eat'
sọgá:ʔah	'anyone', 'someone'
agadekọ́:ni:	'I have eaten'
dwade:kọ́:nih	'let's all eat'
adi:dwá:dọ:t	'we all ate together (yous and I)'
dedwá:dọ:t	'let's eat together'
dagwá:dih	'over here', 'this side'
gyokwái	'food is cooked there'
okwái	'the food is cooked'
gakwí:yoʔ	'nice food'
gakwágʔaọh	'delicious food'
haʔdẹgakwáẹdaʔ	'the food will settle'
gokwayẹdéiʔọ:	'she is a good cook' (literally, 'she knows food')
gonaʔda:yẹdéiʔọ:	'she is a good baker' (literally, 'she knows bread')

Wadewayę́stanih

snʔada:k	'eat the bread'
onaʔdá:gʔaǫh	'delicious bread'
oʔwahagáʔǫh	'delicious meat'
ohǫnʔadágʔaǫh	'delicious potatoes'
oʔnhǫhsagáʔǫh	'delicious eggs'
ohyágʔaǫh	'delicious fruit'
nya:wę́ giʔ gyę:ʔ adi:dwá:dǫ:t	'thank you that we all ate together (yous and I)'
gǫhnǫ́:kseʔ	'I have come after you'
agǫhó:wiʔ	'I told you'
sa:gyahdę́:diʔ	'we two left (s/he and I)'
hekní:yǫh	'let's both go in'
a:yǫkní:nya:k	'we two would marry'
agagyʔadoháesiʔ	'I finished washing my body', 'bathing'
gagę́hjih	'it is old'
tę́ʔ dʔegágęhjih	'it is not old'
tę́ʔ dʔáǫ a:getséiʔ	'I cannot find it'
o:nę́ ęsgahdę́:diʔ	'I'll go home now'
a:yá:węh	'it is hoped'
ęyónisheʔ	'it will be a long time'
hęwágʔidrǫ:ʔ	'it will last me'
dęsgátahahk	'I will walk back'
sǫga:ʔah	'someone', 'anyone'
segę́hjih	'your wife'
degyégahne:ʔ	'she is looking'
hęska:ʔ	'I will take it away again'
gwáhs waʔhétsǫ:	'just now'
hęsé:nǫ:t	'I will feed him there'
śę ní:yǫ:	'how much'
ǫgwa:tsé:nęʔ	'our pet'
tę́ʔ... dʔegę:	'it is not true that...'
dwagrihowánahdǫh	'I think much of it'
godi:howanáhdǫh	'they think the most of it' (females or mixed)
dasá:	'pass it to me'
oʔwáhǫh	'meat'
watǫnʔadǫ́:daʔk	'baked potatoes'
gajíhyo:t	'homemade pan bread'

Wadewayę́stanih

degáhswaʔne:t	'pie'
ohnaʔ	'gravy'
enráhda:s	'lettuce'
oáʔw<u>i</u>hsdaʔ	'peelings'
ęhsátna:	'you will put grease on'
ojihkeʔdá:weht	'it is salty'
nawę́ʔdaweht	'it is sweet'
oʔdá<u>i</u>hę:	'it is hot'
onáʔnu:	'it is cold'
ęhsęniksé'dʔęgoʔ	'you will get a swelled belly'
gaksáhe:ʔ	'dish sitting there'
sędę́o	'you are fortunate'
ahgwih	'don't'
ahgwígwaʔtsǫ: (ahgwih gwaʔ tsǫ:)	'just don't…'
shęh ní:yǫ:	'how much', 'how many'

23

SANAHSGWAĘʔ GĘH SGA̲HOʔDĘːʔĘH?

Wadewayę́stanih

SANAHSGWAĘ? GĘH?

Wadewayę́stanih

SANAHSGWAĘ’ GĘH SGA̲HO’DĘ:’ĘH?

Wadewayęstanih

Wadewayę́stanih

321

Wadewayęstanih

Dehonʔinhęhjędǫ́hǫh.

Hahnih.

Hadę́ganyahs.

Odrę́:no:t.

Godrę́:nǫ:t.

Hodrę́:nǫ:t.

Wadewayę́stanih

HA-/E-/GA-
HA-/Ǫ-/WA-
(He/she/it)

Cayuga speakers generally refer to wild animals as 'it', but often to pets, especially pets they know well, as 'he' or 'she'. Notice that Dave says:

Dęˀ diˀ hoˀdę́ˀ gaya:sǫ́ neˀ so:wa:s?
'What is <u>its</u> name, the dog?'

Pete replies,

Rovér <u>h</u>ayá:sǫh.
'<u>His</u> name is Rover.'

Dave picks up the 'he' and uses 'he' for Rover from then on.

If a verb with 'he' begins with *ha-*, and the same verb with 'she' begins with *e-*, then the verb with 'it' will begin with *ga-*.

hayá:sǫh   'he is called'
eyá:sǫh   'she is called'
gayá:sǫh   'it is called'

Hahnih.   'He is barking.'
Ehnih.   'She is barking.'
Gahnih.   'It is barking.'

nihayˀadóˀdę: 'what he looks like'
niyeyˀadóˀdę: 'what she looks like'
nigayˀadóˀdę: 'what it looks like'

You will find it is very easy to change a verb from 'it' to 'she' to 'he' just by changing the first syllable, from *ga-* to *e-* to *ha-*, or the second.

Some verbs follow a different pattern. You can see this by looking for the form with 'she' or the form with 'it'. If the verb with 'she' begins with *ǫ-*, then the verb for 'it' will begin with *wa-* and the verb with 'he' will have *ha-*, as before.

Hadę́ganyahs.   'He bites.'
Ǫdę́ganyahs.   'She bites.'
Wadę́ganyahs. 'It bites.'

If you know the 'she' form for these, or the 'it' form, it is easy to make up the others, just by changing the beginning, from *ǫ-* 'she' to *wa-* 'it' to *ha-* 'he'.

Wadewayęstanih

SO:WA:S

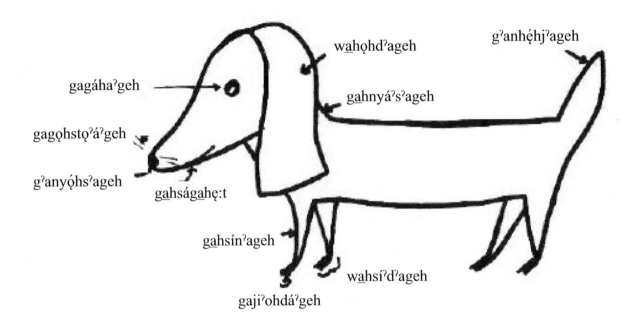

Wadewayęstanih

Practice

Just as with people, the body parts of animals do not usually occur all by themselves. The possessor is referred to. Instead of talking about 'a leg', Cayuga speakers normally say 'its leg', 'his leg', 'her leg', 'my leg', 'your leg', etc. As you can see, the body parts of the dog on the last page all begin with *ga-* or *wa-* 'its'. Now that you know the system, see whether you can talk about the parts of a dog that you know and love, using 'his' or 'her'. If the form for 'it' begins with *ga-*, then you can use *e-* for 'her' and *ha-* for 'his'. If the form for 'it' begins with *wa-*, then you can use *ǫ-* for 'her' and *ha-* for 'his'.

gagáha'geh	'(on) its eye'
egáha'geh	'(on) her eye'
hagáha'geh	'(on) his eye'

wahǫhd'ageh	'(on) its ear'
ǫhǫhd'ageh (ehǫhd'ageh)	'(on) her ear'
hahǫhd'ageh	'(on) his ear'

Now figure out the others on your own.

You can often tell what kind of a pet people have, or how they feel about it, by the beginning of its name. Pete's cat is named after whiskers, *ogǫ́hstǫ'a'*. To show that it was specifically male, female, or neuter, he could have changed the beginning of the name.

Gagǫ́hstǫ'a'	neuter
Egǫ́hstǫ'a'	for a female
Hagǫ́hstǫ'a'	for a male

Wadewayę́stanih

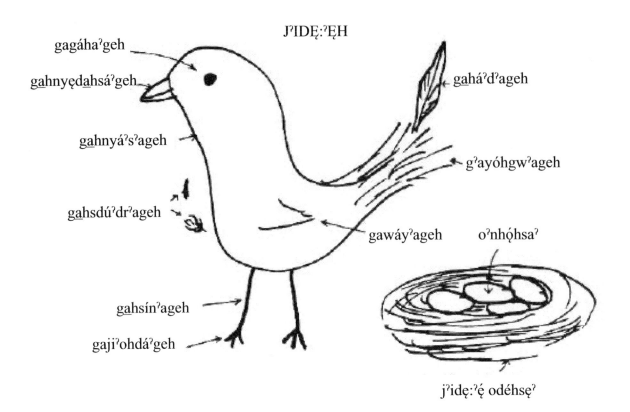

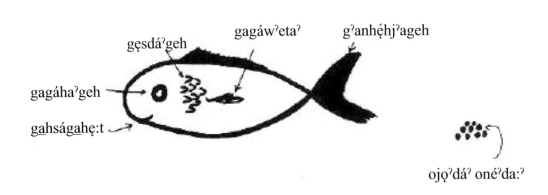

DĘˀ NI:YOHT?
(Why?)

Dave uses a new question in this conversation.

Dęˀ ni:yóht shęh hnyǫˀǫhneha:ˀ?
'Why is it a White (name)?'

Dęˀ ni:yóht shęh né:ˀ gaya:sǫh?
'Why is it called that?'

The *dęˀ ni:yoht* is used to ask 'why?'. As with all questions, *dęˀ ni:yoht* questions remain level in tone at the end, instead of dropping to a lower pitch.

Very often with questions like these, the particle *diˀ* 'then' is added after the first word to show that the question relates to what has just been said.

Dęˀ diˀ ni:yóht shęh hnyǫˀǫhneha:ˀ?
'Well, why is it a White (name)?'

Dęˀ diˀ ni:yóht shęh né:ˀ gaya:sǫh?
'Then why is it called that?'

A LITTLE MORE INCORPORATION

You can see a little more incorporation in this conversation. The root *-hsęn-* is part of several different words.

Hohsęnaęˀ.	'He has a <u>name</u>.'
Ohsęnaęˀ.	'It has a <u>name</u>.'
Tęˀ dˀewadadehsęnaędí:.	'It doesn't know its <u>name</u>.'
A:yagwahsę́:nǫˀ.	'We should give it a <u>name</u>.'

You can see the root *-nahsgw-* 'domestic animal' in part of several different words as well.

Sanáhsgwaęˀ.	'You have a pet.'
Aknáhsgwaęˀ.	'I have a pet.'

Specific words for animals, such as *só:wa:s* and *dagu:s* do not get incorporated. Instead, <u>*-nahsgw-*</u> is incorporated in their place.

Ganasgwiˀyó:	neˀ	só:wa:s.	'It is a good dog.'
it-animal-good	the	dog	

Wadewayę́stanih

HO-/GO-/O-
(He/she/it)

Some verbs use a different set of pronouns for he/she/it. Compare these words:

Hohsę́naę̓.	'He has a name.'
Gohsę́naę̓.	'She has a name.'
Ohsę́naę̓.	'It has a name.'
Hó:ga̓s.	'He likes to eat it.'
Gó:ga̓s.	'She likes to eat it.'
Ó:ga̓s.	'It likes to eat it.'
Hohníhsgǫ:.	'He barks a lot.'
Gohníhsgǫ:.	'She barks a lot.'
Ohníhsgǫ:.	'It barks a lot.'

Usually, if a verb uses *ho-* for 'he', then it will use *go-* for 'she' and *o-* for 'it'. As you can see, it is very easy to learn to shift from one to the other, simply by changing the first sound.

If *hode:kǫ́:ni:* means 'he has eaten', how would you say 'she has eaten'? How about 'it has eaten'?

Practice

Go around the room, asking each person:

Sanahsgwaę̓ gęh sgaho̓dę́:̓ęh?	'Do you have some kind of a pet?'

Answers should be something like:

Ęhę́̓, dagú:s aknáhsgwaę̓.	'Yes, I have a cat.'

Each person should substitute the appropriate animal for *dagu:s*. If you feel you do not have a very interesting pet, go ahead and invent a better answer.

Next, ask the pet's name:

Dę̓ di̓ ho̓dę́̓ gaya:sǫ́ ne̓ dagu:s?	(or whatever pet was mentioned)

Other questions you might ask are these:

Do: niya:gá̓ satse:nę̓?	'How big is your pet?'

Dęʔ hoʔdęʔ snǫ:dę́ satse:nęʔ?   'What do you feed your pet?'
Dęʔ hoʔdę́ʔ nigayʔadoʔdę́: satse:nęʔ?   'What does your pet look like?'
Sanahsgwi:yo: gęh?   'Is it a nice pet?' or 'Is your pet nice?'

Wadewayę́stanih

DO: NIGĘ:NQ:?

sgaya'dá:t dagu:s   sgaya'dá:t só:wa:s

degadiyahsé: dagu:s   degadiyahsé: só:wa:s

ahsę́ nigę:nǫ́: dagu:s

géi nigę:nǫ́: só:wa:s

NEW VOCABULARY

ojǫ́ʔdaʔ	'fish'
ganyáhdę:	'turtle'
jʔidę́:ʔęh	'bird'
ojiʔnǫ́:waʔ	'bug'
sá:no:	'raccoon'
drę́:na:	'skunk'
dagu:s	'cat'
gwáʔyǫʔ	'rabbit'
só:wa:s	'dog'
jinó:wę:	'mouse'
osáisdaʔ	'snake'
satsé:nęʔ	'your pet'
age:tsé:nęʔ	'my pet'
aanáhsgwaęʔ	'you have a pet'
aknáhsgwaęʔ	'I have a pet'
gayá:sǫh...	'its name is...'
hohsę́:naęʔ	'he has a name'
gohsę́:naęʔ	'she has a name'
ohsę́:naęʔ	'it has a name'
tę́ʔ dewadadehsęnaędí:	'it doesn't know its name'
a:yagwahsé:nǫʔ	'we all should give it a name (they and I)'
ganahsgwí:yo:	'it is a nice animal'
ganahsgwahetgęʔ	'it is a bad animal'
ogǫ́hstǫʔaʔ	'whiskers'
degagǫhstǫ́ʔe:s	'its whiskers are long'
hnyǫʔǫhnéha:ʔ	'white style'
dehadawę́:nyeh	'he wanders'
iseʔ	'he is going'
hahníh	'he is barking'
ehníh	'he is barking'
gahníh	'it is barking'
dehonʔinhęhjędǫ́hǫh	'he is wagging his tail'
hadę́ganyahs	'he bites'
odrę́:no:t	'it is singing'

godrę:no:t	'she is singing'
hodrę:no:t	'he is singing'
dę? ho?dę? nigay?ado?dę:?	'what does it look like?'
owahgwáǫnyǫ?	'spots'
dę? ní:yoht?	'why?'
do: niya:ga??	'how big is it?'
nę:hah, gagowané:hah	'fairly big'
níya:gú:?uh	'it is small'
dę? ho?dę? snǫ:dęh?	'what do you feed it?'
knǫ́:dęh	'I feed it'
oji?nǫwahé?da?	'worm'
ohé:tsa?	'sausage'
awęnohgra?sǫ́:?ǫh	'weeds', 'grasses'
o?nhę́hja?	'a tail'
g?anhę́hj?ageh	'its tail' (for an animal)
gagáha?geh	'(on) its eye'
wahǫhd?ageh	'(on) its ear'
gahnyá?s?ageh	'(on) its neck'
gagǫhstǫ?á?geh	'(on) its whiskers'
gahsín?ageh	'(on) its leg'
wahsí?d?ageh	'(on) its paw'
gaji?ohdá?geh	'(on) its claw'
gahságahę:t	'its mouth'
gahnyędahsá?geh	'(on) its beak'
hahnyęd?ageh	'(on) his beak'
g?ayóhgw?ageh	'(on) its tail' (bird's)
gawáy?ageh	'(on) its wing'
gahsdú?dr?ageh	'(on) its feather'
gaha?d?ageh	'(on) its tail feather'
o?nhǫ́hsa?	'egg'
oné?da:?	'fish egg', 'caviar', 'roe'
odéhsę?	'its nest'
gęsdá?geh	'(on) its scales'
gagáw?eta?, egágawe:?	'fin'
tę́? sgaho?dę? d?eǫ́ihǫ:t	'it is useless', 'there is no reason'

Wadewayęstanih

24

O'DRÉHDATGI'

g'adréhda'

g'adréhda'

Wadewayę́stanih

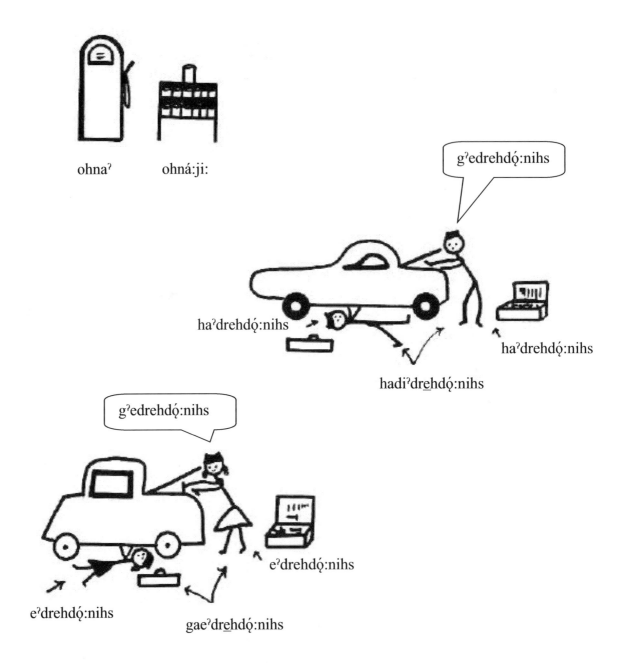

Wadewayę́stanih

OʔDRÉHDATGIʔ

Wadewayę́stanih

Wadewayę́stanih

GO̧-/SG-/SK-/HE-/KE-/HEHS-/SE-...
(How to find out who does what to whom)

Look at these words:

Go̧yę:déi.	'I know you.'
Heyę:déi.	'I know him.'
Sgyędéi.	'You know me.'
Hehsyę:déi.	'You know him.'

The 'know' part of these words is *-yędei*. As you can see, the rest of each verb tells <u>who</u> knows who.

Go̧-	'I/you'
He-	'I/him'
Sg- or Sk-	'You/me'
Hehs-	'You/him'

Cayuga is very different from English in this way. Just one word is a whole statement by itself. Here are some more verbs with *-yędei* you might use:

Keyę:déi	'I know her'	Ke-	'I/her'
Sheyę:déi	'You know her'	Se- or She-	'You/her'

Practice

Practice asking each person in the group one of the questions below, indicating someone else in the room, or a picture. Answer anyone who asks you one of these questions with an appropriate answer, giving a name where the blank is.

Sgyędei gę̨h?	Ęhę́ʔ, go̧yę:déi. --------------- sya:so̧h.
Hehsyę:dei gę̨h?	Ęhę́ʔ, heyę:déi. --------------- haya:so̧h.
Sheyę:dei gę̨h?	Ęhę́ʔ, keyę:déi. --------------- eya:so̧h.

Next, try asking the same questions, but answer in the negative.

Sgyędei gę̨h?	Tę́ʔ. Tę́ʔ gwahs o̧:we dʔego̧yędéi.
So̧: ni:s gwahs nʔaht?	--------------- gyá:so̧h.

(You may notice that some speakers pronounce this verb with I: at the end instead of EI. They would say, for example, *sgyędi:* instead of *sgyędei*. Both are used and both are correct).

Hehsyę:dei gę̨h?	Tę́ʔ. Tę́ʔ gwáhs o̧:wé deheyędéi.
	So̧: diʔ hne:ʔ gwahs nʔaht?
	--------------- hayá:so̧h.

Seyę:dei gęh?   Tę̂ʔ. Tę̂ʔ gwahs ǫ:we dʔekeyędéi.
                                 Sǫ: hne:ʔ gwahs nʔaht?
                                 --------------- eyá:sǫh.

Here are some commands with *hehs-* ('you/him') and *she-* ('you/her'). Remember that all commands contain 'you'.

Hehsnǫ:t.	'Feed him.'	Shé:nǫ:t.	'Feed her.'
Hehsnéganǫ:t.	'Give him a drink.'	Shehnéganǫ:t.	'Give her a drink.'
Hehsyáʔdihsa:k.	'Look for him.'	Seyáʔdihsa:k.	'Look for her.'
Hehsró:wih.	'Tell him.'	Sehó:wih.	'Tell her.'
Hehsyénawaʔs.	'Help him.'	Seyénawaʔs.	'Help her.'

(Some speakers say *hetró:wih* for 'tell him' and *hejénawaʔs* for 'help him'. All are correct.)

TGÁ:GǪ:T
("Yahafta")

The word *tgá:gǫ:t* 'it is necessary' is very useful. You can combine it with any future verb to add the meaning 'must' or 'have to'.

Tga:gǫ́:t   tó   hę́:ge:ʔ.
it-is-necessary there   I-will-go
'I have to go there.'

Tga:gǫ́:t   tó   nęhsye:ʔ.
it-is-necessary there   you-will-do
'You must do it.'

Here are some more *tgá:gǫ:t* expressions you might use.

Tgá:gǫ:t ęgahdę́:diʔ.
'I must go away.'

Tgá:gǫ:t gę ęhsahdę́:diʔ?
'Must you leave?' or 'Do you have to leave?'

NEW VOCABULARY

sʔadrehdahetgʔęse:, esaʔdrehdáhetgęs	'you have car trouble'
agéʔdreʔ	'I am driving'
atgá:daʔ	'it stopped'
satnʔǫhda:	'get in'
ęhsatnʔǫhdá:	'you will get in'
ęgatnʔǫhdáhgoʔ	'I will get out'
dasknʔǫhda:	'you gave me a ride down here'
ęhéhnǫksaʔ	'I will go get him'
ęhé:gęʔ	'I will see him'
heyę:déi	'I know him'
tęʔ dʔeheyędéi	'I do not know him'
gǫyę:déi	'I know you'
tęʔ dʔegǫyędéi	'I do not know you'
hehsyę:déi	'you know him'
sgyędéi	'you know me'
gǫhsęnaędéi	'I know your name'
haʔdrehdǫ́:nihs	'mechanic' (literally, 'he repairs cars')
eʔdrehdǫ́:nihs	'mechanic' (literally, 'she repairs cars')
gaeʔdrehdǫ́:nihs	'mechanics' (literally, 'they repair cars' (females or mixed))
hadiʔdrehdǫ́:nihs	'mechanics' (literally, 'they repair cars' (males only))
tęʔ dehadʔidrehdǫ́:nihs	'they do not repair cars' (males only)
gʔedrehdǫ́:nihs	'I repair cars'
gyę́:gwaʔ	'if'
gʔisęh	'maybe'
nhé:yoht, tsaʔsa:gyę:ʔ	'suddenly'
gwahs ǫ́:weh	'really'
gadó:gę:	'together'
ohnaʔ	'gasoline' (literally, 'grease')
ohná:ji:	'oil'
deyohé:hdahkwaʔ	'horn'
ganaʔjagę́ʔdo:ʔ	'radiator'
gajísdotaʔ	'light'
gʔadrehdáʔ gajísdotaʔ	'headlight' (literally, 'it light-stands up')

Wadewayę́stanih

ę'nísga:'	'wheel'
g'adrehdá' onhóhah	'car door'
knó'sęh	'my uncle'
hyanó'sęh	'your uncle'
hehsá:wahk	'your son'
ǫtnegahní:nǫh	'bar' (literally, 'one sells liquid')
hogyé:sęh	'he is cheap'
agyadadrihǫnyę́:nih	'we two go to school (you and I)'
a:setsę́i'	'you should find'
a:yesay'adágenha'	'she should help you'
e:hya'dagé:nha'	'someone (male) should help you'
o'dréhdatgi'	'a broken down car', 'a bad car' (literally, 'a dirty car')
hehsyénawa's	'help him'
seyénawa's	'help her'
hehsró:wih	'tell him'
sehó:wih	'tell her'
hehsyá'dihsa:k	'look for him'
seyá'dihsa:k	'look for her'
hehsnéganǫ:t	'give him a drink'
sehsnéganǫ:t	'give her a drink'
dę' ho'dę' a:yę́:' n'a:węh?	'what seems to have happened?'
a:yę:' gi' gyę́:' do:gę́hs desęn'ǫáesdǫh	'you sure are using your head, bamboozling'
nya:wę́ gi' gyę́:' sę nyó:' daskn'ǫ́hda:	'thanks for the ride'
to tsǫ: nhé:yoht	'just all of a sudden'

25

DEʔ HOʔDÉʔ NĘHSA:GYE:ʔʔ

Wadewayę́stanih

DĘˀ HOˀDĘ́ˀ NĘHSA:GYE:ˀˀ

Wadewayéstanih

DĘ? NĘHSA:GYE:??
(What will you do?)

This conversation has quite a few more future verbs. You can recognize them by the *ę-* at or near the beginning.

Nęhsá:gye:?.	'You will do it.'
Ęyoyanráhsdǫhǫ:k.	'It will be good.'
Ęgadadekǫnyę?.	'I will cook for myself.'
Ęgǫnhehgǫ́hǫ:k.	'I will live on it.'
Ęsahdęgyǫ́hǫ:k.	'You will be away.'
Ęgeksohaehsǫ́:go?.	'I will finish washing the dishes.'
Ętgǫ́hnǫkse?.	'I will come get you.'
Ętg?nigǫhá:k.	'I will be waiting.'
Dę?ogęnhǫ́:di?.	'It will be summer again.'
Do: nęyonise??	'How long will it be?'
Hęhsę?se:k.	'You will be there.'
Nętge:?.	'I will come from there.'
Dekní: dęyaǫdadogę́hte?.	'It will be two weeks.'
Dęwęhn?idá:ge:.	'It will be two months.'

As you can see, future times are discussed with the future *ę-* as well.

To ask about future plans, you can say:

Dę? ho?dę?   nęhsa:gye:?   o:nę́h   dę?ogęnhǫ:di??
what   you-will-do   when   it-will-be-summer-again
'What will you do this coming summer?'

To ask about other seasons, simply substitute these words for *o:nę́h dę?ogęnhǫ:di?*.

nę:gyę́h gęnęn?agehneh	'this fall'
nę:gyę́h ęyęhsra:t	'this winter'
nę:gyę́h gagwídehneh	'this spring'

To ask about plans for this week, you can substitute these time expressions:

ne? ęwę:dę́:da?	'next Monday (it will be the first)'
ne? dekní: hadǫ?t	'on Tuesday (second)'
ne? ahsę́ hadǫ?t	'on Wednesday (third)'
ne? gei hadǫ?t	'on Thursday (fourth)'
ne? hwíhs hadǫ?t	'on Friday (fifth)'
ne? nakdohaes	'on Saturday'
ne? ęyaǫdadogę́hte?	'on Sunday'

Wadewayęstanih

ne² nakdohaes, ęyaodadogę́hte² hní²	'on the weekend (Saturday and Sunday)'
wá²ne:²	'today', 'now' or 'at this time'
ęyę:ga:	'tonight'
ęyę:hę²	'tomorrow'

Here are some more future verbs you can use to answer questions about your plans.

Ęgęnadáęhna².	'I will go camping.'
Ęgyędagwáha².	'I will go get wood.'
Ęgadahnyęhna².	'I will go fishing.'
Ęgáhyaksa².	'I will go pick berries.'
Ęgadawę́hna².	'I will go swimming.'
Dęgę²nhoksa².	'I will go play ball.'
_____ hę́:²ge:².	'I will go to _____.' (Fill in _____ with a place name.)

Practice

Ask each person in the room about his or her plans for some time in the future. Reply appropriately, if not truthfully, to anyone who is interested, about your own.

NĘH

Pete tells Bessie <u>when</u> things will be good:

Ęyoyanrahsdǫhǫ́:k   nę   dęyogęnhǫ́:di².
it-will-be-good   when   it-will-be-summer
'It will be good when summer comes.'

Bessie tells him <u>when</u> she plans to do nothing:

Ne²   nę   ęgeksohaehsǫ́:go²,   tę²   sgaho²dę²   taosagá:gye:.
the   when   I-will-finish-washing-dishes   not   anything   will-I-do
'When I (will) finish washing dishes, I won't do anything.'

As you can see, to talk about some time in the future speakers can use *nęh* plus a future verb. This *nęh* is short for *ó:nęh*, 'now', 'when', at the time'. This time can come first in the sentence, or second.

Ne²   nę́h   ęgatganǫ́:ni²,   ęge²drehdahní:nǫ².
the   when   I-will-get-rich,   I-will-car-buy
'<u>When I get rich</u>, I will buy a car.'

Ęge²drehdahni:nǫ́²   ne²   nę́h   ęgatganǫ́:ni².
I-will-car-buy   the   when   I-will-get-rich
'I will buy a car <u>when I get rich</u>.'

Wadewayę́stanih

Practice

See how many sentences you can make up that make sense, using the sentence below as a pattern, and fitting different future verbs in place of *ęgyadǫtgá:dǫ:* and *ęhsyǫˀ*. All you have to do is start with one word from the list below, next put *neˀ nę́h* ('when'), then finish with another word from the list. Be sure the sentences make sense!

Sample:
Ęgyadǫtga:dǫ́:   neˀ nę́h   ęhsyǫˀ.
we.two-will-have-fun   when   you-will-come
'We two will have fun when you come.'

Future verbs:

Ęyoyanráhsdǫhǫ:k.	'It will be good.'	Ęgęnadáęhnaˀ.	'I will go camping.'
Dęyogęnhǫ́:diˀ.	'Summer will come.'	Ęgyędagwáhaˀ.	'I will go get wood.'
Ęgeksohaehsǫ́:goˀ.	'I will finish washing the dishes.'	Ęgadahnyęhnaˀ.	'I will go fishing.'
Ęgatganǫ́:niˀ.	'I will get rich.'	Ęgadawę́hnaˀ.	'I will go swimming.'
Ęsgyǫˀ.	'I will return.'	Ęgahyaksaˀ.	'I will go berry picking.'
Ętgǫ́hnǫkseˀ.	'I will come get you.'	Dęgę́ˀnhoksaˀ.	'I will go play ball.'
Hęhseˀse:k.	'You will be there.'	Ęgadekǫ́:niˀ.	'I will eat.'
Ęsahdęgyǫ́hǫ:k.	'You will be away.'	Ękní:nǫˀ.	'I will buy it.'
		Ęgadǫtgá:dǫ:.	'I will have fun.'

GYĘ:GWAˀ
(If)

You can make a lot more sentences from combinations of future verbs by connecting them with *gyę:gwaˀ* 'if'.

Ękni:nǫ́ˀ   gyę:gwáˀ   hęwa:gí:dęˀ.
I-will-buy-it   if   it-will-fit-me
'I will buy it if it fits.'

Practice

See how many 'if' sentences you can make up which make sense, using the pattern above, and future verbs from the list you used before.

HNI?
(Also)

To talk about the weekend, you can just say 'Saturday and Sunday'. Notice that when Cayuga speakers say 'and', the 'and' comes at the end.

nakd<u>o</u>haes,	ẹyaǫdadogẹht<u>e</u>?	hni?	
Saturday,	Sunday (future)	too	'on the weekend (in the future)'

Wadewayęstanih

A:-
(Hopes, options, duties)

You may have noticed that a number of the verbs in this conversation begin with *a:-* (or *ae-* or *aǫ-*).

Gahsga:ne:s a:gęnadáęhna⁷.	'I want to go camping.'
Gahsga:ne:s ne⁷ a:gadáhnyo:⁷.	'I want to fish.'
I:wí: a:gahnyá:ksa⁷.	'I would like to pick fruit.'
A:gagwe:ni⁷.	'It should do.'
Áekne:⁷.	'We two should go (you and I).'
Aegyatgę́⁷seha⁷.	'We two would go see (you and I).'

This *a:-* (or *ae-* or *aǫ-*) adds the meaning 'might', 'could', 'should', or 'would'. It is used when plans are less certain, or they depend on other things. You will hear it a lot with words such as *gahsgá:ne:s* 'I want', 'I wish', and *í:wi:*, 'I hope', 'I want'. You cannot always count on hopes and desires coming true.

The *a:-* also is used with verbs like *a:wa:dǫ⁷*, 'it would be possible'.

A:wa:dǫ́⁷ aegyatgę́⁷seha⁷.	'It would be possible for us to go see.'

Here are some more verbs with *a:-* to use with *gahsgá:ne:s* or *í:wi:* 'I wish'.

Í:wi: / gahsgá:ne:s…	'I wish…'
A:geksa⁷gowágęhę:k.	'I could be handsome.'
A:gogwe⁷dase⁷gęhę:k.	'I could be young.'
A:wagatganǫ́niha:k.	'I could be rich.'
A:wagesgy⁷ǫwátęhę:k.	'I could be thin.'
A:knęyesǫhǫ:k.	'I could be tall.'
A:knǫnyawayę́hǫhǫ:k.	'I could be a good dancer.'
A:gadrę́nota:k.	'I could sing.'
A:gekwawayę́hǫhǫ:k.	'I could be a good cook.'

Wadewayę́stanih

GYĘ́:GWAʔ...
(If...)

You can use the *a:-* 'would' to answer hypothetical questions too, like this one.

Dęʔ hoʔdę́ʔ   na:sagye:ʔ   gyę:gwáʔ   aesahwihsdagaʔdęh?
what   would-you-do if   you-got-a-lot-of-money
'What would you do if you got a lot of money?'

Here are some possible answers. Notice that they all have *a:-* near the beginning.

A:wagatsęnǫ́:niha:k.   'I would be happy.'
Da:gadawęnyeha ʔ.   'I would travel.'
Da:gęnahá:węnye:ʔ.   'I would go crazy.'

The phrase *gyę:ʔǫ hne:ʔ* 'probably then' fits into sentences like these after the first word.

A:gęnihę́:ʔ   gyę:ʔǫ   hne:ʔ   agríhoʔdeʔ.
I-would-stop probably then   I-work
'I would probably quit working.'

A:se:ʔ   gyę:ʔǫ   hne:ʔ   a:kní:nǫʔ   ____.
new   probably then   I-would-buy
'I would probably buy a new ____.'

You can put the name of whatever you would buy in the blank in the last sentence (___).

Practice

Go around asking people what they would do if they were rich. Be ready with answers of your own in case someone asks you. You can use the answers above, or get some from your teacher or another Cayuga speaking friend.

NEW VOCABULARY

sgę̨ꞏǫjih	'things are fine'
swe̱ꞏgeh	'a long time'
sweꞏge̱ꞏhah	'sort of a long time'
gę́ꞏs	'generally'
wáꞏneꞏꞏ	'today', 'now'
ęyę̱ꞏhę̨ꞏ	'tomorrow'
ęyę̨ꞏga	'tonight'
ęwę̨ꞏdę́ꞏdaꞏ	'Monday' (future)
dekníꞏ hadǫꞏt	'Tuesday'
ahsę̨ hadǫꞏt	'Wednesday'
ge̱i hadǫꞏt	'Thursday'
hwíhs hadǫꞏt	'Friday'
nakdo̱haes	'Saturday'
ęyaǫdadogę́hteꞏ	'Sunday' (future)
dęyogę̨nhǫ́ꞏdiꞏ	'it will be summer'
deꞏogę̨nhǫ́ꞏdiꞏ	'it will be summer again'
gęnenꞏage̱hneh	'in the fall'
ęyę̨hsraꞏt	'it will be winter'
gagwíde̱hneh	'in spring'
dekníꞏ dęyaǫdadogę́hteꞏ	'it will be two weeks'
dewęhnꞏidáꞏgeꞏ	'two months'
gagwide̱hꞏíꞏhah	'early spring'
hęhse̱ꞏseꞏk	'you will be there'
ęsahdę̨gyǫ́hǫꞏk	'you will be away'
dętgeꞏ	'I will return'
ęgęnadáę̱hnaꞏ	'I will go camping'
ęgyę́dagwáhaꞏ	'I will go get wood'
ęgada̱hnyę̨hnaꞏ	'I will go fishing'
ęgáhyaksaꞏ	'I will pick berries'
dęgę́ꞏnhoksaꞏ	'I will play ball'
ęgadawę́ꞏnaꞏ	'I will go swimming'
ęgadade̱kǫnyę̨ꞏ	'I will cook for myself'
ęyoyanráhsdǫhǫꞏk	'the conditions will be good'
ęgǫnhehgǫ́hǫꞏk	'I will live on it'
ęgeksohae̱hsǫ́ꞏgoꞏ	'I will finish the dishes'
ętgǫ́hnǫkseꞏ	'I will come get you'

gaęgwaʔnhǫ́:	'somewhere around'
tę:gyęh	'that'
nęh (ó:nęh)	'when'
tgá:gǫ:t	'it is necessary'
otówʔegeh	'north' (where it is cold)
onenʔǫgeh	'south' (where it is warm)
ahí:ʔ	'I thought'
tę́ʔ dʔese:	'you don't want to'
gayáʔtaʔ	'movies'
tgǫ́:gęh	'when I saw you'
do: nęyoniseʔ hęhseʔse:k?	'how long will you be there?'
dęʔ hoʔdę́ʔ nęhsa:gye:ʔ?	'what will you do?'
dęʔ hoʔdę́ʔ nʔasagyehaʔne:?	'what are you going to do?'
tę́ʔ to taǫsagá:gye:	'I won't do it anymore'
í:wi:	'I want', 'I believe'
gahsgá:ne:s	'I wish', 'I would like'
aegyatgę́ʔsehaʔ	'we two would go see (you and I)'
há:ge:ʔ	'I would go there'
hniʔ	'too'
a:gagwé:niʔ	'it would do'
a:wá:dǫʔ	'it would be possible'
a:gęnadáęhnaʔ	'I would go camping'
a:geksaʔgowágęhę:k	'I would be handsome'
a:wagatganǫ́niha:k	'I would be rich'
a:gahyá:ksaʔ	'I would go pick berries'
a:wagesgyʔǫwátęhę:k	'I would be thin'
áekne:ʔ	'we two would go (you and I)'
a:gekwawayę́hǫhǫ:k	'I would cook well'
a:knǫnyawayę́hǫhǫ:k	'I would dance well'
a:knęyesǫhǫ:k	'I would be tall'
a:hahnęyesǫ́hǫ:k	'he would be tall'
a:gǫgweʔdaseʔgęhę:k	'I would be young'
ętkʔnigǫhá:k	'I will be waiting'

26

DEGAHENÁʔTRAʔSE:ʔ

Wadewayęstanih

Wadewayę́stanih

365

Wadewayę́stanih

Wadewayę́stanih

DEGAHENÁʔTRAʔSE:ʔ

DA-/HA²-
(Here and there)

Cayuga commands tell someone what to do. They can also tell someone what direction to do it in. Imagine where you would be standing if you used each of these commands.

Dajǫh.	'Come in.'
Ha²jǫh.	'Go in.'
Dadrá:tęh.	'Climb up here.'
Ha²drá:tęh.	'Climb up there.'
Dasha:.	'Bring it here', 'Pass it.'
Ha²sha:.	'Take it over there.'
Dasa:dó:wih.	'Drive over here, this way.'
Ha²sa:dó:wih.	'Drive over there, that way.'
Dasádawę:.	'Swim this way.'
Ha²sádawę:.	'Swim that way.'
Dasátgahtoh.	'Look here.'
Ha²sátgahtoh.	'Look over there.'

As you can see, commands that begin *da-* mean the action should take place toward the speaker, this way, or over here. Commands that begin *ha²-* mean the action should be directed away from the speaker, away, or over there.

These direction markers show up on a lot of different verbs, in fact, almost any motion verb. You have already seen some in earlier conversations. Sometimes just *t-* or *d-* is used for 'this way' or 'here', and just *h-* is used for 'that way', or 'over there'.

Gaę nhǫ: disahdęgyǫ:?	'Where do you come from?' (literally, 'you come this way')
Tahnawa:dé² dwagáhdęgyǫ:.	'I come from Tonawanda.'
Gaę nhǫ: tohdę:gyǫ:?	'Where does he come from?'
Dagáę².	'They are coming.'
Gaę nhǫ: ha²se²?	'Where are you going?'
Oswe:gę² ha²ge².	'I am going to Canada.'
Hekní:yǫh.	'Let's go in.'
Hęska:².	'I'll take it back there again.'
Hęsge:².	'I'll go back there again.'

Wadewayę́stanih

NEW VOCABULARY

dajǫh	'come in'
haʔjǫh	'go in'
dadrá:tęh	'climb up here'
haʔdrá:tęh	'climb up there'
dasha:	'bring it here', 'pass it'
haʔsha:	'take it', 'take it there'
dasa:dó:wih	'drive over here'
haʔsa:dó:wih	'drive over there'
dasádawę:	'swim this way'
haʔsádawę:	'swim that way'
dasátgahtoh	'look here'
haʔsátgahtoh	'look there'
ętseʔ	'you will come'
ętsha:ʔ	'you will bring it'
ętsáwihdahk	'you will bring it with you'
hęgyǫʔ	'I will arrive there'
hętsha:ʔ	'you will take it back again'
ęgéhsdahsiʔ	'I will finish using it'
a:geníhaʔ	'I would borrow it'
degahenáʔtraʔse:ʔ	'scissors' (literally, 'two cutters, one on top of the other')
sá:węh	'your', 'you own it'
wáʔjih	'after while'
waʔjítsǫ:	'pretty soon'

27

DAJǫH!

Wadewayęstanih

DEYOKYUʔKDÁʔǪH

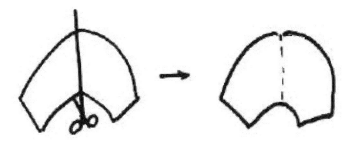

Deyokyuʔkdaʔǫh neʔ degahenáʔtraʔse:ʔ.

Deyokyuʔkdaʔǫh neʔ degahenáʔtraʔse:ʔ.

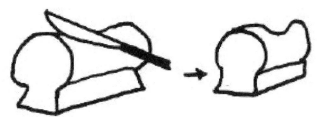

Deyokyuʔkdaʔǫh neʔ gahenʔatraʔ.

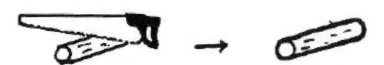

Deyokyuʔkdaʔǫh neʔ deyeǫgyáʔtgahtaʔ / degáyaʔktaʔ.

Wadewayę́stanih

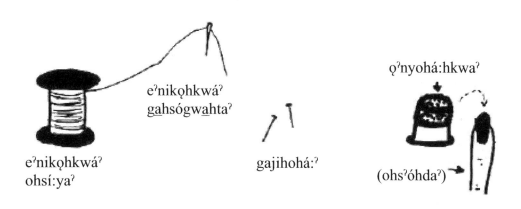

Wadewayę́stanih

DAJQH

Wadewayę́stanih

NIGĘ́ʔǪH/HNIʔ
(Or)

Georgina gives Lila two choices during the visit.

Odí: gęh, kafí nigęʔǫh?
'Tea or coffee?'

Georgina expects her to take one or the other. You can give anyone a choice by following the same pattern. Put *gęh* after the first choice, then *nigęʔǫh* after the second.

_____ gęh, _____ nigęʔǫh?

Here are some more samples.

Ohyáʔ gęh, nawęʔdáʔ nigęʔǫh?
'Fruit or candy?'

Eʔnigǫhkwáʔ gahsógwahtaʔ gęh, gajihohá:ʔ nigęʔǫh?
'Sewing needle or pins?'

The choice can be part of a longer question:

Gaę nhǫ́: haʔse:ʔ, Gahenagǫ: gęh, Taǫdóʔ nigęʔǫh?
'Where did you go, Hamilton or Toronto?'

With another choice Georgina wants to leave Lila the chance to choose either, both, or none. In English, you show this by the tone of voice.

Nawę́ʔdaʔ   gęh,   onǫʔgwáʔ hniʔ?
Sugar   ?   milk ____ also?
'Would you sugar or milk?' (Voice remains high on the end of the English)

The *hniʔ* simply adds the meaning 'too'. It goes at the end of the list.

nawęʔdaʔ onǫʔgwáʔ hniʔ
'sugar and milk' (literally, 'sugar, milk too')

onaʔdá:ʔ owidra:táʔ hniʔ
'bread and butter'

Wadewayę́stanih

You can build more questions on this pattern, when you want to give someone an open choice, letting them choose one, all, or none. Simply put *gęh* after the first choice, then *hniʔ* after the last.

_____ gęh, _____ hniʔ?

Oʔwáhǫ gęh, ohǫnʔadáʔ hníʔ?
'Meat and/or potatoes?'

NEW VOCABULARY

gagyaʔdawiʔtrǫ́:nih	'I am making clothes'
agęnihná:do:k	'I noticed'
deyokyuʔkdáʔǫh	'it is dull'
í:sehs	'use it'
agá:węh	'it is mine', as in *í:ʔ agá:węh*
knináʔda:k	'let us eat bread/baked goods'
agatʔnadáǫt	'I baked'
agatʔnadaǫdá:gwęh	'I have taken the bread/baked goods out'
onáʔnuhsdǫh	'it has cooled'
dejáǫ	'both'
haʔwá:jʔaht	'it is all gone'
kʔnikǫhaʔ	'I am sewing'
eʔníkǫhaʔ	'she is sewing'
eʔníkǫhkwaʔ	'one sews with it'
eʔníkǫhkwaʔ ohsí:yaʔ	'sewing thread'
eʔníkǫhkwaʔ gahsógwahdaʔ	'sewing needle'
gajihohá:ʔ	'straight pins', 'safety pins'
nigahę́:hah	'fabric'
ǫʔnyohá:hkwaʔ	'thimble'
í:se:k	'eat it'
agatsęnǫ́:niʔ	'I became glad'
nǫda:ge:ʔ	'I came'

381

28

GAHÁ:GQ:

Wadewayęstanih

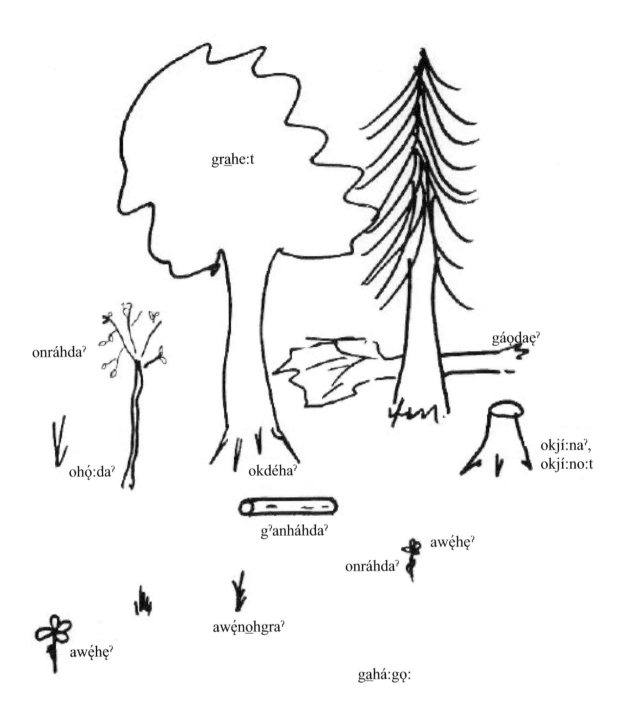

Wadewayęstanih

Wadewayéstanih

<u>A</u>-
(About your past)

The events that Pete describes here are all in the past. You can tell this from the beginning of the verbs. Compare the two verbs below:

Agídagraʔ.	'I fell.'
Ęgídagraʔ.	'I will fall.'

Instead of the future *ę-*, he uses *a-* to show that the actions happened in the past and are over with. Here are some more past verbs.

Agadadé:ʔo:k.	'I cut myself with an axe.'
Asadadé:ʔo:k.	'You cut yourself with an axe.'
Atgadadahjí:yo:ʔ.	'I scratched myself.'
Atsadadahjí:yo:ʔ.	'You scratched yourself.'
Agadadwęʔna̱hsáik.	'I bit my tongue.'
Asadadwęʔna̱hsáik.	'You bit your tongue.'

Wadewayę́stanih

Wadewayęstanih

Agadadejihwęht gehs'óhd'ageh!

Agadadejihwęht gahsí'd'ageh!

ADAT-/ADADE-/ADAD-
(Self)

You may have noticed that a lot of the words in this conversation have the syllables *adat-*, *adad-*, *adade-* in the middle. This is because Pete did all of these things to him<u>self</u>. Compare these:

Atgadadahjí:yoː?.	'I scratched my<u>self</u>.'
Atgahjí:yoː?.	'I scratched it.'
Agadadé:?oːk.	'I cut my<u>self</u> with an axe.'
Agé:?oːk.	'I cut it with an axe.'

As you can see, the *adat-*, *adad-*, *adade-* comes right after the *k-* or *g-* 'I'. Here are some more foolish things you might do to yourself.

Agadadęhsę́:toʔ.   'I kicked myself.'
    (Compare *Agęhsę́:toʔ*, 'I kicked it'.)
Agádatre:ʔ.   'I cut myself.'
    (Compare *Akre:ʔ*, 'I cut it'.)
Agadadéjihwęht.   'I hit myself with a hammer.'
    (Compare *Agéjihwęht*, 'I hit it with a hammer'.)
Agadadé:gęʔ.   'I saw myself.'
    (Compare *Agé:gęʔ*, 'I saw it'.)
Agadadéʔsgotoʔ.   'I burned myself.'
    (Compare *Ageʔsgǫ:daʔ*, 'I burned or roasted it'.)
Agadatnǫʔá:ʔeːk.   'I hit myself in the head.'

Practice

    Go around the room asking each person:

Dęʔ hoʔdę́ʔ nʔa:węh?   'What happened?'

Answer anyone who asks with one of the explanations above, or one of Pete's misfortunes.

GAE̱ NHQ:ʔʔ
(Where?)

You need not be vague when you are complaining. You can combine any of the misfortunes from the last page with a body part, to let your listener know exactly where the damage was done.

Agadade:ʔó:k ga̱hsʔdʔageh.
'I cut myself with an axe on the foot.'

You can combine any of the verbs on the left with any of the body parts on the right.

agadade:ʔó:k	gaho̱hdʔageh
agadadeʔsgo̱tóʔ	kne̱tsáʔgeh
agadatré:ʔ	ge̱hnyáʔsʔageh
agadadeẖjihwe̱ht	ge̱hsʔóhdʔageh
atgadadahji:yó:ʔ	ge̱hsinʔageh
	kyuhsáʔgeh
	ga̱hyagwiyáʔgeh
	ga̱hsíʔdʔageh

(*Agadatno̱ʔá:ʔe:k* 'I hit myself in the head' and *agadadwe̱ʔnahsáik* 'I bit my tongue' already have body parts mentioned in them (*-no̱ʔa-* 'head' and *-we̱ʔnahs-* 'tongue') so it would not make sense to combine them with another body part.)

Wadewayę́stanih

Wadewayę́stanih

S-
(You, of course)

It is very easy to change these verbs with *adat-*, *adad-*, *adade-* 'self' from 'I' did something to myself to 'you' did something to yourself. Just change *k-* or *g-* 'I' to *s-* 'you'.

Agadadé?sgǫto?.	'I burned myself.'
Asadadé?sgǫto?.	'You burned yourself.'

Of course being able to talk about your hearer's misfortune is very useful if you want to ask polite or impolite questions. Just put a *gęh* after the 'you' form.

Asadadęhsę́:to?   gęh?
you-kicked-yourself   ?
'Did you kick yourself?'

You can even match the appropriate body part to the person with the same kind of change.

Asádatre:?   gęh   s<u>e</u>hs?ohd?ageh?
you-cut-yourself   ?   on-your-hand
'Did you cut your hand?'

Practice

Now, let everyone in the room pretend to be in pain. Go to each person in turn, maintaining your painful image, and try to guess the cause of his or her discomfort. Keep asking until you get it right. Here is a sample approach:

Dę? ho?dę́? n?a:węh?   Asadadéj<u>i</u>hwęht gęh?
'What is the matter?'   'Did you hit yourself with a hammer?'

Asadadé?sgǫto? gęh, syuhsa?geh?
'Did you burn your elbow?'

If you can come up with them, offer a few comforting comments about bad luck.

Wadewayę́stanih

HA-/Ǫ-

(His and her misfortunes)

Once you know how to talk about your own accidents, it is very easy to talk about others. To talk about a man, simply put *h-* 'he' in place of *k-/g-* 'I'.

Agadadęhsę́:toʔ.	'I kicked myself.'
Ahadadęhsę́:toʔ.	'He kicked himself.'
Aʔǫdadęhsę́:toʔ.	'She kicked herself.'
Agadadwęʔna̲hsáik.	'I bit my tongue.'
Ahadadwęʔna̲hsáik.	'He bit his tongue.'
Aʔǫdadwęʔna̲hsáik.	'She bit her tongue.'
Awadadwęʔna̲hsáik.	'It bit itself.'
Awadatgaiʔ.	'She bit herself.'

To talk about a woman or girl, simply put *ǫ-* in place of the *ha-* 'he'.

Ahadadęhsę́:toʔ.	'He kicked himself.'
Aʔǫdadęhsę́:toʔ, Aǫdadęhsę́:toʔ.	'She kicked herself.'
Ahadatnǫʔá:ʔe:k.	'He hit himself in the head.'
Aǫdatnǫʔá:ʔe:k.	'She hit herself in the head.'
Awadatnǫʔá:ʔe:k.	'It hit itself in the head.'

Total Disaster

Now let everyone circulate around the room, moaning and showing visible discomfort. Ask each person about someone else in the room. For males, you can ask:

Dęʔ hoʔdę́ʔ nʔahoyʔada:węh?
'What happened to him?'

For females, you can use:

Dęʔ hoʔdę́ʔ nʔagoyaʔdawęh?   (from *nʔaagoyaʔdawęh*)
'What happened to her?'

To ask people about themselves, you can use:

Dęʔ hoʔdę́ʔ nʔesayaʔda:węh?
'What happened to you?'

To ask about yourself, you can use:

Dęʔ hoʔdę́ʔ nǫgyaʔdáwęh?
'What happened to me?'

Answer all questions that come your way in as much detail as you can manage.

NEW VOCABULARY

ohǫ́:daʔ	'sapling', 'whip'
onráhdaʔ	'leaf'
okdéhaʔ	'root'
gáǫdaʔ	'tree' (usually fallen)
gáǫdaęʔ	'fallen tree'
gra̲he:t	'standing tree'
gʔanháhdaʔ	'log'
okjí:naʔ	'stump'
okjí:no:t	'standing tree trunk'
awę́hęʔ	'flower'
ga̲ha:gǫ:	'in the bush', 'in the woods'
hegéʔsę̲hę:ʔ	'I have been there'
ga̲he:tgęʔ	'it is bad'
dewagę́:sǫ:	'I have shoes on'
wa̲hdáhgwadę:s	'thick shoes'
daga:yé:na:ʔ	'it grabbed it'
agídagraʔ	'I fell down', 'I tripped'
ęgídagraʔ	'I will fall down', 'I will trip'
agadadé:ʔo:k	'I cut myself with an axe'
asadadé:ʔo:k	'you cut yourself with an axe'
atgadadahjí:yo:ʔ	'I scratched myself'
atsadadahjí:yo:ʔ	'you scratched yourself'
agadadwęʔna̲hsáik	'I bit my tongue'
asadadwęʔna̲hsáik	'you bit your tongue'
ahadadwęʔna̲hsáik	'he bit his tongue'
agadadéʔsgǫtoʔ	'I burned myself'
asadadéʔsgǫtoʔ	'you burned yourself'
ahadadéʔsgǫtoʔ	'he burned himself'
agádatre:ʔ	'I cut myself'
asádatre:ʔ	'you cut yourself'
akre:ʔ	'I cut it'
agé:gęʔ	'I saw it'
agadadé:gęʔ	'I saw myself'
agéji̲hwęht	'I hit it with a hammer'

Wadewayęstanih

agadadéjihwęht	'I hit myself with a hammer'
agęhsę́:toʔ	'I kicked it'
agadadęhsę́:toʔ	'I kicked myself'
asadadęhsę́:toʔ	'you kicked yourself'
ahadadęhsę́:toʔ	'he kicked himself'
aʔǫdadęhsę́:toʔ	'she kicked herself'
awadadęhsę́:toʔ	'it kicked itself'
agadatnǫʔá:ʔe:k	'I hit myself in the head'
asadatnǫʔá:ʔe:k	'you hit yourself in the head'
ahadatnǫʔá:ʔe:k	'he hit himself in the head'
aʔǫdatnǫʔá:ʔe:k	'she hit herself in the head'
awadatnǫʔá:ʔe:k	'it hit itself in the head'
sadraʔswahé:tgęʔ	'you have bad luck'
esadrʔaswahetgęʔnheʔ	'your luck turned bad'
agę́nʔewa:ʔ	'I was startled'
ǫknehá:goʔ	'I was surprised'
dǫgáhsiʔgyaʔk	'I stubbed my foot'
ohdrǫht	'it is scary'
a:gyędá:goʔ	'I would go get wood'
sʔnigóha:g	'watch out'
dęʔ hoʔdę́ʔ nʔa:węh?	'what happened?'
dęʔ hoʔdę́ʔ nʔa:węh?	'what happened to you?'
dęʔ hoʔdę́ʔ nʔahoyʔada:węh?	'what happened to him?'
dęʔ hoʔdę́ʔ nʔagoyaʔdawęh?	'what happened to her?'
dęʔ hoʔdę́ʔ nesaʔadá:węh?	'what happened to you?'
dęʔ hoʔdę́ʔ nʔahsye:ʔ?	'how did you do that?', 'what did you do?'
shęh niyó:	'until', 'as far as', as in *shęh niyó: nʔadǫ:dá:ge:ʔ* 'on my way back here'
shęh nʔesayʔadá:węh	'what happened to you', as in, *tę́ʔ dʔeoyanreʔ sę nʔesayʔadá:węh*, 'it is not good, what happened to you'
ahgwíh ǫ:sesáhnǫhnyaʔk	'don't get hurt again'
aʔonhiʔdrǫ́:nyǫ:ʔ	'many mistakes'

29

ĘYAGWA̱HDÉ:DIʔ

Wadewayęstanih

ĘYAGWAHDÉ:DIʔ

Wadewayę́stanih

Wadewayę́stanih

Wadewayẹ́stanih

Ẹ-
(About the future)

    Sam and Junior are talking about their future plans, so this conversation has a lot of future verbs in it. Before reading further, look back through the conversation to see how many future verbs you can identify. There are about thirty.

Nẹswá:gyẹ:ʔ.	'Yous will do.'
Dẹyogẹnhǫ́:diʔ.	'It will be summer.'
Ẹyagwahdẹ́:diʔ.	'We all will go away (they and I).'
Hẹswe:ʔ.	'Yous will go there.'
Hẹyá:gweːʔ.	'We all will go there (they and I).'
Ẹyǫgwahdẹ́gyǫhǫ:k.	'We all will be gone.'
Hẹyǫgwagyaʔdanúhsdǫhǫ:k.	'We all will be cooling off there.'
Hẹyagwadáhnyo:ʔ.	'We all will fish there (they and I).'
Hẹyagwá:yǫʔ.	'We all will arrive there (they and I).'
Ẹyǫgwadáhnyo:k.	'We all will be fishing.'
Ẹyagyǫnhéhgǫhǫ:k.	'We all will live on it (they and I).'
Ẹyagwatsẹ́iʔ.	'We all will find it (they and I).'
Ẹji:swá:yǫʔ.	'Yous will return.'
Dẹdwa:tó:wa:t.	'It will begin to get cold again.'
Dẹgyagwahdẹ́:diʔ.	'We all will leave from there (they and I).'
Ẹjagwagyẹ́daẹʔ.	'We all will get stove wood for ourselves (they and I).'
Ẹyagwadehsrǫnyáhno:ʔ.	'We all will prepare ourselves (they and I).'
Ẹswahdẹgyǫ́hǫ:k.	'You will be away.'
Ẹyagwʔẹdrǫ́:daʔk.	'We all will stay home (they and I).'
Ẹyagwayẹ́twahsǫ:ʔ.	'We all will plant things (they and I).'
Ẹwadohsrá:tight.	'It will be a bad winter.'
Ẹyǫgwadẹnʔatrágʔade:k.	'We all will have lots of food.'
Ẹswadǫhswéʔdẹʔ.	'Yous will get hungry.'
Ẹgwadẹnáʔtranǫ:t.	'We will give you food.'
Ẹyǫgwayẹ́:daʔk.	'We all will have (they and I).'

Do you notice a trend?

H-
(Away)

A lot of verbs in this conversation begin with *h*. This is the same *h-* that you saw earlier. It means that the activity is directed away from the speaker or that it takes place in a distant location. Look at these:

Hęyǫgwadáhnyǫ:k.	'We all will be fishing there (they and I).'
(Compare *ęyǫgwadáhnyǫ:k,*	'We all will be fishing (they and I)'.)
Hęyá:gwe:ʔ.	'We all will go away (they and I).'
Hęya:gwá:yǫʔ.	'We all will get there (they and I).'
Hęyǫgwagyaʔdanúhsdǫhǫ:k.	'We all will be cooling off there.'
Hęswe:ʔ.	'Yous will go away.'

SWA-
(How to talk to a group)

In most of the questions, Junior is asking about Sam's whole family, not just Sam alone. He shows this by using *sw-* 'yous' instead of just *s-* 'you' (alone). This is the same *sw(a)-* you saw earlier for commands addressed to a group of people.

Ęswahdęgyǫ́heʔ.	'Yous are going away.'
Ęswadǫhswéʔdę́ʔ.	'Yous will get hungry.'
Ędí:sweʔ.	'Yous will come.'
Hęswe:ʔ.	'Yous will go there.'

Wadewayéstanih

409

Wadewayęstanih

YAGWA-/YǪGWA-

Sam is discussing what he and his family are planning to do together. You can tell that he is talking about more than just himself by the *yagwa-* or *yǫgwa-* on his verbs. It means 'they and I'.

Ęyagwahdę́:diʔ.	'We all will go away (they and I).'
Hęyá:gwe:ʔ.	'We all will go there (they and I).'
Hęya:gwá:yǫʔ.	'We all will arrive there (they and I).'
Ęyagwatsę́iʔ.	'We all will find (they and I).'
Nęya:gwá:ye:ʔ.	'We all will do it (they and I).'
Dęgyagwahdę́:diʔ.	'We all will leave from there (they and I).'
Ęyagwadehsrǫnyáhnǫ:ʔ.	'We all will prepare (they and I).'
Ęyagwʔędrǫ́:daʔk.	'We all will stay home (they and I).'
Ęyagwayę́twahsǫ:ʔ.	'We all will plant (they and I).'
Ęyǫgwahdę́gyǫhǫ:k.	'We all will be gone (they and I).'
Ęyǫgwadáhnyo:k.	'We all will be fishing (they and I).'
Ęyǫgwadęʔatrágʔade:k.	'We all will have lots of food (they and I).'
Ęyǫgwayę́:daʔk.	'We all will have it (they and I).'
Hęyǫgwagyaʔdanúhsdǫhǫ:k.	'We all will be cooling off there (they and I).'

(Notice that most verbs with *yagwa-* talk about some kind of action, while most verbs with *yǫgwa-* just talk about a continuing state.)

Activities

Go around the room, asking each person what they and their families plan to do this summer.

Gwé:, dęʔ ní:s hwaʔ hoʔdę́ʔ nęswa:gyę́:ʔ nę:gyęhwaʔ dęyogęnhǫ:diʔʔ?

In case someone asks you, here are some possible answers.

O:, ęyagwahdę́:diʔ ní:ʔ hwaʔ.	'Oh, we all will go away this time (they and I).'
Ęyagwadáhnyo:ʔ.	'We all will fish (they and I).'
Ęyagwadá:wę:ʔ.	'We all will swim (they and I).'
Ęyagwahyá:goʔ.	'We all will pick berries (they and I).'
Ęyagwadríhoʔda:t.	'We all will work (they and I).'
Ęyagwęnádaęʔ.	'We all will camp (they and I).'
Ęyagwanǫhsǫ́:niʔ.	'We all will build a house (they and I).'
Ęyagwʔędrǫ́:daʔk.	'We all will stay home (they and I).'
Ęyagwayę́twahsǫ:ʔ.	'We all will plant (they and I).'
Dęyagwʔęnho:k.	'We all will play ball (they and I).'

Wadewayęstanih

Of course if you tell someone that you are going away, you had better be prepared to tell them where you plan to go.

In case you are curious about people's fall plans, here is how to ask them:

Gwe:, dę' ní:s hwa' ho'dę' nęswa:gye:' nę:gyęhwa' ęgęnęna'ge'nhe'?
'What are yous going to do next fall?'

Here are a couple of answers.

Ęyagwanrahdáohe:k.	'We all will rake leaves (they and I).'
Ęyagwahnyo'gwanǫ́hgwa:s.	'We all will pick up nuts (they and I).'
Ęyagwagyędáohe:k.	'We all will gather our wood/ stock up on wood (they and I).'

If you would like to ask about spring plans, here is how:

Gwé:, dę' ní:s hwa' ho'dę' nęswa:gyé:' nę:gyę́hwa' ęgagwidé'nhe'?
'Well, what are yous going to do next spring?'

Here are some answers to that:

Ęyagwahgaodǫ́:nyǫ:'.	'We all will tap trees (they and I).'
Ęyagwawęhęyétwahsǫ:'.	'We all will plant flowers (they and I).'
Dęyagwatnǫhsohdá:', Dęyagwatnǫ́hsahsnye'.	'We all will clean house (they and I).'
Ęyagwahgwęnyahní:nǫnyǫ:'.	'We all will buy clothes (they and I).'

You might as well ask about winter plans while you are at it. Here is how:
Gwé:, dę' ní:s hwa' ho'dę' nęswa:gyé:' nę:gyę́hwa' ęyohsra:t?
'Well, what are yous going to do next winter?'

Here are a couple of winter possibilities:

Ęyagwadó:wa:t.	'We all will hunt (they and I).'
Ęyagwadríhsdaę', Ęyagwadrihdáęshǫ', Ęyagwadrihsdáędǫnyǫ'.	'We all will trap (they and I).'
Ęyagwagyęhsrǫnyáhnǫ:'.	'We all will make quilts (they and I).'

Can you keep this all straight? If you would like a snappy reply to someone's plans, you can tell them what they should plan to do instead. Simply change *ęyagwa-* ('we all will') to *aeswa-* ('yous should'). The rest of the word can stay exactly the same.

Aeswanrahdáohe:k.	'Yous should rake leaves.'
(Compare *Ęyagwanrahdáohe:k,* 'We all will rake leaves'.)	
Aeswadó:wa:t.	'Yous should hunt.'
(Compare *Ęyagwadó:wa:t,* 'We all will hunt'.)	

Wadewayęstanih

NEW VOCABULARY

nęswá:gye:ʔ	'yous will do'
dęyogęnhǫ́:diʔ	'it will be summer'
ęyagwahdę́:diʔ	'we all will go away (they and I)'
hęyá:gwe:ʔ	'we all will go there (they and I)'
hęya:gwá:yǫʔ	'we all will arrive there (they and I)'
ęyagwatsę́iʔ	'we all will find (they and I)'
nęya:gwá:ye:ʔ	'we all will do it (they and I)'
dęgyagwahdę́:diʔ	'we all will leave from there (they and I)'
ęyagwadehsrǫnyáhnǫ:ʔ	'we all will prepare (they and I)'
ęyagwʔędrǫ́:daʔk	'we all will stay home (they and I)'
ęyagwayę́twahsǫ:ʔ	'we all will plant (they and I)'
ęyǫgwahdę́gyǫhǫ:k	'we all will be gone (they and I)'
ęyǫgwadáhnyo:k	'we all will be fishing (they and I)'
ęyǫgwadęʔatrágʔade:k	'we all will have lots of food (they and I)'
ęyǫgwayę́:daʔk	'we all will have it (they and I)'
hęyǫgwagyaʔdanúsdǫhǫ:k	'we all will be cooling off there (they and I)'
ęyagwadáhnyo:ʔ	'we all will fish (they and I)'
ęyagwadá:wę:ʔ	'we all will swim (they and I)'
ęyagwahyá:goʔ	'we all will pick berries (they and I)'
ęyagwadríhoʔda:t	'we all will work (they and I)'
ęyagwęnádaęʔ	'we all will camp (they and I)'
ęyagwanǫhsǫ́:niʔ	'we all will build a house (they and I)'
dęyágwʔęnho:k	'we all will play ball (they and I)'
ęyagwanrahdáohe:k	'we all will rake leaves' (they and I)
ęyagwahnyoʔgwanǫ́hgwa:s	'we all will gather nuts (they and I)'
ęyagwagyę́daęʔ	'we all will gather wood (they and I)'
ęyagwahgaodǫ́:nyǫ:ʔ	'we all will tap trees (they and I)'
ęyagwawęhęyę́twahsǫ:ʔ	'we all will plant flowers (they and I)'
ęswahdęgyǫ́heʔ	'yous are all going away'
ęswadǫhswéʔdęʔ	'yous will get hungry'
ędí:sweʔ	'yous will all come'
hęswe:ʔ	'yous will all go there'
ęgęnęnáʔgʔenheʔ	'it will become fall'
ęgagwidéʔnheʔ	'it will become spring'

Wadewayę́stanih

ęyóhsra:t	'it will become winter'
tę́ˀ taeswayę́twahsǫ:	'yous will not plant things'
ęyagyǫnhéhgǫhǫ:k	'we all will live on it (they and I)'
ganyoˀsǫ:ˀǫh	'game'
a:yagwadekǫ́:niˀ	'we all would eat it (they and I)'
odǫtgá:deˀ	'it is fun'
odǫtga:déˀǫh	'it should be fun, I bet'
dędwa:tó:wa:t	'it will get cold again'
ęjóhsra:t	'it will be winter again'
ęwadohsrá:tgiht	'it will be a bad winter'
sá:dǫh	'you are saying'
ęgwadęnáˀtranǫ:t, ęgwákwanǫ:t	'we all will feed you (they and I)'
dęyagwatnǫhsohdá:ˀ, dęyagwatnǫ́hsahsnyeˀ	'we all will clean house (they and I)'
ęyagwahgwęnyahnínǫnyǫ:ˀ	'we all will buy clothes (they and I)'
ęyagwadó:wa:t	'we all will hunt (they and I)'
ęyagwadríhsdaęˀ	'we all will trap (they and I)'
ęyagwagyęhsrǫnyáhnǫ:ˀ	'we all will make quilts (they and I)'
aeswanrahdáohe:k	'yous should rake leaves'
aeswadó:wa:t	'yous should hunt'

30

ĘSWAYĘTOˀ GĘH?

Wadewayę́stanih

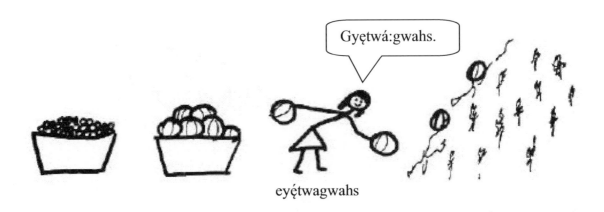

Wadewayęstanih

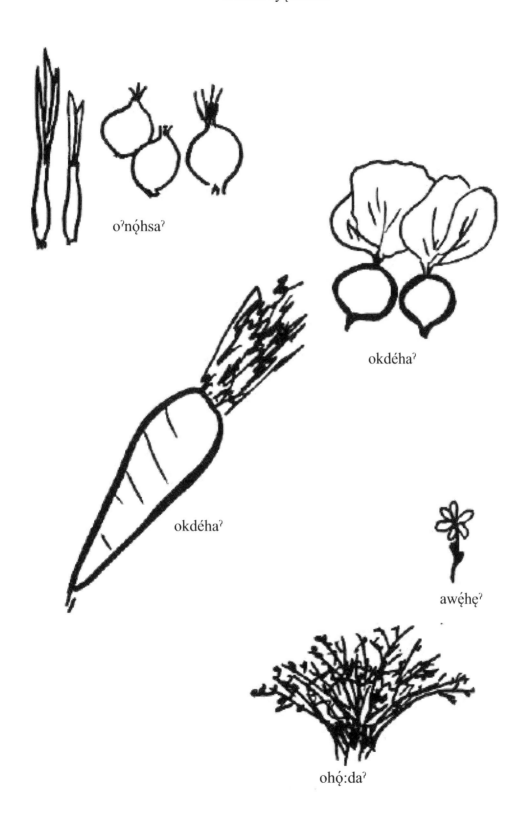

Wadewayę́stanih

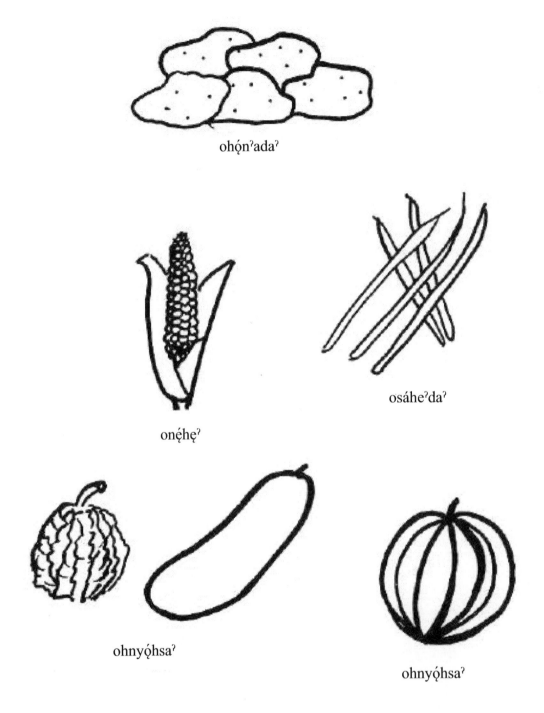

Wadewayęstanih

ĘSWAYĘTO' GĘH?

Ęswáyęto' gę' ní:s hwa' gagwidehji:hah?

Ęhę́', né:' gi' agwe:.

Dę' di' ní:s ho'dę́' gwahs ęswayętwahso:'?

A:yę́:' agwé: onęhę́' osahe'dá' ohǫn'adá' ǫhni',

gwahs i:só:'ah ęyagwayę́twahso:', tréhs a:yę́:' o:nę́ do:gę́hs ganǫ́:' ohǫ́n'ada'.

Wadewayę́stanih

Wadewayęstanih

Wadewayęstanih

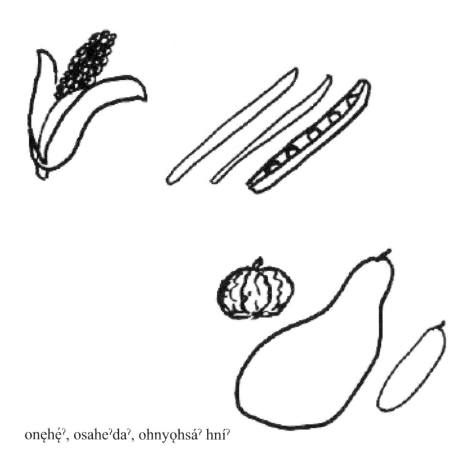

onęhę́ʔ, osaheʔdaʔ, ohnyǫhsáʔ hníʔ

HNI̱ʔ
(As well, also)

When Georgina wants to list a number of vegetables, she just lists them, then says *hniʔ* at the end. You can do this with any list of objects or activities in Cayuga.

Onęhęʔ osaheʔdáʔ hníʔ	'Corn and beans'
Onaʔdá:ʔ owidra:táʔ hníʔ	'Bread and butter'
Onaʔdá:ʔ owidra:táʔ otsesdáʔ hníʔ	'Bread, butter, and honey'

See whether you can tell someone in good Cayuga exactly what is in each picture on the next page. Be sure to use *hniʔ* for each.

Wadewayę́stanih

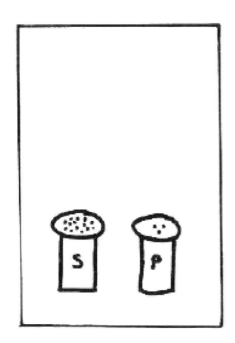

Wadewayęstanih

Wadewayéstanih

DĘꞌ HOꞌDĘ́ꞌ ĘHSYĘ:TOꞌꞌ

Wadewayę́stanih

Wadewayęstanih

SWA-
(Yous)

Lila asks Georgina about their family plans for the garden. You can tell that she means to include Georgina's whole family because she uses *swa-* 'yous'.

Ęswáyęto?.	'Yous will plant.'
Ęswayętwáhso:?.	'Yous will plant a lot of things.'
Swahǫn?adáyętwęh.	'Yous planted potatoes.'

This is the same *swa-* that you saw earlier for talking to a group, giving commands to several people at once, and talking about body parts.

(Y)AGWA-
(They and I)

Georgina wants to tell Lila about her whole family's plans. You can tell that she means to include at least two other people when she says 'we' because she uses *(y)agwa-* 'they and I'.

Ęyagwayętwahsǫ:?.	'We will plant various things (they and I).'
Hęyágwahge:t.	'We will stop by there.' or 'We will go and return (they and I).'
Agwayę:twá:go?.	'We harvested (they and I).'
Agwe:.	'We think (they and I).'

(The first Y is dropped at the beginning of words). Watch future conversations to see whether you can tell how many people are involved when a Cayuga speaker says 'we' or 'you'.

Wadewayę́stanih

Wadewayę́stanih

Ę̨-
(More future plans)

You can probably recognize future verbs with no trouble by now. Count the number of future verbs in this conversation. Did you come up with these?

Ęswáyęto².	'Yous will plant.'
Ęswáyętwáhsǫ:².	'Yous will plant a variety of things.'
Ęyagwayę́twahsǫ:².	'We all will plant a variety of things (they and I).'
Ęshehní:nǫ².	'I will buy from him again.'
Ęsgahdę́:di².	'I will go home.'
Hęyágyahge:t.	'We two will stop by there (they and I).'

A:-
(More possible plans)

This conversation has a few more verbs with *a:-* instead of *ę-*, for possible events.

A:yohǫn²adá:tgęh.   'The potatoes would rot.'
(Compare *Ęyohǫn²adá:tgęh,* 'The potatoes will rot'.)

A:gagwé:ni².   'It should do.', 'It should be enough.'
(Compare *Ęga:gwé:ni²,* 'It will be enough'.)

A:sní:nǫ².   'You should buy it.'
(Compare *Ęhsní:nǫ²,* 'You will buy it'.)

-HSǪ:²
(Varieties)

When Cayuga speakers talk about objects, the words normally do not change, no matter how many objects are involved.

ohǫ́n²ada²	'potato' or 'potatoes'
osáhe²da²	'bean' or 'beans'

If a speaker wants to emphasize that a lot of objects or activities are involved, particularly a variety of different ones, he or she can add *-hsǫ:²* to the end of the word. Compare these:

Ęswáyęto².	'You will plant.'
Ęswayętwáhsǫ:².	'You will plant them.' or 'You will plant them a variety of things.'

Wadewayęstanih

DĘʔ HOʔDĘʔ ĘHSYĘTWAHSǪ:ʔ?
(What kinds of things will you plant?)

      To answer this question, you can just put your crop, the most important information first, then *ęgyę:toʔ* 'I will plant'.

Onęhę́ʔ   ęgyę́:toʔ.
corn   I-will-plant
'I will plant corn.'

Ohǫnʔadáʔ   ęgyę́:toʔ.
potatoes   I-will-plant
'I will plant potatoes.'

Ohnǫhsáʔ   ęgyę́:toʔ.
squash   I-will-plant
'I will plant squash.'

This is how Georgina answers Lila's question.

      Lila asks about planting in a different way later on.

Swahǫnʔadáyętwę   gęh?
you-potato-plant   ?
'Did you plant potatoes?'

The potatoes are right inside of the word. If you would like to be fancy, and incorporate your crop into your planting word, here are some helpful hints. Notice that the planting part of the words stay about the same, but the crop changes.

Ęknęhęyę́:toʔ.	'I will plant corn.'
Ęgesahe̱ʔdayę́:toʔ.	'I will plant beans.'
Ęgehnyǫhsáyęto ʔ.	'I will plant squash (pumpkins, etc.).'
Ękǫnadáyętoʔ.	'I will plant potatoes.'
Ęknʔǫhsayę́:toʔ.	'I will plant onions.'
Ęgekde̱háyętoʔ.	'I will plant carrots/beets/turnips (any roots).'
Ęgwęhęyę́:toʔ.	'I will plant flowers.'
Ękǫdayę́:toʔ.	'I will plant shrubs.'
Ęgyęʔgwayę́:toʔ.	'I will plant tobacco.'

NEW VOCABULARY

ęhsyę́:to?	'you will plant'
ęhsyętwahso:?	'you will plant a lot'
ęyagwayętwahso:?	'we all will plant a lot (they and I)'
swah<u>o</u>n?adáyętwęh	'yous planted potatoes'
ogwáyętwęh	'we all have planted (they and I)'
ęknęhęyę́:to?	'I will plant corn'
ęges<u>a</u>he?dayę́:to?	'I will plant beans'
ękon?adáyęto?	'I will plant potatoes'
ękn?ohsayę́:to?	'I will plant onions'
ęgekd<u>e</u>háyęto?	'I will plant carrots/beets/turnips, etc.'
ęgwęhęyę́:to?	'I will plant flowers'
ękodayę́:to?	'I will plant (a) shrub'
ęgyę?gwayę́:to?	'I will plant tobacco'
ohnyóhsa?	'squash, pumpkin'
ohnyohs?áoweh	'hubbard squash'
onę́hę?	'corn'
osáhe?da?	'beans'
okdéha?	'root', 'carrot', 'beet', 'turnip', etc.
awę́hę?	'flower'
ohó:da?	'shrub', 'sapling'
o?nóhsa?	'onion'
ohón?ada?	'potatoes'
a:y<u>o</u>hon?adá:tgęh	'potatoes would rot'
oyę́?gwa?	'tobacco'
hohon?adág?ade?	'he has a lot of potatoes'
agwayętwá:go?	'we all harvested (they and I)'
agatehdó:ni:	'I have prepared the land'
sgagáhatwęh	'it has been ploughed again'
degahehdáwęnyeh(s)	'it stirs the field', 'cultivator'
atkehdawę́:nye:?	'I hoed', 'I stirred the field'
tsigę́:nheh, tsiganęna?geh	'last summer'
agasda:nohwé?nhe?, agasdáowanaht	'it rained a lot'
agétsahni?k	'I got scared of it'

Wadewayę́stanih

í:wi:	'I want', 'I think'
ǫ́:wi:	'I would think so'
agyę'	'I have'
gagwide̲hjí:hah	'in spring'
agwe:	'we all think (they and I)'
hwa'	'this time'
í:so'	'much', 'a lot', 'many'
gwé:gǫh	'all'
dó:gwa'?	'how?'
ní:yǫ:	'amount', 'so much'
dají:hah	'a little while'
hę́'hne:'	'also'
ogá:ę'	'it is worth it'
ęshehní:nǫ'	'I will buy from him again'
a:sní:nǫ'	'you should buy it'
sa̲hwihsdagá'de'	'you have a lot of money'
ęhsátga̲hto'	'you will see'
ęsayená:wa's	'it will help you'
ęhsatędǫ́:ni'	'you will garden'
tgá:gǫ:t	'it is necessary', 'must'
a:gagwé:ni'	'it should do', 'it should be possible'
gaiho'dęhsrowá:nęh	'it is a lot of work', 'big job'
ęsgahdę́:di'	'I will go home'
hęyágwa̲hge:t	'we all will stop by (they and I)'
do: di' ni:yǫ'...?	'then how much...?', 'then how many...?'
ahsę́ niga:yá:ge:	'three bags'
géi n'adew'enya:w'é: sigwa:dí:hah niga:nǫ́:'	'a little more than four hundred it costs'
ęswáyęto'	'yous will plant'
ęswayętwáhsǫ:'	'you will plant a lot of things'

31

DWĘNQHSANÉKAHQ?

Wadewayęstanih

Wadewayę́stanih

Wadewayę́stanih

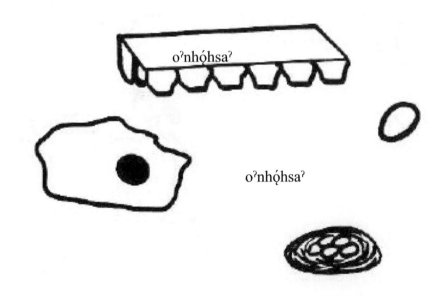

Wadewayéstanih

DWĘNOHSANÉKAHǪ'

Wadewayęstanih

Wadewayę́stanih

Wadewayęstanih

-OʔKD- / -OʔKT-
(Run out of)

Lila runs out of a number of crucial ingredients. She announces this to Sam with verbs containing -*oʔkd-* 'run out of' near the end. She can emphasize the missing ingredient by putting it at the beginning of the sentence:

Oteʔtráʔ   agadʔokdáʔǫh.
flour   I-have-run-out-of
'I have run out of flour.'

She can also incorporate the missing ingredient right into the verb.

Agadeteʔtroʔkdáʔǫh.   'I have run out of flour.' or 'I am out of flour.'

Good speakers tend to incorporate quite often. If you would like to impress people with your Cayuga, try working a few of these into your conversation:

Agadranawʔędóʔkdʔaǫh.	'I have run out of sugar.'
Agadediʔtroʔkdáʔǫh.	'I have run out of tea.'
Agatǫnaʔdʔokdáʔǫh.	'I have run out of potatoes.'
Agadejikeʔdóʔkdʔaǫh.	'I have run out of salt.'
Agadwidra:toʔkdáʔǫh.	'I have run out of butter.'
Agatnʔadaʔokdáʔǫh.	'I have run out of bread.'
Agadʔenhǫhsʔokdáʔǫh.	'I have run out of eggs.'
Agadęnaʔtroʔkdáʔǫh.	'I have run out of food.'
Agatnadʔókdaʔǫh.	'I have run out of gas.'
Agatnʔokdáʔǫh.	'I have run out of oil.'
Agadmajisdʔokdáʔǫh.	'I am out of matches.'

(or, *Ǫdegʔadahkwáʔ agadʔokdaʔǫh.*)

If you look closely at these words, you can see glottal stops (ʔ) hopping left in odd-numbered syllables.

T-/H-
(Here and there)

Lila and Sam use more words in this conversation with the *t(a)-* that means 'here', 'this way', or 'at the place'.

Dajǫh.	'Come in.'
Tganǫ́hsǫ:t	'The house standing there, at that place'

In some future verbs, this *t-* comes after the future *ę-*.

Ęt̨gaǫdekǫnyáhneʔ.	'They will come here and eat.'
Dętseʔ.	'You will come back.'
Ętgáęʔ.	'They will come here.'

They use a few others with the *h(aʔ)-* that means 'there' or 'away'.

Haʔsátgahtoh.	'Look over there.'
Haʔgáhge:t.	'I went there.'
Hesge:.	'Let me go back there.'

There is also a word which begins *haʔde-*. This means 'all sorts of'. Here are some examples of it.

Haʔdé:yǫ:	'Many different things'
Haʔdeyǫgwéʔdage:	'All sorts of different people'
Haʔdegadiyʔadá:ge:	'All sorts of different animals'
Haʔdeganǫ́hsage:	'All sorts of different houses'
Haʔdegáǫdage:	'All sorts of different trees'

S-
(More commands)

Lila asks Sam to do a number of things. Here are some of the commands she uses. You can recognize them by the *s-* 'you' at the beginning.

Sekdǫ́hnah.	'Go and see.'
Sęníhahsah	'Go and borrow'
Seteˀtraníhahsah.	'Go and borrow flour.'

Sam tells Lila to bake:

Satnaˀdáǫdęh.	'Go and bake.'

Requests can be made a little more polite if you use the future instead of a straight command.

Ęhsę́ni̱haˀ.	'(You will) Borrow it.'
Ęhsní:nǫˀ.	'(You will) Buy it.'
Ęsníˀyǫˀ.	'(You two will) Arrive.'
Ęgasehǫ́gaǫˀ.	'(You will) Give them an invitation.'
Gǫdagyéˀ dętseˀ.	'(You will) Come back right away.'

You can make a suggestion even more polite with the *a:-* 'should', 'might' at the beginning.

A:snˀadáǫniˀ.	'You should bake.', 'You might bake.' or 'Would you bake?'
A:sˀenhǫhsaníhaˀ.	'You could/might borrow some eggs.'

Sometimes a suggestion gets better results than a crisp order.

-HNA/-SAH/-HA
(Go and...)

     Some of the commands ask people to <u>go and</u> do something. This 'go and' is right at the end of the command. It is usually *-hna*, *-hsa*, or *-ha*.

Sekdǫ́hnah.	'Go and see.'
Sęníhahsah	'Go and borrow'
Seteʔtraníhahsah.	'Go and borrow flour.'

Here are some more commands with this 'go and'.

Sninǫ́hah	'Go and buy'

          (Compare *sní:nǫh,* 'buy')

S<u>a</u>hyá:ksah.	'Go and pick (eat) berries.'
Segwáhah	'Go and get'
Seyǫʔs<u>e</u>há sanó:haʔ.	'Go visit your mother.'

(You probably recall that sentences ending in a single, short vowel get an automatic H at the end. That is why the last command can change.

Seyǫʔs<u>e</u>há.	'Go and visit her.'
Seyǫʔs<u>e</u>há sanó:haʔ.	'Go and visit your mother.'

You are probably adding those breaths automatically at the end of sentences by now.)

NEW VOCABULARY

haʔsátgahtoh	'look over there'
Satgáhtoh	'look'
gonęnadínyʔǫdǫh	'they've moved in' (females or mixed)
gęnadinyǫ́ʔtaʔ	'I am moving in'
agaǫnádinyǫʔt	'they moved in'
sekdǫ́hnah	'go and see'
ęgasehǫ́gaǫʔ	'you will give them an invitation'
ętgaǫdekǫnyáhneʔ	'they will come and eat' (females or mixed)
ęyǫgwadó:gęhs	'we all will know'
dętseʔ	'you will come back'
dewagʔedráihęhs	'I am in a hurry'
a:wagęnǫhdǫ́ʔnheʔ	'I would find out'
haʔgáhge:t	'I stopped by there'
ętgáęʔ	'they will come'
ęsgadrihóʔdataʔ	'I will go back to work'
ędwa:k	'we all will eat it (yous and I)'
agadranawʔędóʔkdʔaǫh	'I am out of sugar'
agadeteʔtróʔkdaʔǫh	'I am out of flour'
agadediʔtroʔkdáʔǫh	'I am out of tea'
agatǫnaʔdʔokdáʔǫh	'I am out of potatoes'
agadejikeʔdóʔkdʔaǫh	'I am out of salt'
agadwidra:toʔkdáʔǫh	'I am out of butter'
agatnʔadaokdáʔǫh	'I am out of bread'
agadʔenhǫhsʔokdáʔǫh	'I am out of eggs'
agatnʔokdáʔǫh	'I am out of gas/oil/lard'
agadęnaʔtroʔkdáʔǫh	'I am out of food'
otéʔtraʔ	'flour'
agadʔokdáʔǫh	'I am out of it'
sadóʔkdʔaǫh	'you are out of it'
godóʔkdʔaǫh	'she is out of it'
tę́ʔ dʔeá:gyęʔ	'I don't have any'
tę́ʔ dʔeǫgwadęnʔatráęʔ	'we all have nothing to eat'
ęhsę́niha ʔ	'you will borrow it'
ęgę́nihaʔ	'I will borrow it'
seteʔtraníhahsah	'go and borrow flour'
geteʔtraníhahseʔ	'I come to borrow flour'

Wadewayę́stanih

a:sʔenhǫhsaníhaʔ	'you should borrow eggs'
a:gʔenhǫhsaníhaʔ	'I should borrow eggs'
satnaʔdáǫdęh	'bake bread'
a:yǫtnaʔdáǫdęʔ	'she could bake'
a:snʔadáǫniʔ	'you should make bread'
nę:	'say', 'look'
do:gaʔ	'I don't know'
gǫ́dagyeʔ	'immediately'
wáʔjih	'after while', 'a while ago'
haʔdé:yǫ:	'many things'
haʔdeyǫgwéʔdage:	'all sorts of people'
haʔdegadiyʔadá:ge:	'all sorts of animals'
haʔdeganǫ́hsage:	'all sorts of houses'
haʔdegáǫdage:	'all sorts of trees'
ǫgenhaʔǫhǫ́gyeʔ	'she hired me'
daǫgadę́nyeht	'she sent me'
tę́ʔ dʔeagatrehnagáʔtsǫ:	'I have not unpacked'
wadá:nyǫʔ	'they are in it' (animals)
gyagonehdáhgǫh	'they believe' (females or mixed)
gyǫgwéhdahgǫh	'we all believe'
sǫknʔígǫhęh	'I forgot'
agádehęh	'I was ashamed'
tę́ʔ dʔáǫ daǫsagǫʔniʔgǫ́haęʔ	'I won't bother you again'
dęyǫgwadagyʔadagenhę́hę:k,	'we all will help each other'
dędwadagyénʔawaʔs	'we all will help each other (they and I)'
shęh ní:yoht	'the way'
hesge:	'let me go there again'
sʔesgę́hę:ʔ	'you were here'
ęgíhsa:k	'I will look for it'
naǫdáęʔ	'she could come here'
sahsyǫʔ	'you have returned'
ęsní:yǫʔ	'you two will arrive'
sninǫ́hah	'go and buy it'
segwáhah	'go and get it'
sahyá:ksah	'go and pick berries'

32

OYĘHSRA'

OYĘHSRAʔ

-OʔDĘʔ
(Kinds of things)

Georgina and Lila spend a lot of time talking about the kind of quilt Lila is making with her mother. A number of words in their discussion end with *-oʔdęʔ* or *-oʔdę:*. Words with *nʔa...oʔdęʔ* refer to a kind, type, breed, or make of something.

Dęʔ   hoʔdęʔ   nʔagadiyaʔdʔodęʔ   jʔidę:ʔęh?
what   kind   so-their-body-breed   bird
'What kind of birds are they?'

Here are some more:

Dęʔ   hoʔdęʔ   nʔagaʔdrehdoʔdęʔ?
what   kind   so-car-make
'What make car is it?'

Dęʔ   hoʔdęʔ   nʔaohsohgoʔdęʔ?
what   kind   so-colour-type
'What type of colour is it?' or 'What kind of paint is it (oil paint, fast drying paint, etc.)?'

Words with *ni...oʔdę:* refer to appearance, or other, similar description.

Dęʔ   hoʔdęʔ   niyoyęhsroʔdę:?
what   kind   so-blanket-appearance
'What does the quilt look like?'

Dęʔ   hoʔdęʔ   niyohsohgoʔdę:?
what   kind   so-colour-appearance
'What colour is it?' or 'What does the colour look like?'

Hehsʔáęʔ   niyohsohgóʔdę:.
brown   so-colour-appearance
'It is brown (coloured).'

Dęʔ   hoʔdęʔ   nigaʔdrehdoʔdę:?
what   kind   so-car-appearance
'What does the car look like?'

To talk about the appearance of several things, *ni...oʔdęʔs* can be used.

Dęʔ   hoʔdęʔ   niyohsohgoʔdęʔs?
what   kind   so-colour-appearance-s
'What colour is it?' or 'What colours are they?'

Wadewayęstanih

-I:YO:
(Nice)

One kind of answer to *dę? ho?dę?* questions about appearance is words ending with *-i:yo:* 'nice'. You already know a few words like this from earlier sections.

sǫgwe?dí:yo:.	'You are a nice person.'
gahen?atrí:yo:	'a good cutter', 'a good saw' or 'a good blade'
ganahsgwí:yo:	'a good pet' or 'a nice pet'
agya?dawi?trí:yo: or wagya?dawi?trí:yo	'a good dress'
węhnisrí:yo:	'a nice day'

You can see the same ending on several words from this conversation.

ohsohgwí:yo:	'nice colour'
oyęhsrí:yo:	'nice blanket' or 'nice quilt'

To talk about several nice things at once, you can simply use *-i:yo?s* instead of *-i:yo:*.

ohsohgwí:yo?s	'nice colours'
oyęhsrí:yo?s	'nice blankets' or 'nice quilts'

Could you imagine how to say 'nice dresses', or 'good saws'?

The word below can act as a whole statement.

Sagya?dawi?trí:yo:.	'Your dress/coat/shirt is nice.'

Can you imagine what these words mean?

Satna?tsotrí:yo:
Sanahaotrí:yo:
Satna?gwihtrí:yo:
Sadahd?itrí:yo:
Sahdahgwí:yo:
S?ęnyo:trí:yo:

Wadewayę́stanih

Wadewayę́stanih

Wadewayę́stanih

J-
(Both of yous)

Compare these commands:

Satgyę́:.	'Sit down (to one person).'
Jatgyę́:.	'Sit down, both of yous (to two people).'
Satgáhtoh.	'Look (to one person).'
Jatgáhtoh.	'Look, both of yous (to two people)'

As you can see, Cayuga speakers pay attention to how many people they are ordering around. The *s-* is used to one person, and the *j-* to two.

Georgina uses this *j-* 'you two' while she is talking to Lila, because she is asking about two people, Lila and her mother.

Jagyęhsrǫ́:nih   'You two are making a blanket.'
(Compare *Sagyęhsrǫ́:nih*, 'You (alone) are making a blanket'.)

To change a command that begins *sa-* to apply to two people, all you have to do is substitute *ja-*.

Satgę́h. 'Get up (to one person).'   Jatgę́h. 'Get up, you two.'

Practice

Imagine you are talking to two children. Can you choose the commands below so that they would apply to both? (Just change the *sa-* to *ja-*.)

Sade:kǫ́:nih.	'Eat.'	Jadekǫ́:nih.	'Eat, you two.'
Satgohsoháe.	'Wash your face.'	?	'Wash your faces, you two.'
Satgę́ʔse:.	'Have a look.'	?	
Sahjóhae:.	'Wash your hands.'	?	
Satnuʔjoháe.	'Brush your teeth.'	?	
Sadeʔnyę́:dęh.	'Try it.'	?	
Satrǫ́:nih.	'Get dressed.'	?	
Satnaʔtsó:we:k.	'Put your pants on.'	?	
Sadahdʔitrǫ́:da:.	'Put your socks on.'	?	
Sanaháowe:k.	'Put your hat on.'	?	
Sadó:wih.	'Drive.'	?	

The 'you' may not always come right at the beginning of the word, but it will be near the beginning. Could you tell two people to tidy up?

Desadohdá:.   'Tidy up.'   ?   'Tidy up, you two.'

Wadewayęstanih

Wadewayęstanih

Wadewayę́stanih

SNI-
(Another both of yous)

Some verbs use *sni-* for 'you two'.

Syadǫ́:.	'Write (to one person).'
Sn<u>i</u>hyá:dǫ:.	'Write, you two.'
Seksoháehǫ:.	'Wash the dishes (to one person).'
Sniksoháehǫ:.	'Wash the dishes, you two.'
Seksagewáhǫ:.	'Dry the dishes (to one person).'
Sniksagewáhǫ:.	'Dry the dishes, you two.'

If a command to one person begins with *s-* then *is followed by* a consonant (consonants are H, K, N, R, S, T, W, Y, ʔ), the *s-* changes to *sni-*, to order two people around.

Sn<u>o</u>háehǫ:. 'Do the washing (alone).'   Sninoháehǫ:. 'Do the washing, you two.'

If a command to one person begins with *se-*, just change the *se-* 'you' to *sni-* 'you two' to order two people around.

Sejisdó:deh. 'Turn on the light   Snijisdó:deh. 'Turn on the light, you two
   (to one person).'   (to two people).'

Georgina uses some words with this *sni-* when she is talking to Lila about herself and her mother.

Ęsniwayę:nę́:daʔ.   'You two will finish it.'

Practice

The commands below will let you order one person around. Can you change them to order two people around at once?

Snǫ́:dęh.	'Feed it.'
Senhóha:.	'Close the door.'
Senhodǫ́:goh.	'Open the door.'
Seję́hęh.	'Go get water.'
Sekǫ́:nih.	'Cook.'
Segahoʔjí:yaʔk.	'Cut the grass.'
Segwáhah.	'Go get it.'
Setsę́i.	'Find it.'
Segáʔtsih.	'Take it off.'

Wadewayęstanih

Wadewayę́stanih

Wadewayę́stanih

SWA-
(Yous)

As you can see by now, Cayuga speakers pay very close attention to exactly how many people they are ordering around. Once you know how to talk to two people, using *tsa-* or *sni-*, it is very easy to change any word to apply to a larger group. Simply substitute *swa-* 'yous' for *tsa-* or *sni-* 'you two'.

Jagyę:.	'Sit down, you two.'
Swagyę:.	'Sit down, yous.'
Jatgáhtoh.	'Look, you two.'
Swatgáhtoh.	'Look, yous.'
Snihyá:dǫ:.	'Write, you two.'
Swahyá:dǫ:.	'Write, yous.'
Sn<u>i</u>hnég<u>e</u>hah.	'Drink, you two.'
Sw<u>a</u>hnég<u>e</u>hah.	'Drink, yous.'

You have already run across this *swa-* 'yous' a number of times, for example in the section on body parts. It can also mean 'your'.

S<u>a</u>hǫhda'geh.	'On your ear (to one person).'
Sw<u>a</u>hǫhda'geh.	'On your ears (to two or more people).'

This *swa-* will work when talking to any group of people of three or more.

Practice

See whether you could change the commands you know for two people to commands for a whole group. See how many correct group orders you can come up with. Go ahead and look back at the last few pages for inspiration.

(Y)AKNI-
(Both of us)

When Lila talks about herself and her mother, she cannot use just *k(e)* 'I'. To show she is including her mother, she uses a special form for 'we two', *yakni-* or *akni-*. Compare the words below.

Ęgewayę:nę́:daʔ.	'I will finish it.'
Ęyakniwayęnę́:daʔ.	'We two will finish it (she and I).'
Ęyagwawayęnę́:daʔ.	'We all will finish it (they and I).'
Agehsrǫnyáhnǫ:ʔ.	'I made things.'
Aknihsrǫ́nyahnǫ:ʔ.	'We two made things (she and I).'
Agwahsrǫ́nyahnǫ:ʔ.	'We all made things (they and I).'
Akʔníkǫnyǫ:ʔ.	'I sewed.'
Aknʔiníkǫnyǫ:ʔ.	'We two sewed (she and I).'
Agwʔaníkǫnyǫ:ʔ.	'We all sewed (they and I).'

As you can see, the difference between 'we two' and 'we all' is really just one syllable, *ni-* or *wa-*. If you know the form of a verb for 'we two', which contains *akni-*, you can easily change it to a verb for 'we all' by substituting *agwa-*.

H-
(Away)

A number of verbs in this conversation begin with *h-*, because Lila is discussing what she did while she was away.

Heséʔsgęhę:ʔ.	'You were there.'
Hęsge:ʔ.	'I will go back there.'
Hęyakniwayęnę́:daʔ.	'We two will go back to it (he or she and I).' or 'We two will finish it over there (he or she and I).'

The *h-* on the beginning of the word shows that the action or event was or will be away somewhere. It means 'there' or 'away'. Can you imagine how to say, 'we all will go back to it'?

NEW VOCABULARY

dagatwęnǫ́daʔ	'I called up'
tę́ʔ dʔesíʔdrǫʔ	'you weren't home'
gyʔedrǫʔ	'she is/was home there'
eʔdrǫʔ	'she is/was home'
itgeʔs	'I am/was there'
agagyʔǫséhǫhk	'I had gone to visit'
agáhdęgyǫ:	'I had gone away'
hęsge:ʔ	'I will go back there'
nʔejá:gye:ʔ	'you two did it'
nʔeswá:gye:ʔ	'yous did it'
esniwayę:nę́:daʔ	'you two finished it'
eswawayę:nę́:daʔ	'yous finished it'
jagyęhsrǫ́:nih	'you two are making a blanket'
swagyęhsrǫ́:nih	'yous are making a blanket'
jagyę́:	'sit down, both of you'
swagyę́:	'sit down, yous'
jatgáhtoh	'look, both of you'
swatgáhtoh	'look, yous'
sn<u>i</u>hnég<u>e</u>hah	'drink, you two'
sw<u>a</u>hnég<u>e</u>hah	'drink, yous'
jatgę́h	'get up, you two'
swatgę́h	'get up, yous'
hęyakniwayęnę́:daʔ	'we two will finish over there, then (he/she and I)'
tę́ʔ gwáhs dʔeǫkniwayęnę́dʔaǫʔ	'we two didn't quite finish'
aknʔiníkǫnyǫ:ʔ	'we two sewed things (he/she and I)'
agwʔaníkǫnyǫ:ʔ	'we all sewed things (they and I)'
akn<u>i</u>hsrǫ́ny<u>a</u>hnǫ:ʔ	'we two made things (he/she and I)'
agwahsrǫ́ny<u>a</u>hnǫ:ʔ	'we all made things (they and I)'
té:dęʔ	'yesterday'
aǫhę́:ʔęh	'it is alone'
oyę́hsraʔ, oyę́hzraʔ	'blanket', 'quilt'
dáonǫ:ʔ	'it lacked'
gadiyʔadáǫnyǫʔ	'pictures' (literally, 'their bodies are on it')

Wadewayę́stanih

nʔagadiyáʔdʔodę́ʔ	'kind of bodies', 'breed'
degá:gyaʔs	'parrot(s)' (literally, 'it breaks shells')
haʔdey<u>o</u>hsóhgwage:	'many different colours'
g<u>a</u>hsdúʔdrʔageh	'on its feathers'
degáy<u>e</u>hsdǫh	'it is mixed'
oyę̨hsrí:yo:, oyę̨hzrí:yo:	'nice quilt', 'nice blanket'
niyoy<u>ę</u>hsróʔdę:, niyoy<u>ę</u>hzróʔdę:	'kind of quilt', 'kind of blanket'
gyagodʔedrá:dǫʔ	'she has it framed'
tgayę̨hsraní:yǫ:t	'the blanket is hanging there'
oya:nré:ʔah	'it is sort of nice'
á:gehs	'for me to use'
nʔagaʔdrehdóʔdę:	'make of car'
nʔaohs<u>o</u>hgóʔdę:	'type of paint', 'kind of colour'
niyoyę̨hsróʔdę:	'kind of blanket', 'appearance'
ohsohgwí:yo:	'nice colour'
ohsohgwí:yoʔs	'nice colours'
sagyaʔdawiʔtrí:yo:	'your dress/coat/shirt is nice'
ne:ʔ hó:niʔ	'that is why'
aǫhę:ʔę̨ ohsohgwí:yoʔs	'outstanding colours'
ę̨yakn<u>i</u>hnég<u>e</u>haʔ	'he/she and I will drink'
ę̨yagw<u>a</u>hnég<u>e</u>haʔ	'we will drink (they and I)'

33

DĘDWAʔĘNÁĘʔ

Wadewayéstanih

479

Wadewayę́stanih

Wadewayęstanih

DĘDWAʔĘNÁĘʔ

Wadewayę́stanih

Wadeway:ęstanih

<u>J-/SN(I)-/ or SWA-</u>
(Yous)

    You can tell how many people Sam is talking to by looking at the pictures, or by listening to how he says 'you'. When he is talking to just two people, he uses *j-* or *sn(i)-* 'both of yous'.

Dajagyęhę́:toh.	'You two, pull.'
Hęsnóʔkdęʔ.	'You two will get to the end.'
Heʔsniǫdíʔdre:.	'You two, drag the log over there.'
Dędisniǫ́dʔidre:ʔ.	'You two will drag the log back here.'

When he is talking to a larger group, he uses *sw(a)-* 'yous'.

Swáǫgyʔagǫh.	'Yous have cut the log.'
Swáǫdahęh.	'Put the log up..., yous.'
Ęswagyadǫ́:niʔ.	'Yous will make a track.'
Ędiswahsá:węʔ.	'Yous will start.'

Wadewayę́stanih

Wadewayę́stanih

DW(A)-/YAGW(A)-
(You and I/They and I)

English really has only one way of saying 'we': *we*. You have seen that Cayuga speakers distinguish whether two people are involved or more, (*yakni-* 'we two', *yagwa-* 'we all'). Cayuga makes another distinction: whether the hearer is included or not. So far, in earlier conversations, the speaker never included the hearer. Sam told Junior about his family's plans to go away for the summer (Junior was not going along), Georgina told Lila about her family's garden (Lila was not going to help), and Lila told Georgina about her and her mother's quilt (Georgina was not with them). Whenever these people said 'we', they meant 'those people and I'.

On this outing, Sam wants to include the people he is talking to.

Dędwaʔęnáęʔ.	'We will play snowsnake (yous and I).'
Ędwagyadǫ́:niʔ.	'We will build a track (yous and I).'
Ędwaǫdíʔdre:ʔ.	'We will drag a log (yous and I).'
DwʔagranhohsrÓ:dęh.	'Let's all pile this snow (yous and I).'
Ędwawayę:nę́:daʔ.	'We all will finish (yous and I).'
Dęjidwadá:tgęʔ.	'We will see each other again (yous and I).'

A few times, he excludes the person he is talking to. These times, instead of using *twa-* 'yous and I', as he did in the words above, he uses *yagw(a)-* 'they and I'.

Ęyagwʔagranhohsró:dęʔ.	'We all will pile the snow (they and I).'
Hęyá:gwe:ʔ.	'We will go over there (they and I).'
Eyagwagya:dǫ́:niʔ.	'We all will make a track (they and I).'

If you compare the two pairs below, you can see that it is just the part that means 'we' that changes.

Ędwagyadǫ́:niʔ.	'We all will build a track (yous and I).'
Ęyagwagya:dǫ́:niʔ.	'We all will build a track (they and I).'
Dwʔagranhohsró:dęh.	'Let's all pile this snow (yous and I).'
Ęyagwʔagranhohsró:dęʔ.	'We will all pile this snow (they and I).'

These inclusive 'you and I' forms are useful for proposing things to do or for invitations.

Ędwe:ʔ gęh?	Gayaʔtaʔgé hedwe:.
you-all-and-I-go ?	movies-to let-us-go-there
'Will you come with us?'	'Let's go to the movies.'

Wadewayęstanih

Dwagyę:.   'Let's sit down.'   Jidwahdę:dih. 'Let's go home.'

Dwade:kǫ́:nih. 'Let's eat.'   Dwahnégehah. 'Let's drink.'

NEW VOCABULARY

dędwaʔęnáę́ʔ	'we all will play snowsnake' (yous and I)
ędwagyadǫ́:niʔ	'we all will build a track' (yous and I)
ędwaǫdíʔdre:ʔ	'we all will drag the log' (yous and I)
dwʔagranhohsró:dęh	'let us pile up snow' (yous and I)
ędwawayę:nę́:daʔ	'we all will finish' (yous and I)
dejidwadá:tgęʔ	'we all will see each other again' (yous and I)
ęyagwʔagranhohsró:dęʔ	'we all will pile snow' (they and I)
ęyagwagya:dǫ́:niʔ	'we will make a track' (they and I)
ękne:ʔ	'we two will go together (you and I)'
hękní:yǫʔ	'we two will arrive there (you and I)'
ędwadagwáisiʔ	'we all will do it straight' (yous and I)
hęyá:gwe:ʔ	'we all will go there' (they and I)
hędwe:ʔ	'we all will go there' (yous and I)
swáǫgyʔagǫh	'yous have cut the log'
ędiswahsá:węʔ	'yous will start'
hęwáhsawęʔ	'it will start from there'
ęswagyadǫ́:niʔ	'yous will make a track'
swáǫdaę	'yous lay the log here'
dajagyę̣hę́:toh	'you two pull'
heʔsniǫdíʔdre:	'you two, drag the log away'
hęsnóʔkdęʔ	'you two will get to the end over there'
dędisniódʔidre:ʔ	'you two will drag the log back here'
ęjisnʔokdęʔ	'you two will end it back here'
heyó:doʔk	'it ends over there', 'it runs out over there'
dęhęnʔáęnaęʔ	'they will play snowsnake' (males only)
sigwa:dí tgá:yęʔ	'it is laying over there'
gaę diʔ nyó: hęyá:gwe:ʔ?	'how far do we go?'
ó:, ęga:gwe:niʔ gyę́:ʔǫ hne:ʔ	'I suppose it will do'
oyánrahsdǫh	'it is ideal'
oʔgraęʔ	'snow on the ground'
oyá:deʔ	'track'

Wadewayę́stanih

dagwá:dih	'over here'
sigwá:dih	'it is laying there'
tgá:yę²	'it will be first'
gyonǫdahe²ge:	'to the big hill'
oyánragye²	'it is going well'
odęháiyo:	'the sun is bright'
awa²graná:wę²	'snow melted'
ęga:gwé:ni²	'it is enough', 'it will do'
niyó:we²	'distance'
sę n(i)yó:we²	'up to there', 'until'
niyowęyǫhgá:ge:	'that many inches'
nęgayadáha²k	'track will be set up from the ground'
awadewayęnę́:da²	'it got finished'
dehá:da²	'let him stand'
dekda²s	'I stand'
dehá:da²s	'he stands'
deyé:da²s	'she stands'
oyádagǫ:	'in the track'
gáǫd²ageh	'on the log'
grǫdí²dre²	'I am pulling the log'
o²ę́:na², deyǫ²ęnaędáhkwa²	'snowsnake'
dega²ęnáęhę²	'I am a snowsnake player'
deha²ęnáęhę²	'he is a snowsnake player'
deyǫ²ęnáęhę²	'she is a snowsnake player'
onódahǫ²	'hills'
dwagagyęhę́:twęh	'I am pulling'
gyagogyęhę́:twęh	'she is pulling'
togyę́hętwęh	'he is pulling'
gyagonagyę́hętwęh	'they are pulling'
ha²dewagáhja:²	'I am pushing'
ha²deyagáhja:²	'she is pushing'
ha²déhohja:²	'he is pushing'
shęh niyo:yá:de:s	'how deep the track is'
ętęnahsá:wę²	'they will begin' (males only)

34

ĘKNÍYĘTO?

Wadewayéstanih

ĘKNIYĘTOʔ

Wadewayę́stanih

Wadewayę́stanih

-KN(I)-
(You and I will)

Making plans to plant together, Pete and Sam use a lot of words which begin *kni-* 'you and I'.

Ękníyęto⁷.	'You and I will plant.'
Ęknihona⁷dayę́:to⁷.	'You and I will plant potatoes.'
Ęknihona⁷dayę́twahsa⁷.	'You and I will go plant potatoes.'
Ękni:yę́twahsǫ:⁷.	'You and I could plant things.'
Hęknéhdahk.	'You and I will go there.'

The *kn(i)-* shows that just two people, the speaker and the hearer, are involved.

GǪ-/SG-/SK-
(I for you and you for me)

There are a number of things Pete offers to do <u>for</u> Sam, some that Sam will do <u>for</u> Pete, and some that one does <u>to</u> the other. Look at these words.

A**gǫ́**:gę⁷.	'<u>I</u> saw <u>you</u>.'
Ęs**gǫ́**:gę⁷.	'<u>I</u> will see <u>you</u> again.'
Ęs**gǫ́**⁷drǫhna⁷.	'<u>I</u> will take <u>you</u> back again.'
A:**gǫ**yénawa⁷s.	'<u>I</u> could help <u>you</u>.'
Hę**gǫ**hawíhdę⁷.	'<u>I</u> will carry it there for <u>you</u>.'

As you can see, the *gǫ-* adds the meaning 'I...you'.

Now look at these words:

Sa**sg**í⁷drǫ:⁷.	'<u>You</u> brought <u>me</u> back.'
Ę**sg**yénawa⁷s.	'<u>You</u> will help <u>me</u>.'
Hę**sk**áwihdę⁷.	'<u>You</u> will carry it there for <u>me</u>.'
A**sg**é:gę⁷.	'<u>You</u> saw <u>me</u>.'
A:**sg**yená:wa⁷s.	'Could <u>you</u> help <u>me</u>.'

As you can see, the *sg-* or *sk-* adds the meaning 'you...me'.

Some of the verbs also have a part which shows that the action is for the other person's benefit. This part is the *-⁷s* on the end of the words about helping and *-ę* on the end of the verbs about carrying.

GǪ-/DAG-/DAK-

You can also command someone to do something for you, or offer to do something for them. Compare the commands here:

Dagyénawaʔs.	'Help me.'
Gǫyénawaʔs.	'Let me help you.'
Dagékǫnyęh.	'Cook for me.'
Gǫkǫ́:nyęh.	'Let me cook for you.'
Dakyádǫhahs.	'Write it for me.'
Gǫhyádǫhahs.	'Let me write it for you.'

As you can see, to change a command to an offer, you can simply change *dag-* or *dak-* ('you for me') to *gǫ-* ('I for you'). Try changing the commands below to offer to help.

Dagadadríhǫnyęʔs.   'Read it to me.'

Dagadahǫhsí:yohs.   'Listen to me.'

Sometimes the first syllable of an offer is whispered, as in 'let me write it for you'. This is because the first syllable ends in *h*. See whether you can predict how to say 'let me buy one for you' and 'let me follow you' from the commands below.

Dakní:nǫʔs.	'Buy it for me.'	(*dak-hní:nǫ-ʔs*)
Daknǫ́:dręh.	'Follow me.'	(*dak-hnǫ:dręh*)

Both of the offers should begin with a whispered syllable.

NEW VOCABULARY

desawayęnhá:ʔǫh	'you are busy', 'you were busy'
dewagewayęnháʔǫh	'I am busy', 'I was busy'
syętwáhsǫh	'you are planting things'
gyętwáhsǫh	'I am planting things'
agǫ́:gęʔ	'I saw you'
asgé:gęʔ	'you saw me'
ihse:	'you think'
tę́ʔ gęh dʔese:ʔ	'don't you think?'
a:gǫyénawaʔs	'I could help you'
a:sgyená:waʔs	'you could help me'
dagyénawaʔs	'help me'
gyętwáhsǫh	'let me help you'
ęsgyénawaʔs	'you will help me'
aekniyętwahsǫ:ʔ	'you and I could plant'
ękniho̜naʔdayę́:toʔ	'you and I will plant potatoes'
ękniho̜naʔdayętwahso:ʔ	'you and I will plant lots of potatoes'
ękníyętoʔ	'you and I will plant'
hękǫnʔadáyętoʔ	'I will plant potatoes there'
ęgadehsrǫ́nyahnǫ:ʔ	'I will prepare'
hęgǫhawíhdęʔ	'I will take it for you'
hęskáwihdęʔ	'you will take it for me'
hęknéhdahk	'you and I will go there together'
ęságaę	'you will be willing'
ęsgǫ́ʔdrǫhnaʔ	'I will take you back'
dǫdasgʔidrǫ́hnah	'you take me back'
sasgíʔdrǫ:ʔ	'you have brought me back'
ęsgǫ́:gęʔ	'I will see you again'
dagékǫnyęh	'cook for me'
gǫkǫ́:nyęh	'let me cook for you'
dakyádǫhahs	'write it for me'
gǫhyádǫhahs	'let me write for you'
dakní:nǫʔs	'buy it for me'
dagadadríhǫnyęʔs	'read it to me'
dagadahǫhsí:yohs	'listen to me'

Wadewayęstanih

daknǫ:dręh	'follow me'
ǫhnyá²geh	'on the river flats'
saná:kdo:t	'you have time (space)'
hęgyę²tsǫ²	'never mind'
sedjí:hah	'early in the morning'
gǫ́dagye²	'right away'
sadę́n²atra²	'your lunch', 'your groceries'
sǫ́:de²	'last night'

35

AQHDĘGYǪHEʔ

Wadewayęstanih

ohwę'gá:' deyagonęhsóweksǫ' / deyagonę́hsǫ'

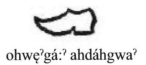

ohwę'gá:' ahdáhgwa'

Wadewayęstanih

Wadewayéstanih

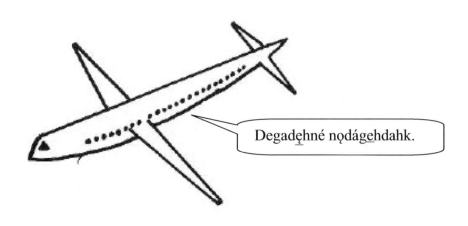

506

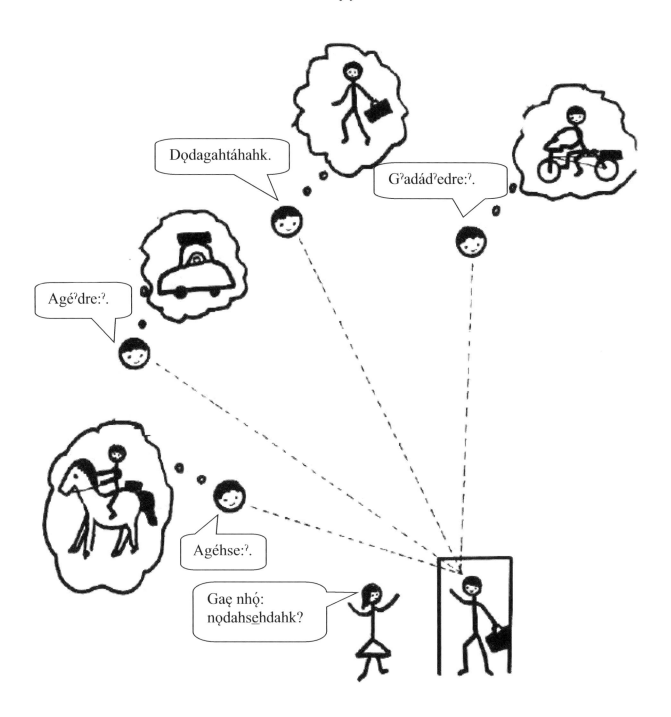

Wadewayęstanih

AǪHDĘGYǪHEʔ

Wadewayę́stanih

Wadewayę́stanih

GAE-/GAĘ-
(Those women)

In this conversation Helen and Pete are talking about the two women together. You can see that more than one person is involved from the beginning of the verb. The *kae-* or *gaę-* means 'they' (females or mixed) and is the same form you saw earlier in the conversation about the twin neighbors.

Tgáenagreʔ.	'They live there.'
Haʔgáęʔ.	'They went there.'
Hegáęʔs.	'They are there.'
Haʔgáęhdahk...	'They went by way of...'

YAGODI-/YAGON-

Another form which means 'they' (females or mixed) is *yagodi-* or *yagon-*.

Heyagodí:yǫ:.	'They arrived there.'
Deyagonęhsówieksǫʔ.	'They are wearing shoes.'

When this is at the beginning of the word, the first syllable is dropped, leaving *godi-* or *gon-* for 'they'.

Goné:nǫhk.	'They had gone together.'
Gonáhdęgyǫ:.	'They are gone.'

There are a lot of ways to say 'they' in Cayuga, and these are used only for the women! A good goal for now is just to remember these forms: *gae-*, *gaę-*, *yagodi-*, *yagon-*, *godi-*, and *gon-* so that you will recognize them when they appear, and will know that several people are involved.

AE-/AʔE-
(She did)

Notice that when Pete asks whether Lila enjoyed her trip, he says, *aénǫhweʔ* 'she liked it', but when Helen replies, she uses the word *aʔénǫhweʔ* 'she liked it'. The second word has a catch between the first two syllables. Both forms are used, and you will hear this difference a lot with words meaning 'she did something'. The first way, without the catch, is less formal.

Wadewayę́stanih

H-/D-/T-
(More there and here)

You may have noticed that a number of verbs in this conversation begin with the *h-* that means 'away', or 'over there', since Helen and Pete are discussing a trip and a foreign country.

Heyę́ʔsgęhę:ʔ.	'She was there.'
Hé:yęʔs.	'She was/is there.'
Hegáęʔs.	'They were/are there (females or mixed).'
HaʔgáęhdahkЕ	'They went by means ofЕ' or 'They went by (females or mixed)Е'
Heyagodí:yǫ:.	'They arrived there (females or mixed).'

The conversation also has a few verbs with *t-* or *d-* 'here', 'this way', or 'in this or that place'.

D<u>a</u>heʔ.	'He is coming (this way).'
Tgáenagreʔ.	'They live there (females or mixed).'

SATSĘ:NǪ:NI: GĘH?
(Are you glad?)

Helen tells Pete that her father was happy to have her mother home.

Ahatsęnǫ:níʔ neʔ o:nę́ saeyǫʔ.	'He was happy when she returned.'

If you would like to tell someone you are glad about something, you can use the word *agatsęnǫ́:ni:* 'I am glad'. (Notice that the ending is *-i:* for the present.)

Agatsęnǫ:ní: ahsyǫʔ.	'I am glad you came.'
Agatsęnǫ:ní: adigyadá:tgęʔ.	'I am glad we saw each other.'
Agatsęnǫ:ní: nę:tv nǫda:ge:ʔ.	'I am glad I came.'

TĘ́ʔ GĘH?
(When you suspect the worst)

Cayuga speakers can ask negative questions too. They usually use these when they suspect the answer is 'no'.

Tę́ʔ gęh dʔesa:tǫ́:deʔ?   'Don't you hear it?'
   (Compare *Satǫ́:deʔ gęh?*, 'Do you hear it?'.)

As you can see, negative questions begin *tę́ʔ gęh...*, with 'not' and the question marker, then the negative verb.

Tę́ʔ gęh dʔesatsęnǫ́:ni:?   'Aren't you glad?'

Tę́ʔ gęh dʔesadǫhswéʔdanih?   'Aren't you hungry?'

Tę́ʔ gęh dʔehesé:gę:?   'Didn't you see him?'

Negative questions usually have negative answers.

Tę́ʔ dʔeagadǫhsweʔdá:nih.   'No, I'm not hungry.'

Try making negative questions out of these negative statements.

Tę́ʔ dʔesé:gę:.   'You didn't see it.' (Didn't you see it?)

Tę́ʔ dʔesátsęhdǫh.   'You aren't tired.'

Tę́ʔ dʔesahwihsdáęʔ.   'You don't have any money.'

Answers to these are most likely to be the following.

Tę́ʔ, tę́ʔ dʔegé:gę:.

Tę́ʔ, tę́ʔ dʔeagatsę́hdǫh.

Tę́ʔ, tę́ʔ dʔeakwihsdáęʔ.

GAĘ HESEʔSGĘHĘ:ʔ?
(Where were you?)

You can easily answer a question like this using place names from earlier conversations in this book.

Gaę heseʔsgęhę:ʔ?	'Where were you?'
_____ hegéʔsgęhę:ʔ.	'I was in _____.'
Taǫdǫ́ʔ hegéʔsgęhę:ʔ.	'I was in Toronto.'

GAĘ NHǪ: HAʔSEHDAHK?
(How did you get there?)

Pete asks Helen whether the women went to Europe by boat.

Gahǫwagǫ́:   gęh   haʔgáęhdahk?
in-a-boat   ?   they-went-there-with
'Did they go by boat?'

She replies that they went by airplane.

Degadęhné   haʔgáęhdahk.
on-it-flies   they-went-there-with
'They went by airplane.'

To ask someone how they traveled somewhere, you can just ask:

Gaę nhǫ́: haʔsehdahk?	'How did you go?'
or	
Gaę nhǫ́: nǫdahsehdahk?	'How did you get here?'

Here are some answers.

Atgátahahk.	'I walked.'	Dǫdagatáhahk.	'I walked here.'
Gʔadádʔedreː?.	'I rode a bike.'		
Agéhseːʔ.	'I rode horseback.'		
Agéʔdreːʔ.	'I drove.' or 'I rode.'		

⎧ gʔadrehdowanęhné   (on a train) ⎫   ⎧ haʔgéhdahk   (I went by) ⎫
⎨ degadęhné   (on a plane) ⎬   +   ⎨ nǫdágehdahk   (I came by) ⎬
⎩ gahǫwagǫ́:   (in a boat) ⎭   ⎩   ⎭

DO: NʔAONISHEʔ?
(How long did it take?)

Pete is having a hard time understanding time. Some of the questions he asks are below. His voice stays level in tone throughout.

Do: diʔ nʔaonishéʔ to he:yęʔs?
'Then how long was she there?'

Do: diʔ gę nʔaonishéʔ to nyó:ʔ haʔgaęʔ?
'Then how long did it take for them to get there?'

You can see that to ask how long something lasted, you just ask:

Do: (diʔ) nʔaonisheʔ...

Here are some more samples:

Dó: nʔaoniséʔ sahdę:gyǫ:?   'How long were you away?'

Dó: nʔaoniséʔ hehseʔs?   'How long were you there?'

You can also use this expression to ask how long it took someone to do something.

Dó: nʔaoniséʔ esagyena:wáht...?
'How long did it take you...?'

Here are some samples of that:

Dó: nʔaonishéʔ esagyena:wáht asehsrǫ:niʔ?
'How long did it take you to make it?'

Dó: nʔaonishéʔ esagyena:wáht sasehsrǫ:ni?
'How long did it take you to fix it?'

Sometimes the phrase *dó: nʔaonishéʔ esagyena:wáht* is shortened to:

Dó: esagyena:wáht...?
'How long did it take you...?'

O̧GAGYENÁ:WAHT
(It took me…)

In case someone asks you how long it took you to do something, here are some answers you can use.

Sgá:t agahwihsdaʔé:k o̧gagyená:waht.
'It took me one hour.'

Dekní: atgahwihsdaʔé:k o̧gagyená:waht.
'It took me two hours.'

Ahsę́ nʔatgahwihsdaʔé:k o̧gagyená:waht.
'It took me three hours.'

For four hours or more, just substitute the number for *ahsę*.

Géi nʔatgahwihsdaʔé:k o̧gagyená:waht.
'It took me four hours.'

Degró̧ʔ nʔatgahwihsdaʔé:k o̧gagyená:waht.
'It took me eight hours.'

If it took you longer, you might want to talk in terms of days.

Swę́hnihsrá:t o̧gagyená:waht.
'It took me one day.'

Dewęhnihsra:gé: o̧gagyená:waht.
'It took me two days.'

Ahsę́ niwęhnihsra:gé: o̧gagyená:waht.   (For more days, just substitute the number
'It took me three days.'   you want for *ahsęh*.)

Géi niwęhnihsra:gé: o̧gagyená:waht.
'It took me four days.'

Perhaps you did not put in full time on your project, and you want to talk in terms of weeks.

Sgá:t ao̧dadogę̱htéʔ o̧gagyená:waht.
'It took me one week.'

Dekní: agyao̧dadogę̱htéʔ o̧gagyená:waht.
'It took me two weeks.'

Ahsę́ nʔao̧dadogę̱htéʔ o̧gagyená:waht.   (For more weeks, substitute the number
'It took me three weeks.'   you want for *ahsęh*.)

If you were really slow, you might need these.

Swęni'dá:t ǫgagyená:waht.
'It took me one month.'

Dewęhn'ida:gé: ǫgagyená:waht.
'It took me two months.'

Ahsę́ niwęhn'ida:gé: ǫgagyená:waht. (For four or more months, substitute the
'It took me three months.' appropriate number for *ahsę*.)

Géi niwęhn'ida:gé: ǫgagyená:waht.
'It took me four months.'

Gyohdǫ́: niwęhn'ida:gé: ǫgagyená:waht.
'It took me nine months.'

If you are both slow and patient, you might find these useful.

Johsrá:t ǫgagyená:waht.
'It took me one year.'

Deyohsragé: ǫgagyená:waht.
'It took me two years.'

Ahsę́ niyohsragé: ǫgagyená:waht. (For four or more years, substitute the
'It took me three years.' appropriate number for *ahséh*.)

Hwíhs niyohsragé: ǫgagyená:waht.
'It took me five years.'

Ja:dáhk niyohsragé: ǫgagyená:waht.
'It took me seven years.'

You can use these times to talk about the length of any activity in the past. Simply substitute the verb you want in place of *ǫgagyená:waht*. Here are some samples.

Hwíhs niyohsragé: n'etóh agadrihó'da:t.
'I worked there for five years.'

Hwíhs niyohsragé: n'etóh tg'idrǫ'.
'I lived there for five years (I live somewhere else now).'

Hwíhs niyohsragé: tsigi'drǫ' nę:toh.
'I have lived here for five years (and still do).'

HWĘ:DQH?
(When?)

You can ask someone when a particular past event took place with the word *hwę:dǫh* 'when'.

Hwę:dǫ́ jisa:yǫ:?
'When did you get back?'

Here are some answers to that question.

Waʔhe haʔtsǫ́: swagyǫ:.	'I just returned.'
Tsigaǫhyahę́ swagyǫ:.	'I returned at noon.'
Wa̱hsǫ:tę́ swagyǫ:.	'I returned at midnight.'
Sgá:t tsijohwi̱hsdaʔe: swagyǫ:.	'I returned at one o'clock.'
Ahsę́ tsijohwi̱hsdaʔe: swagyǫ:.	'I returned at three o'clock.'
Géi tsijohwi̱hsdaʔe: swagyǫ:.	'I returned at four o'clock.'

etc.

These times specify that the moment is past. Here are some days of the week for the same kind of answer, again about a past event.

Tsiyonakdóhaes	'Saturday (past)'
Tsiaǫdadogę́hdǫh	'Sunday (past)'
Tsaʔwę:dę́:daʔ	'Monday (past)'
Dekní: hadǫ́ʔtgęhę:ʔ	'Tuesday (past)'
Ahsę́ hadǫ́ʔtgęhę:ʔ	'Wednesday (past)'
Géi hadǫ́ʔtgęhę:ʔ	'Thursday (past)'
Hwíhs hadǫ́ʔtgęhę:ʔ	'Friday (past)'

Wadewayę́stanih

Your latest fling

      Go around the room, asking each person where they were on some particular day. (You can use the days just listed.)

Gaę heseʔsgę̱hę:ʔ tsiaǫdadogę̱hdǫh?
etc.

Next, ask how they got there:

Gaę nhǫ́: haʔsehdahk?

Now, ask how long it took to get there:

Dó: nʔaonishéʔ esagyena:wáht haʔsyǫʔ?

Find out how long they were there:

Dó: diʔ nʔaonishéʔ hehseʔs?

See whether they enjoyed it:

Asnǫ́hweʔ gę̱h?

Finally, ask when they returned:

Hwę:dǫ́ jisa:yǫ:?

      Answer any questions that come your way with the most preposterous story you can think of. Here are some words that might be useful:

_____ hegéʔsgę̱hę:ʔ.	'I was in _____.'
_____ hé:geʔs.	'I was there for _____.'
_____ haʔgéhdahk.	'I went by _____.'

NEW VOCABULARY

eʔdrǫʔ	'she is home'
jagó:yǫ:	'she arrived back home'
heyę́ʔsgę̱hę:ʔ	'she was there'
sganyada:digó:wah	'Europe' (literally, 'beyond the ocean')
tgáenagreʔ	'they live there'
de̱honę:sowé:ksǫʔ	'they wear shoes' (male only)
gonę:nǫhk	'they went together'
deyagonę̱hsóweksǫʔ	'they wear shoes' (females or mixed)
nʔaeyʔadóʔdę̱ʔ	'the kind of person she is'
hegáę̱ʔs	'they are there'
agyaǫdadogę́hteʔ	'it was two weeks'
nʔagahwi̱hsdáʔe:k	'it was several hours'
gonáhdę̱gyǫ:	'they were away'
asehsrǫ́:niʔ	'you made it'
tgaí:ʔ	'it is correct'
gahwísdʔaes	'time', 'clock'
ahoʔnigǫháę̱daʔ	'he understood'
tę́ʔ dehoʔnigǫháę̱daʔ	'he does not understand'
dę̱ʔ niyó:gyę:	'what is happening'
tę́ʔ desa:tǫ́:deʔ	'you do not hear it'
ahatsę̱nǫ́:niʔ	'he became happy'
agatsę̱nǫ́:ni:	'I am glad'
satsę:nǫ́:ni:	'you are glad'
tse̱hawinǫ́:gyeʔ	'she brought back things'
ǫkihawíʔse̱heʔ	'she brought for us'
sǫwahawíʔse̱heʔ	'she brought back for him'
esagyená:waht	'it took you time'
nʔesagyená:waht	'it took you so much time'
ǫgagyená:waht	'it took me time'
waʔhétsǫ:	'just now'
agę̱ʔ	'it is said'
to niyo:	'that far'
sedjí:hah	'early in the morning'
odǫgo̱hdǫ́ gáǫhya̱hę̱h	'in the afternoon'

Wadewayéstanih

aʔénǫhweʔ	'she liked it'
haʔgáęhdahk…	'they went by…'
haʔgáęʔ	'they went' (females or mixed)
gonáhdęgyǫ:	'they left'
heyagodí:yǫ:	'they arrived there'
hé:yęʔs	'she is there'
ohwę́ʔga:ʔ	'wooden'
sanó:haʔ	'your mother'
ga<u>h</u>ǫwagǫ:	'in a boat'
swęníʔda:t	'one month'
dewęhnʔidá:ge:	'two months'
____ niwęhnʔidá:ge:	'__ months' (three or more people)
j<u>o</u>hsra:t	'one year'
deyóhsrage:	'two years'
____ niyóhsrage:	'__ years' (three or more people)
agadr<u>i</u>hóʔda:t	'I worked'
tgʔidrǫʔ	'I lived there'
tsigíʔdrǫʔ	'I have lived (and still do) somewhere'

Wadewayę́stanih

36

DIALOGUES WITH TRANSLATIONS

Chapter 3 SGĘ:NQ̨ʔ

SGĘ:NQ̨ʔ (Cayuga) p. 32

Pete:	Sgę́:nǫʔ
Bessie:	Ęhę́ʔ, ne:ʔ giʔ á:yę:ʔ.
Pete:	Węhnihsri:yó: wáʔne:ʔ.
Bessie:	Ęhę́ʔ, węhnihsrí:yo:.

SGĘ:NQ̨ʔ (English) p. 32

Peter:	Hello, how are you?
Bessie:	Not bad, I guess.
Pete:	Nice day today.
Bessie:	Yes, in fact it is.

Chapter 4 ĘYOSDAQDIʔ

ĘYOSDAQDIʔ (Cayuga) p. 38

Bessie:	Sgę́:nǫʔ.
Pete:	Ęhę́ʔ, ne:ʔ giʔ á:yę:ʔ.
Bessie:	Węhnihsri:yó: wáʔne:ʔ.
Pete:	Ęhę́ʔ, węhnihsrí:yo:.
Pete:	A:yę:ʔtsǫ́: ohjíʔgreʔ.
Pete:	Ęyosdaǫdíʔ gʔishę́ hwaʔ.
Bessie:	Gaę nǫdáhse:ʔ?
Pete:	Ganadagǫ́: nǫdá:ge:ʔ.
Pete:	Gaę diʔ haʔseʔ?
Bessie:	Ganadagǫ́: haʔgeʔ.

ĘYOSDAQDIʔ (English) p. 38

Bessie:	Hello, how are you?
Pete:	Not bad, I guess.
Bessie:	Nice day today.
Pete:	Yes, it is a nice day.
Pete:	It just seems a bit cloudy.
Pete:	Perhaps it will rain.
Bessie:	Where did you come from?
Pete:	I came from town.
Pete:	Where are you going?
Bessie:	I am going to town.

Chapter 5 DĘ' HO'DĘ' SYA:SQH?

DĘ' HO'DĘ' SYA:SQH? (Cayuga) p. 47

Pete:	Sgę́:nǫ'.
Myrtle:	Ęhę́', ne:' gi' á:yę:'.
Pete:	Dę' ho'dę' syá:sǫh?
Myrtle:	Myrtle gyá:sǫh.
Pete:	Péte ní:' gyá:sǫh.
Pete:	Gaę nhǫ́: disahdęgyǫ:?
Myrtle:	Tahnawa:dé' dwagáhdęgyǫ:.
Myrtle:	Nę' ne' i:s?
Pete:	Ohswe:gę́' ní:' dwagáhdęgyǫ:.
Pete:	Sha'da:tęhs gęh?
Myrtle:	Ęhę́', a:yę́:' ka'dá:tęhs.
Pete:	Dę' ho'dę' ęhsnegeha'?
Myrtle:	Ohnegaga'ǫ́ ęknégeha'.
Pete:	Hao' d'ęnyóh.
Myrtle:	Háo'. Desa'dráihęh.

DĘ' HO'DĘ' SYA:SQH? (English) p. 47

Pete:	Hello, how are you?
Myrtle:	Hello, how are you?
Pete:	what is your name?
Myrtle:	Myrtle is my name.
Pete:	My name is Pete.
Pete:	Where do you come from?
Myrtle:	I am from Tonawanda.
Myrtle:	How about you?
Pete:	I am from Six Nations.
Pete:	Are you thirsty?
Myrtle:	Yes, it seems like I am.
Pete:	What will you drink?
Myrtle:	I'll drink some pop.
Pete:	OK.
Myrtle:	OK. Hurry.

Chapter 6 SQ: HNE:' N'AHT TO:GYĘH?

SQ: HNE:' N'AHT TO:GYĘH? (Cayuga) p. 61

Pete:	Né:dá gí' gyę:', snegéhah.
Myrtle:	Nyá:węh.
Myrtle:	Oga'ǫ́ nę:gyę́ ohnegagá'ǫh.
Pete:	Gwe:gǫ́ gę gasheyędei?
Myrtle:	Tę́' tóne:'.
Myrtle:	Sǫ hne:' n'áht to:gyę́ eksa:'ah?

Pete:	Bessie eyá:sǫh.
Myrtle:	Ó:ò:, gaę nhǫ́: gyagohdęgyǫ:?
Pete:	G'ada:gra'sgęhę:' gyagóhdęgyǫ:.
Myrtle:	Ǫhǫ:ká' gę ǫgwehǫ́:weh?
Pete:	Oihwi:yó' hne:'.
Myrtle:	Ó:ò:, sǫ: hne:' n'áht to:gyę́ haksa:'ah?
Pete:	Ne:' gi' David hayá:sǫh.
Myrtle:	Ó:ò:, gaę nhǫ́: tohdę:gyǫ:?
Pete:	Tayędane:gę́' tohdę́:gyǫ:.
Myrtle:	Ó:ò:,hahǫ:ká' gę́ ǫgwehǫ:weh?
Pete:	Oihwi:yó' hné:'.
Bessie:	Ó:ò:. Sǫ: hne:' n'áht to:gyę́ eksa:'ah?
Pete:	Ne:' gi' Barb eyá:sǫh.
Myrtle:	Ó:. Gaę nhǫ́: gyagohdęgyǫ:?
Pete:	Gwehsahsné gyagohdęgyǫ:.
Myrtle:	Gwé:, sǫ: hne:' n'áht to:gyę́ haksa:'ah?
Pete:	Ne:' gi' Neil hayá:sǫh.
Myrtle:	Ó:ò:, gaę nhǫ́: tohdę:gyǫ:?
Pete:	Ohnyahę́ tohdę́:gyǫ:.
Myrtle:	Ó:ò:, hahǫ:ká' gę́ ǫgwehǫ:weh?
Pete:	Tę' hne:' dehahǫká' ǫgwehǫ́:weh, ho'nigǫhaęda's hné:'.
Myrtle:	Wa'hé hę' ní:' agadewayęsdǫ́hǫgye'.
Pete:	Ó:ò:, o:nę́ gi' a:yę́:' swęní:yo:!

SǪ: HNE:' N'AHT TO:GYĘH? (English) p. 61

Pete:	Here it is, drink.
Myrtle:	Thank you.
Myrtle:	This pop is delicious.
Pete:	Do you know everyone?
Myrtle:	Not really.
Myrtle:	Who is that girl?
Pete:	Here name is Bessie.
Myrtle.	Oh. Where does she come from?
Pete:	She comes from Cattaraugus.
Myrtle:	Does she speak Indian?
Pete:	She certainly does.
Myrtle:	Oh. Who is that boy?
Pete:	That one is called David.
Myrtle:	Oh. Where does he come from?
Pete:	Deseronto. He comes from there.
Myrtle:	Oh. Does he speak Indian?
Pete:	He certainly does.
Bessie:	Oh. Then who is that girl?
Pete:	That one is called Barb.
Myrtle:	Oh. Where does she come from?
Pete:	She comes from Akwesasne.

Myrtle:	Well, who is that boy?
Pete:	That one is called Neil.
Myrtle:	Oh. Where does he come from?
Pete:	He comes from Oneida.
Myrtle:	Oh. Does he speak Indian?
Pete:	He doesn't speak Indian, but he does understand.
Myrtle:	I myself am just learning also.
Pete:	Oh, you already seem to speak well!

Chapter 8 EKSA?GÓ:WAH

EKSA?GÓ:WAH (Cayuga) p. 88

Pete:	Sǫ: hne:? n?áht to:gyęh?
Pete:	A:yę́:? do:gę́hs eksa?gó:wah.
Junior:	Né:? gi? deyagyanǫhsané:gę:. Deliláh eyá:sǫh.
Pete:	Sǫ: hne:? n?áht to:gyęh, dahoyagę?ǫhǫ:gyé? tganǫhso:t?
Junior:	Né:? gi? né? ho:?.
Pete:	Ó:. Dę? ho?dę́? haya:sǫh?
Junior:	Sampsón hayá:sǫh.
Pete:	Sǫ: hne:? n?áht to:gyę́ gaeks?ashǫ:?ǫh?
Junior:	Né:? gi? Sampsón, Deliláh hni? gaǫdatáwahksǫ?. Ahsę́ nigá:gǫ:.
Pete:	Dę? ho?dę́? gaeyasǫ??
Junior:	Junior, Helen, Hercules hni'.
Pete:	A:yę́:? do:gę́hs ǫ odǫtga:dé? shę gá:gǫnhe?.
Pete:	He?no:sháhs to:gyę́ hǫgweh, shę nyo:wé ni:yeks?ago:wá né? ho:?.
Pete:	Sǫga:?á gę́ ne? gagǫgwé swęnǫhsanekahǫ́? ne? tę́? de?agonya:gǫh?
Junior:	Ęhę́?, degaeyáhshe: degaǫdęhnǫdé:?ah.
Junior:	Jeya?dá:t gonǫhgę́:t, tohgé jeya?dá:t gogéaji:
Junior:	Ne:? tsǫ: shę degaejáǫ gaeks?agó:wah.
Pete:	Dę? ho?dę́? gaeya:sǫh?
Junior:	Elsie eya:sǫ́ ne? gonǫhgę́:t, Ester hné:? eya:sǫ́ ne? gogé?aji:.
Pete:	Gaę nhǫ́? tgae?drǫ??
Junior:	Johahadí shę nhǫ:wé agwę́?drǫ?.
Pete:	Ga:gǫgwe?di:yo: gę́h?
Junior:	Ęhę́?, ga:gǫgwe?dí:yo:.
Pete:	Da:sgadagyędeihdę́? gyę:? nęne:?.
Junior:	Si gi? gyę:? dagáę? ó:nęh!
Pete:	Ne:? di? gęh? A:yę́:? hné:? gáegęhjih.
Junior:	Ęhę́? né:?.
Junior:	Tę́? gyę:? d?esgahǫ:dǫ́? dó: niyagonohsriyá?gǫh.
Pete:	Do: di? niyagonohsriya?gǫh?
Junior:	Degrǫ́? niwahshę́:… hwíhs niyagonohsriyá?gǫh. Degaeké? gyę:?.
Pete:	Sǫgwe?di:yó: gi? hné:; né:? tsǫ́: shęh tę́? gwahs ǫ:wé d?eaknǫhwe?ǫ́:? shę nhó: snagre?,
Pete:	tréhs a:yę́:? ǫk?nigǫhsá:dǫ?k.

EKSAʔGÓ:WAH (English) p. 88

Pete:	Who is that?
Pete:	She sure looks pretty.
Junior:	That's my neighbor. She is called Delilah.
Pete:	Who is that coming out of the house?
Junior:	That is her husband.
Pete:	Oh. What is his name?
Junior:	He is called Sampson.
Pete:	Then who are those children?
Junior:	Those are Sampson and Delilah's children. There are three of them.
Pete:	What are they called?
Junior:	Junior, Helen, and Hercules.
Pete:	It sure seems enjoyable, the way they live.
Pete:	I envy that man, the way his wife is so pretty.
Pete:	Do you have any women neighbors who are not married?
Junior:	Yes, two of them, sisters.
Junior:	One is fair, the other has dark hair.
Junior:	But both are pretty.
Pete:	What are they called?
Junior:	The fair one is named Elsie, and the dark one is Esther.
Pete:	Where do they live?
Junior:	Across the street from where we live.
Pete:	Are they nice women?
Junior:	Yes, they are nice women.
Pete:	You should introduce me, you know.
Junior:	Well here they come now!
Pete:	Is that them? They look old!
Junior:	Yes, that is them.
Junior:	You didn't ask me who old they are.
Pete:	Well how old are they?
Junior:	Eighty-five years old. They are twins.
Pete:	Well you are a nice person, but I don't really like your neighborhood.
Pete:	I seem to get too lonesome.

Chapter 11 SATGĘH

SATGĘH (Cayuga) p. 142

Sam:	Haoʔ desaʔdraihę́ satgę́h!
Helen:	Do: diʔ niyohwihsdaʔé: o:nęh?
Sam:	O:nę́ hné:ʔ to:há ja:dáhk niyohwihsdáʔe:.
Sam:	O:nę́ gę satgę́hǫh?
Helen:	Tę́ʔ ahsǫ́ dʔeagatgę́hǫh.
Sam:	Desaʔdráihęh, satgǫhsohae!
Sam:	O:nę́ gę satgǫhsohaeʔ?
Helen:	Tę́ʔ ahsǫ́ dʔeagatgǫhsoháeʔ.

Sam:	Desaʔdraihę́ giʔ gyę:ʔ!
Sam:	O:nę́ gokwai̱hsé: sanó:haʔ.
Sam:	Sade:kǫ́:nih desaʔdráihęh!
Sam:	Waʔji tsǫ́: o:nę́ ęgyahdę́:diʔ.
Sam:	Gaę hne:ʔ sagyaʔdawiʔtraʔ?
Helen:	Tę́ʔ dʔeagęnǫhdǫ́ʔ gaę nhǫ́: nigá:yę́ʔ.
Sam:	Gaę hne:ʔ sanahaotraʔ?
Helen:	Tę́ʔ dʔeagęnǫhdǫ́ʔ gaę nhǫ́: nigá:yę́ʔ.
Helen:	Si gʔishę́ hwaʔ gwa:dí gʔato:há tganí:yǫ:t.
Sam:	Gwé: o:nę́ gę́h?
Helen:	Tę́ʔ ahsǫ́ dʔeakwę́dʔaǫh.
Sam:	Haoʔ gya̱hdę́:dih.
Sam:	O:nę́ hné:ʔ to:há degrǫ́ʔ niyohwi̱hsdáʔe:.
Sam:	Desaʔdraihę́ giʔ gyę:ʔ.
Helen:	Haoʔ dʔęnyó ó:nęh, o:nę́ agekwędáʔǫh.
Helen:	Háoʔ gya̱hdę́:dih.

SATGĘH (English) p. 142

Sam:	Come on, hurry, get up!
Helen:	Well what time is it now?
Sam:	It is now almost seven o'clock.
Sam:	Are you up now?
Helen:	I'm not yet up.
Sam:	Hurry, wash your face!
Sam:	Have you washed your face now?
Helen:	I haven't washed my face yet.
Sam:	Hurry up then!
Sam:	Your mother has the meal cooked already.
Sam:	Eat. Hurry!
Sam:	You and I will leave pretty soon.
Sam:	Where is your coat?
Helen:	I don't know where it is.
Sam:	Where is your hat?
Helen:	I don't know where it is.
Helen:	Maybe it is hanging somewhere over there.
Sam:	Well, are you ready now?
Helen:	I haven't finished eating yet.
Sam:	Come on, let's go.
Sam:	It is almost eight o'clock already.
Sam:	Hurry up then.
Helen:	O.K., I have finished now.
Helen:	Come one, let's go.

Wadewayęstanih

Chapter 12 ENQHSQNYAʔDAʔSQ:ʔQH

ENQHSQNYAʔDAʔSQ:ʔQH (Cayuga) p. 159

Sam:	Swa:yę́ʔ gę nęʔ gajihwaʔ? Gajihwáʔ gihsa:s.
Salesman:	Ęhęʔ.
Sam:	Do:diʔ niga:nǫ́:ʔ nę:gyę́ gajihwaʔ?
Salesman:	Ó:, wagye:sę́:ha giʔ.
Salesman:	Degyahdihahnǫ́ʔ giʔ shę niga:nǫ́:nyǫʔ.
Salesman:	Né:ʔ giʔ nę:gyę́ nigajihyu:ʔúh í:soʔ degahwihsda:gé: niga:nǫ́ʔ
Salesman:	né neʔ nę:gyę́ gajihyowa:nę́ ahsę́ hneʔ nigahwihsda:gé: nigajihwa:nǫ́:ʔ
Salesman:	tohgé nę:gyę́ gwahs gajihyowa:nę́ heyóhe:. Hwíhs hné:ʔ nigahwihsda:gé: nigajihwa:nǫ́:ʔ.
Sam:	Ęhéʔ. Né:ʔ giʔ gyę:ʔǫ́ nę:gyę́ néʔ. Degahwihsda:gé: nigajihwa:nǫ́:ʔ. Né:ʔ ękní:nǫʔ.
Salesman:	Sgahoʔdé:ʔę gę o:yáʔ desadǫhwę:jo:nih?
Sam:	Ęhęʔ. Enesdanyaktáʔ giʔ hniʔ dewagadǫhwęjó:nih.
Salesman:	O:.
Sam:	Né:ʔ giʔ dewagadǫhwęjo:ní neh gwáhs ohyuʔtí:yeht. Gahenʔatri:yó: gyęgę́:s hó:dęʔ.
Salesman:	Haoʔ dʔenyóh. Dá giʔ gwa:díh tgahǫʔ ne:ʔ gwahs oyá:nreʔs, gahenhatri:yóʔs hóʔdęʔ.
Salesman:	Nę:dá giʔ gyę:ʔ sgá:t gaheʔ.
Salesman:	Né:ʔ nę:gyę neʔ gwahs aǫhę:ʔę́ gahenʔatri:yó: enesdanyáʔktaʔ.
Salesman:	Né:ʔ gwʔató gyaǫhę:ʔę tganǫ́:ʔ. Gyę:gwáʔ né:ʔ desadǫhwę:jó:nih.
Sam:	Do:diʔ niga:nǫ:ʔ?
Salesman:	Né:ʔ giʔ nę:gyę́ hwaʔ neʔ degrǫ́ʔ nigahwihsda:gé: niga:nǫ́:ʔ.
Sam:	Degrǫ́ʔ nigahwihsdá:ge:?
Salesman:	Ęhę́ʔ, degrǫ́ʔ nigahwihsdá:ge:.
Sam:	A:yę́:ʔ do:gę́hs ganǫ́:ʔ.
Salesman:	Ęhę́ʔ, ganǫ́:ʔ, né:ʔ tsǫ: shę oya:nréʔ giʔ gyę:ʔ gwʔatoh.
Salesman:	Ǫgwa:yę́ʔ giʔ hné:ʔ neʔ wagye:sę́ heyóhe:, wagyesęhsǫ́:ʔǫh.
Salesman:	Ahsę́ nigahwihsdá:ge:, né:ʔ aǫhę́:ʔę wagyé:sęh,
Salesman:	né:ʔ tsǫ́: shę tę́ʔ giʔ gyę́:ʔ hné:ʔ gwʔató gwahs to niyó: dʔeóyanreʔ. Ohsno:wéʔ gę:s adwákyuʔkdęʔ.
Sam:	Neʔ giʔ gyę:ʔǫ ękni:nǫ́ʔ neʔ gwáhs gahenʔatri:yó: enesdanyáʔktaʔ.
Sam:	Degrǫ́ʔ nigawihsda:gé: sa:dǫ́ niga:nǫ:ʔ gę́h?
Salesman:	Haoʔ dʔisah, né:ʔ toh.
Salesman:	Sgahoʔdé:ʔę gę o:yáʔ desadǫhwę:jo:nih?
Sam:	A:yę́:ʔ toʔǫtsǫ: ni:yó: gwahs dewagadǫhwęjó:nih, nę:gyę́ neʔ gajihwáʔ né:ʔ neʔ enesdanyáʔktaʔ.
Sam:	Dó: diʔ niga:nǫ́:ʔ neʔ hegwe:gǫh?
Salesman:	Ó:, agiʔ giʔ gyę:ʔ a:yę́:ʔ degrǫ́ʔ nigahwihsda:ge: gęh, gʔató:hah neʔ enesdanyaʔktaʔ tohgé degahwihsda:gé: hne:ʔ neʔ gajihwaʔ.
Salesman:	Wahshę́ giʔ gyę́:ǫ nigahwihsda:gé: hegwé:gǫh.
Sam:	Haoʔ dʔenyóh.

ENQHSQNYA'DA'SQ:'QH (English) p. 159

Sam:	Do yous have a hammer? I am looking for a hammer.
Salesman:	Yes.
Sam:	How much is a hammer?
Salesman:	Oh, fairly cheap.
Salesman:	There is a variety of price.
Salesman:	The smaller hammer costs two dollars,
Salesman:	while the larger hammer costs three dollars.
Salesman:	and the biggest hammer costs five dollars.
Sam:	Yes. I guess I will buy the two-dollar hammer.
Salesman:	Is there something else you want?
Sam:	Yes, I also want a saw.
Salesman:	Oh.
Sam:	I want the very sharpest, the good, cutting kind.
Salesman:	All right. Over here are the best cutters.
Salesman:	Take this one over here.
Salesman:	It's the best log cutter.
Salesman:	This is also the most expensive, if that is what you want.
Sam:	How much is it then?
Salesman:	This one here costs eight dollars.
Sam:	Eight dollars?
Salesman:	Yes, eight dollars.
Sam:	It sure seems expensive.
Salesman:	Yes, it is expensive, but it is a good one.
Salesman:	But we do have cheaper ones, the cheaper kind,
Salesman:	three dollars is the cheapest,
Salesman:	but then it isn't much good. It gets dull fast.
Sam:	Then I guess I'll buy the best cutting saw.
Sam:	Eight dollars did you say it cost?
Salesman:	Yes, that's it.
Salesman:	Was there anything else you wanted?
Sam:	That seems to be all I want, really, this hammer and the saw.
Sam:	How much is the whole thing?
Salesman:	Oh, I guess I said eight dollars for the saw, didn't I, and two dollars for the hammer.
Salesman:	I guess ten dollars for the whole thing.
Sam:	O.K.

Chapter 13 GATGWĘ'DA'

GATGWĘ'DA' (Cayuga) p. 184

Pete:	Háe Sam.
Sam:	Háe.
Pete:	Ni: gę: tóne:' ǫgahdǫ́:' ne' agétgw'ęda'.
Pete:	Tę́' ní:s g'ató d'ese:gę:?

Sam:	Tęˀ tóne:ˀ gˀató dˀegé:gę:.
Sam:	Gaę diˀ nhǫ́: a:yę́:ˀ desahdǫ:ˀ?
Pete:	O:, tęˀ giˀ gwahs a:yę́:ˀ dˀeagenǫhdǫ́ˀ gaé nhǫ́: dǫgáhdǫ:ˀ, gaęgwáˀ giˀ nhǫ́: nę́:toh.
Sam:	Tęˀ giˀ níːˀ dˀege:gę́: gaéˀǫ nhǫ́: desáhdǫ:ˀ.
Pete:	Iheˀs dˀigę́ hné:ˀ dejadęhnǫ:de:ˀ?
Sam:	Tęˀ hné:ˀ dˀeheˀs. Honǫhǫkda:ní gyę́:ˀgęˀ stǫ:hǫ́ hotowinyǫˀsé: gyę́:ˀǫh. Haˀjoh.
Pete:	O:. Gyę́:gwaˀ giˀ gyę́:ˀ ęga:she:gę́ˀ sǫgá:ˀa, ęgasheho:wíˀ shę ǫgetgwˀędáhdǫ:ˀ.

GATGWĘˀDAˀ (English) p. 184

Pete:	Hi Sam.
Sam:	Hi.
Pete:	Mind you, I lost my wallet.
Pete:	You haven't seen it?
Sam:	No, I really haven't seen it.
Sam:	Where do you think you lost it?
Pete:	Oh, I don't really seem to know where I lost it, somewhere.
Sam:	Well, I didn't see where you lost it.
Pete:	Well is your brother there?
Sam:	No he isn't. He seems to be sick, a bit of a cold, I guess. Go in.
Pete:	Oh. Well, if you see anyone, tell them I lost my wallet.

Chapter 16 SATRǪ́:NIH

SATRǪ́:NIH (Cayuga) p. 212

Mother:	Satgę́h!
Mother:	Haoˀ satrǫ́:nih!
Son:	Dęˀ ni:yoht?
Mother:	Ganadagǫ́: hękne:ˀ.
Mother:	Háoˀ, satnaˀtsó:we:k
Mother:	desatnˀagwihdrę́: hniˀ gaoˀ shę nyó: ęsatnˀatsó:tręˀs.
Mother:	Sagyáˀdawiˀt…
Mother:	sadahdˀitrǫdá: desęhso:wé:k hniˀ.
Son:	O:nę́ giˀ aga:trǫ́:niˀ!
Mother:	Sanaháowe:k, sagyaˀdawíˀt hniˀ.
Mother:	O:, tréhs giˀ gyę́:ˀ agayeshaˀ, osdaǫgyǫ́: hnéːˀ ó:nęh.
Mother:	Sasanahaowé:ksih, sasagyˀadawihsí hniˀ.
Mother:	Sasatnˀatsóweksih, dǫsasatnaˀgwihdręhsí hniˀ.
Mother:	Sasadahdiˀtradáhgoh, ahgwí ęjisˀanígǫhę sasęhso:tsí hniˀ.
Mother:	Gwé:, o:nę́ gęh, gwe:gǫ́ sasatrǫnyahsiˀ?
Son:	O:nę́ gwe:gǫ́ sagatrǫnyáhsiˀ.
Mother:	Haoˀ dˀęnyóh. Sasędˀadrá giˀgyę́:ˀ hya:.
Mother:	Ęyosdaędˀaǫhǫ́:k gˀishę́hwaˀ hne:ˀ nę́ ętsyeh.
Mother:	Haoˀ, sasa:tgę́ ó:nęh.
Mother:	O:nę́ agasdáędaˀ. Ęwa:dǫ́ˀ ganadagǫ́: hękné: ó:nęh.

Mother:	Háoʔ, sasa:trǫ́:nih!
Mother:	Sasagyʔada:wíʔt sasatnʔatso:wé:k hniʔ.
Mother:	dǫsasatnáʔgw<u>i</u>hdrę:, sasad<u>a</u>hdiʔtrǫdá:
Mother:	dǫsasę:so:wé:k hniʔ.
Mother:	Sasan<u>a</u>háowe:k sasagyʔada:wíʔt hniʔ.
Mother:	Gwé: o:nę́ gęh, sasa:trǫ:niʔ?
Son:	O:nę́ gwe:gǫ́ saga:trǫ́:niʔ.
Mother:	Háoʔ giʔ gyę́:ʔ ganadagǫ́: hekné: ó:nęh.
Mother:	O:o:, tę́ʔ dʔeakw<u>i</u>hsdáę́ʔ!
Mother:	Sasatrǫnyáhsih...

SATRǪ́:NIH (English) p. 212

Mother:	Get up!
Mother:	Come on, get dressed!
Son:	Why?
Mother:	We'll go to town.
Mother:	Come on, put your pants on,
Mother:	your belt, too, so that your pants won't fall down.
Mother:	Put your shirt on
Mother:	and your socks and shoes.
Son:	Now I'm dressed.
Mother:	Put your hat and coat on!
Mother:	Oh, that's too bad, it's raining now.
Mother:	Take your hat back off, and take your coat back off too.
Mother:	Take your pants back off, and take your belt back off.
Mother:	Take your socks back off, and don't forget to take your shoes back off.
Mother:	Well, are you all undressed now?
Son:	I'm all undressed now.
Mother:	O.K. Go back to bed.
Mother:	Perhaps the rain will have stopped when you wake back up.
Mother:	Come on, get back up now.
Mother:	Now the rain has stopped. We can go to town now.
Mother:	Come on, get dressed again.
Mother:	Put your shirt back on, and put your pants back on.
Mother:	Put your belt back on, put your socks back on,
Mother:	and put your shoes back on.
Mother:	Put your hat back on, and put your coat back on.
Mother:	Well, are you dressed again now?
Son:	I'm all dressed again now.
Mother:	Come on, let's go to town now.
Mother:	Oh, I don't have any money!
Mother:	Get undressed again...

Chapter 17 AGYAʔDAWÍʔTRAʔ

AGYAʔDAWÍʔTRAʔ (Cayuga) p. 225

Lila:	Háe
Salselady:	Sgę́:nǫʔ
Saleslady:	Gwé:, dęʔ hoʔdę́ʔ a:yę́:ʔ ihse: a:sni:nǫʔ?
Lila:	Ó:, agyaʔdawiʔtráʔ giʔ a:yę́: gihsá:s a:kní:nǫʔ.
Saleslady:	Do: niyohshe:dę́ sehstaʔʔ?
Lila:	Ó:, gaęgwaʔ nhǫ́: neʔ géi sgaheʔ ǫ niyohshé:dęh.
Saleslady:	Né:ʔ gę neʔ gwahs ǫ:wé oya:nréʔ desadǫhwę:jó:nih,
Saleslady:	né:ʔ nigę́ʔǫ́ neʔ haʔdewęhnihsragehká:ʔ tsǫ: hoʔdę́ʔ ęhsehs?
Lila:	A:yę́ʔ giʔ ahí:ʔ né:ʔ gwahs agyaʔdawiʔtri:yó: hoʔdę́ʔ a:kní:nǫʔ.
Lila:	Dęʔ diʔ hoʔdę́ʔ niyohsohgoʔdę́ʔs swa:yę́ʔ?
Saleslady:	Ó:, haʔdeyohsóhgwage:, otgwęhjʔiaʔ, ǫhyʔáęʔ, swęʔdʔáęʔ, nrahdʔáęʔ,
Saleslady:	dewagyehsdǫ́ hniʔ neʔ gę:ʔgę́: niyohsohgoʔdęʔs.
Saleslady:	Dęʔ diʔ hoʔdę́ʔ niyohsohgoʔdę́: neʔ shǫhweʔs?
Lila:	Ó:, a:yę́:ʔ ní:ʔ né:ʔ gwahs knǫhweʔs neʔ hehsʔáęʔ niyohsohgoʔdę́:,
Lila:	né:ʔ gʔishę́ neʔ ojiʔtgwa:gę́ʔdʔah, jiʔtgwá:ʔ gʔishęh, otgwęhjʔia:gę́ʔt gʔishęh.
Lila:	Gaęgwáʔ giʔ ni:gá: nę́:gyęh.
Saleslady:	Nę:dá giʔ gyę́:ʔ gwa:dí gani:yǫ́:t sgá:t. Né:ʔ sadeʔnyę:dęh.
Saleslady:	Né:ʔ a:yę́:ʔ dekní: sgaheʔ niyohshé:dęh.
Saleslady:	Gwé:, heʔsai:dęʔ gęh?
Lila:	Tę́ʔ. Tręhs hne:ʔ a:yę́:ʔ niwú:sʔuh. A:yę́:ʔ tę́ʔ daę ha:wagí:dęʔ.
Saleslady:	Da: giʔ gyę́:ʔ gwa:dí gani:yǫ́:t né:ʔ hęʔ hne:ʔ. Otgwęhjʔia:gę́ʔt niyohsohgóʔdę:. Sadeʔnyę:dę́ giʔ gyę́:ʔ.
Saleslady:	Gwé:, heʔsai:dęʔ?
Lila:	Tęʔ, Tręhs do:gęhs a:yę́:ʔ gowá:nęʔs.
Saleslady:	Dagwa:dí gani:yǫ́:t gę:ʔgę́: niyohsohgoʔdę:.
Saleslady:	A:yę́:ʔ neʔ to:há tsaʔde:yóht nę́:gyęh. Né:ʔ sadeʔnyę́:dęh.
Saleslady:	Géi sgaheʔ niyohshé:dęh.
Saleslady:	Gyę:gwáʔ hne:hwáʔ stǫ:hǫ́ degyáhdihęh, shę ní:waʔs.
Saleslady:	Sadeʔnyę:dę́ giʔ gyę́:ʔ.
Saleslady:	Gwé:, heʔsai:dęʔ?
Lila:	Ęhę́ʔ, a:yę́:ʔ giʔ né:ʔ hǫʔgí:dęʔ.
Lila:	A:yę́:ʔ haʔga:í:t, né:ʔ tsǫ́: shę tę́ʔ giʔ gwahs dʔeknǫ́hweʔs neʔ gę:ʔgę́: niyohsohgóʔdę:,
Lila:	tręhs gę:s wagyesʔagé aʔosdagwá:ęh.
Lila:	Gyę́:gwaʔ tsigaihwá:ʔa neʔ ǫhyʔáęʔ niyohsohgoʔdę́:, sá:yę nę:gyę tsaʔdeyohshé:dęh, né:ʔ nę:gyę́ a:kní:nǫʔ.
Saleslady:	Waʔgyę́diʔ gihsá:kah.
Saleslady:	Ó:, a:yę́:ʔ ǫgadrʔaswíyohsdęʔ.
Saleslady:	Age:tsę́iʔ sgá:t neʔ tsaʔdegadi:yáǫʔdʔoję:. Nę:gyę́ tsaʔdé:yoht.
Lila:	Do: diʔ niga:nǫ:ʔ?
Saleslady:	Hwíhs sgaheʔ nigahwihsda:gé: niga:nǫ́:ʔ.
Lila:	A:yę́:ʔ do:gę́hs ganǫ́:ʔ.
Saleslady:	A:yę́:ʔ gyę́:ʔ stǫ:hǫ́ ganǫ́:ʔ. Neʔ tsǫ́: shę oya:nréʔ sʔegyę́: hné:ʔ gwʔatoh.

Lila:	Tę́ʔ dʔáǫ a:wadahsgwʔitrǫ́:niʔ, hę:gyę: neʔ haesatronihá:k aesę́:daʔ.
Lila:	Haoʔ dʔisáh, ękni:nǫ́ʔ giʔ gyę́:ʔǫh.
Saleslady:	Sgahoʔdę́:ʔę́ dʔigę́ o:yáʔ desadǫhwę:jo:nih?
Lila:	Ęhę́ʔ, a:yę́:ʔ anahaotráʔ hniʔ í:wi:, ęʔnyo:tráʔ hniʔ.
Lila:	Ne:ʔ giʔ gwʔató ęgę:né:ʔ nę:gyę niyohsohgóʔdę:ʔ.
Saleslady:	Haoʔ dʔisáh.
Saleslady:	Da: giʔ gyę:ʔ gwa:dí wanaháotrahǫʔ.
Saleslady:	Nę:dá giʔ gyę:ʔ ǫhyʔáéʔ niyohsohgoʔdę: anaháotra. Sadeʔnyę́:dęh.
Saleslady:	Gwé:, heʔsai:dęʔ?
Lila:	Ęhę́ʔ, né:ʔ giʔ nę:gyę́ a:yę́:ʔ haʔga:í:t.
Lila:	Né:ʔ a:yę́:ʔ tohjí shę níːwaʔs.
Lila:	Né:ʔ gyę:ʔǫ́ nę:gyę́ a:yę́:ʔ ękní:nǫʔ.
Saleslady:	Tę́ʔ gęh taʔdesadǫhwęjo:ní sgahoʔdę:ʔę́ o:yaʔ?
Saleslady:	Adáhdʔitraʔ ahdahgwáʔ gʔishęh?.
Lila:	Tę́ʔ, ęga:gwe:níʔ a:yę́:ʔ ó:nęh.
Saleslady:	Hnaʔgǫhkáːʔ gʔishę́ sgahoʔdę:ʔęh?.
Lila:	Tę́ʔ hę́ʔ hne:ʔ. A:yę́:ʔ o:nę́ gwé:gǫh.
Lila:	Do: diʔ niga:nǫ́:ʔ neʔ gwe:gǫh?
Saleslady:	Ó:, a:yę́:ʔ degrǫ́ʔ sgahe ʔ nigahwihsdá:ge:.
Lila:	Haoʔ dʔisáh.
Saleslady:	Dędi:snéʔ giʔ gyę́:ʔ é:ʔ.
Lila:	Haoʔ dʔęnyóh. O:nę́ gʔihya:!
Saleslady:	Haoʔ dʔęnyóh.

AGYAʔDAWÍʔTRAʔ (English) p. 225

Lila:	Hi.
Saleslady:	Hello.
Saleslady:	Well, what would you like to buy?
Lila:	Oh, I guess I am looking for a dress to buy.
Saleslady:	What size do you wear? (What number do you use?)
Lila:	Oh, somewhere around size fourteen.
Saleslady:	Do you want a really good one,
Saleslady:	or will you just use the everyday kind?
Lila:	Oh, it seems I thought I would buy a really good dress.
Lila:	What colors do yous have?
Saleslady:	Oh, all sorts of colors, red, blue, black, green,
Saleslady:	and then some that are white.
Saleslady:	What color do you like?
Lila:	Oh, the one I like the best is brown,
Lila:	or perhaps a light yellow, or maybe yellow, or maybe pink.
Lila:	Anyway, one of these.
Saleslady:	Try this one hanging over here.
Saleslady:	It seems to be a size twelve.
Saleslady:	Well, does it fit you?
Lila:	No. It seems to be too small for me. It doesn't seem to fit me.
Saleslady:	There is a pink one hanging over here. Try this one.

Wadewayęstanih

Saleslady:	Well, does it fit you?
Lila:	No. It really seems to be too big for me.
Saleslady:	There is a white one hanging over here.
Saleslady:	It seems to be the same style as the one you were trying on.
Saleslady:	It is a size fourteen.
Saleslady:	Maybe they are a little different in size.
Saleslady:	Try this on then.
Saleslady:	Well, does it fit you?
Lila:	Yes, this one does seem to fit me.
Lila:	It seems to fit, but I don't really like the white color,
Lila:	because it gets dirty too easily.
Lila:	If you even had a blue one in the same size, I would buy it.
Saleslady:	Let me go look for it.
Saleslady:	Oh, I seem to have gotten lucky.
Saleslady:	I found one that is the same shape, just like this one.
Lila:	How much does it cost then?
Saleslady:	It costs fifteen dollars.
Lila:	That certainly seems expensive.
Saleslady:	It seems a little expensive, but it is a good one.
Lila:	It won't wrinkle, even if you sleep with your clothes on.
Lila:	O.K., I guess I'll buy it then.
Saleslady:	Was there anything else that you wanted?
Lila:	Yes, I believe I want a hat too, and gloves,
Lila:	that will go with these colors.
Saleslady:	O.K.
Saleslady:	Over here are the hats.
Saleslady:	Here is a blue hat. Try it on.
Saleslady:	Well, does it fit you?
Lila:	Yes, this one does seem to fit me.
Lila:	It seems to be just the right size.
Lila:	I guess I'll buy this one.
Saleslady:	There wasn't anything else you wanted?
Saleslady:	Stockings, or shoes?
Lila:	No, that will do for now, I guess.
Saleslady:	Underclothes or something?
Lila:	No, not that either. This seems to be all for now.
Lila:	How much is that in all?
Saleslady:	Oh, it seems to be eighteen dollars.
Lila:	O.K.
Saleslady:	Come back again.
Lila:	O.K. Goodbye.
Saleslady:	Bye.

Chapter 19 GAHWAJIYÁ:DEʔ

GAHWAJIYÁ:DEʔ (Cayuga) p. 257

Myrtle:	Hae Pete!
Pete:	Hae Myrtle!
Pete:	Gwé:, o:nę gę sha:wíʔ neʔ swayaʔdá:ʔ sahwa:ji:yaʔ?
Myrtle:	Ęhéʔ, o:nę giʔ ká:wiʔ.
Pete:	Sahwajiyówanę diʔ gęh?
Myrtle:	Ęhéʔ, gwáhs giʔ ǫgwatgʔadé:ʔah.
Myrtle:	Nę:dáʔ giʔ gyę:ʔ satgę:ʔsé: agwáyʔada:ʔ.
Pete:	Sǫ́: hne:ʔ nʔaht nę:gyęh?
Myrtle:	Ne:ʔ giʔ hne:ʔ haʔní nę:gyę́ hayáʔda:ʔ.
Pete:	Ó:, né:ʔ hyʔanih.
Pete:	Sǫ́: diʔ hne:ʔ nʔaht nę:gyęh? Né:ʔ gę sano:haʔ?
Myrtle:	Ęhéʔ, né:ʔ kno:háʔ né:gyęh.
Pete:	Da hniʔ gwa:dí nę:gyę́ gáet, hǫgwéh agǫ:gwé hniʔ, sǫ́: hne:ʔ nʔaht?
Myrtle:	Ne:ʔ gʔihęʔ hné:ʔ deyagwadęhnǫdrǫʔ.
Myrtle:	Né:ʔ giʔ nę:gyę́ hǫgwé iha:t, né:ʔ hęʔ hné:ʔ deyagyadęhnǫ́:de:ʔ. Né:ʔ hehjíʔah.
Myrtle:	Tohgé neʔ agó:gwéh, né:ʔ hęʔ hné:ʔ deyagyadęhnǫ́:de:ʔ. Né:ʔ hęʔ hné:ʔ kehjíʔah.
Pete:	Sǫ́: diʔ nʔaht nę:gyę́ niga:gu:sʔú hne:ʔ?
Myrtle:	Ó:, né:ʔ giʔ hęʔ hné:ʔ deyagwadęhnǫdrǫʔ.
Myrtle:	Ne:ʔ hné:ʔ gakeʔgʔęshǫ́:ǫh.
Myrtle:	Ne:ʔ hné:ʔ nę:gyę́ gwa:dí ihá:t neʔ hne:ʔ heʔgę́:ʔęh.
Pete:	Ó:, né:ʔ heseʔgę́:ʔęh.
Pete:	Né:ʔ diʔ gę sheʔgę:ʔę́ nę:gyę́ niya:gu:uh?
Myrtle:	Né:ʔ keʔgę́:ęh.
Pete:	Sǫ:, dʔihne:ʔ nʔáht nę:gyę́ dagwa:dí gaet?
Pete:	A:yę́:ʔ do:gę́hs gaegęhjí ǫ hne:ʔ
Myrtle:	Ó:o né:ʔ giʔ nę:gyę́ gakehsotsǫ́ʔ gáet.
Myrtle:	Né:ʔ giʔ nę:gyę́ gwai iha:t ne:ʔ hne:ʔ hehso:t,
Myrtle:	tohgé neʔ gado:gę́: gaet kehsó:t hné:ʔ.
Pete:	A:yę́:ʔ gwe:gǫ́ʔǫ swayáʔda:ʔ. Swatgaʔdéʔ giʔ gyę:ʔ.
Myrtle:	Ęhéʔ, ǫgwatgaʔdéʔah. Swahwajiyowanę dʔigęʔ hęʔ ni:s?
Pete:	Ęhéʔ, agwahwajiyowa:nę́:ha giʔ hę́ʔ ni:ʔ.
Myrtle:	Hwę:dǫ́ gwaʔ giʔ gyę:ʔ hęʔ ní:s ętsa:wíʔ neʔ swayaʔdá:ʔ ęgatgę:ʔséʔ hę́ʔ ni:ʔ.
Myrtle:	Ęgatgę:ʔséʔ dó: ni:s niswahwají:yaʔ.
Pete:	Haoʔ dʔęnyóh.
Myrtle:	O:nę́ giʔ gyę:ʔǫ́ hya:.

GAHWAJIYÁ:DEʔ (English) p. 257

Myrtle:	Hi Pete!
Pete:	Hi Myrtle!
Pete:	Well, have you brought your family's pictures?
Myrtle:	Yes, I've brought them now.
Pete:	So do you have a big family?
Myrtle:	Yes, there are quite a few of us.

Myrtle:	In fact here, have a look at our pictures.
Pete:	Who is this?
Myrtle:	That's my father's picture.
Pete:	Oh, that's your father.
Pete:	And who is this? Is that your mother?
Myrtle:	Yes, that is my mother.
Pete:	And these people standing over here, a man and a woman, who is that?
Myrtle:	Those are my brothers and sisters.
Myrtle:	This man standing here, he is my brother. That is my older brother.
Myrtle:	And the woman, she is my sister. That is my older sister.
Pete:	But then who are these little ones?
Myrtle:	Oh, they are also my brothers and sisters.
Myrtle:	They are my younger brothers and sisters.
Myrtle:	And this one standing over here is my younger brother.
Pete:	Oh, that is your younger brother.
Pete:	Then is this your sister, the small one?
Myrtle:	That is my younger sister.
Pete:	So then who is this standing over here?
Pete:	They look old.
Myrtle:	Oh, those are my grandparents.
Myrtle:	This one standing over here is my grandfather,
Myrtle:	and these standing together, that is my grandmother.
Pete:	It seems like you all got your picture taken. There are a lot of yous.
Myrtle:	Yes, there are a lot of us. Do you have a big family too?
Pete:	Yes, we have a fairly big family too.
Myrtle:	Sometime you bring a picture of all of you, and <u>I</u> will look at it.
Myrtle:	I will see how big <u>your</u> family is.
Pete:	O.K.
Myrtle:	So long for now.

Chapter 20 Q̲DWE̲NQDÁHTA'

Q̲DWE̲NQDÁHTA' *(Cayuga) p. 279*

Sam:	Sgé:nǫ'. De̲' ho'de̲' nihsagyeha'?
Pete:	A:ye̲:' gi' hne:' te̲' gwáhs sgaho'de̲'. De̲' di' ho'de̲' ihse:?
Sam:	Ahí:' se' ao̲dasagy'o̲sehá' daedwá:do̲:t.
Pete:	Hao' d'e̲nyóh. Do: di' niyohwihsda'é: e̲dwadeko̲:ni'?
Sam:	Ó:, hyei'shó̲:'o̲ áo̲dahse'.
Sam:	One̲'o̲ eyagokwaihséha:k.
Pete:	E̲tsgihno̲ksé' gi' gye̲:', tréhs te̲' d'eag'edréhdae̲'.
Sam:	Hao' d'isháh, e̲tgo̲hno̲ksé' gi' gye̲:' dó:ge̲hs.
Sam:	E̲sadehsro̲nis'o̲hó̲:k gi' gye̲:', ó:, hyei'só̲:'o̲h.
Pete:	O:ne̲' gi' hya:.
Sam:	Ha:o'.

ǪDWĘNǪDÁHTAʔ (English) p. 279

Sam:	Hello. What are you doing?
Pete:	Oh, nothing much, I guess. What do you want?
Sam:	I thought you would come and visit, and we would eat together.
Pete:	O.K. What time will we eat?
Sam:	Oh, you should come around six-ish.
Sam:	She should have the food cooked by then.
Pete:	Will you come and get me, because I don't have a car?
Sam:	O.K., sure, I'll come get you.
Sam:	Be ready around six-ish, then.
Pete:	So long for now.
Sam:	Bye.

Chapter 22 DWADE:KǪ:NIH

DWADE:KǪ:NIH (Cayuga) p. 294

Sam:	Gwé:, o:nę́ gę́ sadehsrǫnihsʔǫh?
Sam:	O:nę́ gǫhnǫ́:kseʔ, neʔ ęhsadekǫ́nyahnaʔ.
Pete:	Ęhę́ʔ, o:nę́ giʔ akdehsrǫ́nihʔǫh.
Pete:	Gwahs waʔheʔtsǫ́: agagyʔadoháesiʔ.
Sam:	Haoʔ dʔisáh, gyahdę́:dih.
Sam:	Onę́ʔǫ hnéːʔ gyokwái.
Pete:	A:ya:wę́ giʔ dó:gęhs.
Pete:	O:nę́ do:gęhs agadǫhsweʔdanih.
Pete:	Sadǫhsweʔda:ní diʔ gęʔ ni:s?
Sam:	Ęhę́ʔ, a:yę́:ʔ giʔ o:nę́ agadǫhswéʔdanih.
Sam:	Ó:, degyegahné:ʔ giʔ.
Sam:	O:nę́ gyę́:ʔǫ ǫkwái.
Sam:	Sá:gaʔs diʔ gę ní:s sohǫ:t?
Pete:	Ęhę́ʔ, giʔ gyę:gwá: tę́ʔ dʔegágęhjih.
Sam:	Hekni:yǫ́: giʔ gyę:ʔ.
Sam:	Haoʔ giʔ gyę:ʔ sagyę́: sade:kǫ́:nih. Sagyę́:, dedwá:dǫ:t.
Pete:	Dęʔ diʔ hoʔdę́ʔ nę:gyę́ gaksaheːʔ?
Pete:	A:yę́:ʔ onrahdáʔ ǫ́ hne:ʔ.
Lila:	Né:ʔ onráhdaʔ. Sá:gaʔs diʔ gę nę:gyę́ enrahda:s?
Pete:	Tę́ʔ ní:ʔ dʔea:gé:gaʔs.
Pete:	Tę́ʔ ní:ʔ gwaʔyǫ́ʔ dʔegę:.
Lila:	Da giʔ gyę:ʔ gwa:dí gaksahé:ʔ watǫnʔadǫ́:daʔk.
Lila:	Sá:ga:s gę́ hne:ʔ?
Pete:	Ęhę́ʔ, giʔ hné:ʔ gę:s a:yę:ʔ.
Pete:	Ne:ʔ tsǫ́: neʔ oaʔwisdáʔ tę́ʔ ní:ʔ dʔege:s.
Pete:	Gwisgwís gyę:ʔ hné:ʔtsǫ́: ga:dí:s neʔ oáʔwisdaʔ.
Sam:	Hęská:ʔ gyę́:ʔ ǫ́ hné:ʔ tsǫ́:.
Sam:	Hęshe:nǫ́:t neʔ ǫgwa:tse:nę́ʔ gwísgwis.
Sam:	Oʔwáhǫ gęh?

Pete:	Haoʔ dʔęnyó dó:gęhs.
Pete:	Ohsi:náʔ giʔ níːʔ ę́:ge:k.
Pete:	Ohsi:náʔ gyę́:ʔ nęne:ʔ níːʔ aǫhę́:ʔę dwagrihowánahdǫh.
Pete:	Onaʔdáːʔ giʔ gyę́:ʔ hníʔ dasha:.
Pete:	A:yę́:ʔ gajihyó:t hoʔdę́ʔ neʔ onáʔda:ʔ.
Sam:	Né:ʔ tó ne:ʔ do:gę́hs hoʔdę́ʔ.
Sam:	Gonaʔda:yędeiʔǫ́ gyę́:ʔ kegę́jih.
Pete:	Swá:yę́ʔ dʔegę hné:ʔ neʔ ohnaʔ?
Lila:	Ęhę́ʔ dagwa:dí gaksáhe:ʔ.
Lila:	Ęhsátna: diʔ gęh?
Pete:	Haoʔ dʔęnyó dó:gęhs. Oihwi:yóʔ shę gakwágʔaǫh.
Pete:	A:yę́:ʔ giʔ o:nę́ tó:ha ęwágahdaʔ.
Pete:	Swá:yę́ʔ diʔ hne:ʔ sgahoʔdę́:ʔę degáhswaʔne:t?
Lila:	Ęhę́ʔ, ohya:jíʔ hoʔdę́ʔ degahswaʔne:t ǫgwá:yę́ʔ.
Lila:	Nę:dah giʔ gyę́:ʔ snʔadá:k.
Lila:	Ahgwigwaʔ tsǫ́: ęhsęniksé:dʔęgoh.
Pete:	Óː, onaʔda:gʔáǫ giʔ gyę́:ʔ dó:gęhs.
Sam:	Ęhę́ʔ. Agǫho:wíʔ gyę́:ʔ hné:ʔ shę gokwayędeiʔǫ́: kegęhjih.
Pete:	O:, sędę:ʔǫ́: giʔ gyę́:ʔ ní:s.
Pete:	Eksa:gó:wah, gokwayędeiʔǫ́: hniʔ neʔ shegę́hjih.
Pete:	Daʔ níːʔ gwá:dih, tę́ʔ níːʔ dʔáǫ a:getsę́iʔ sǫgá:ʔa a:yǫkní:nya:k.
Pete:	Ji gʔishę hwaʔ tę́ʔ dʔeagʔedréhdaę́ʔ.
Pete:	A:yę́:ʔ neʔ aǫhę́:ʔę godi:howanahdǫ́ wáʔne:ʔ.
Sam:	Nya:wę́ giʔ gyę́:ʔ adi:dwá:dǫ:t.
Pete:	Ęyonishéʔ hęwagʔidrǫ́:ʔ shę niyo:weʔ gakwi:yó: agadekǫ́:niʔ.
Pete:	O:nę́ giʔ ęsgahdę́:diʔ.
Pete:	Hęgyę́ʔ tsǫ́: dęsgátahahk.
Pete:	Haʔdęgakwaędáʔ stǫ́:hǫh, shę niyó: hęsge:ʔ.
Sam:	Haoʔ.
Lila:	Dętséʔ giʔ gyę́:ʔ e:ʔ.
Pete:	O:nę́ giʔ hya:.

DWADE:KǪ:NIH (English) p. 294

Sam:	Well, are you ready now?
Sam:	I have come after you to come and eat.
Pete:	Yes, I am ready now.
Pete:	I just finished having a bath.
Sam:	All right then, let's go.
Sam:	The food should be cooked.
Pete:	I hope so.
Pete:	I am so hungry now.
Pete:	Are you hungry?
Sam:	Yes, I am.
Sam:	Oh, she is looking out.
Sam:	The food must be cooked now.
Sam:	Do you like turkey?

Pete:	Yes, if it's not too old.
Sam:	Let's go in.
Sam:	Go ahead, sit down. Eat. Sit down, let's eat.
Pete:	What is this dish sitting here?
Pete:	It looks like leaves.
Lila:	Yes, those are leaves. Do you like lettuce?
Pete:	No, I don't like it.
Pete:	I'm no rabbit, you know.
Lila:	Then over here there is a dish of baked potatoes.
Lila:	Do you like those?
Pete:	Yes, I guess I like them.
Pete:	It's just the peelings that I don't eat.
Pete:	It's only pigs that eat the peelings.
Sam:	I guess I'll just take the peelings away.
Sam:	I will feed our pet pig.
Sam:	Meat?
Pete:	All right, sure.
Pete:	I'll eat the leg.
Pete:	Legs are something I think a lot of.
Pete:	Pass the bread, too.
Pete:	It looks like homemade biscuits.
Sam:	They sure are.
Sam:	She is a good baker, my wife.
Pete:	Do yous have any gravy?
Lila:	Yes, the dish is sitting over there.
Lila:	Do you want to put on some grease?
Pete:	All right. Oh, it sure is good food.
Pete:	I seem to be just about full.
Pete:	Do yous have any kind of pie?
Lila:	Yes, we have blueberry pie.
Lila:	Here then, eat this pie.
Lila:	Just don't get a swelled belly.
Pete:	This pie sure is delicious.
Sam:	Yes, didn't I tell you what a good cook she is, my wife?
Pete:	Oh, you are sure lucky.
Pete:	She is pretty, and she is a good cook, too, your wife.
Pete:	As for me, I can't find anyone to marry me.
Pete:	Maybe it is because I don't have a car.
Pete:	It seems like that is what they think the most of nowadays.
Sam:	Thank you that we ate together.
Pete:	It will last me a long time, how much good food I ate.
Pete:	I guess I'll go home now.
Pete:	I will just walk.
Pete:	My meal will settle a little as I go.
Sam:	Bye.
Lila:	Come again.

Pete: Goodbye for now

Chapter 23 SANAHSGWAĘʔ GĘH SGAHOʔDĘ:ʔĘH?

SANAHSGWAĘʔ GĘH SGAHOʔDĘ:ʔĘH? (Cayuga) p. 317

David: Háe Pete.
Pete: Háe.
David: Gwé:, í:s gę satse:nę́ʔ to:gyę́ so:wa:s?
Pete: Ęhę́ʔ, i:ʔ age:tsé:nęʔ.
David: Sgahoʔdę:ʔę diʔ gę o:yáʔ sanáhsgwaęʔ?
Pete: Ęhę́ʔ, dagú:s giʔ hníʔ aknáhsgwaęʔ.
Pete: Gwaʔyǫ́ʔ hníʔ gwʔáe aknahsgwáęʔ hę́ʔ hne:ʔ.
Pete: Tó gʔi ní:ʔtsǫ: ni:yǫ́ʔ aknáhsgwaęʔ, nę:gyę́ ne:ʔ so:wá:s, dagú:s gwaʔyǫ́ʔ hniʔ.
David: Dęʔ diʔ hoʔdęʔ gaya:sǫ́ neʔ so:wa:s?
Pete: Rover hayá:sǫh.
David: Mmm. Dęʔ diʔ ni:yóht shę hnyǫʔǫhneha:ʔ?
David: Hohsęnaęʔ dʔi gę hne:ʔ ǫgwehǫwehneha:ʔ?
David: Dęʔ diʔ hoʔdę́ʔ haya:sǫ́ ǫgwehǫwehneha:ʔ?
Pete: Dehadawę:nyéʔ haya:sǫ́ ǫgwehǫwehneha:ʔ, Gyotgǫ́:t gyę:ʔ nę́ne:ʔ ę:tsǫ́: isheʔ dehadawę́:nyeh.
Daivd: Ǫ́:. Nę néʔ dagu:s, dęʔ hneʔ hoʔdę́ʔ gaya:sǫh?
Pete: Ogǫhstǫʔáʔ hne:ʔ gayá:sǫh. Ogǫ́hstǫʔaʔ.
David: Dęʔ diʔ ni:yóht shę néʔ gaya:sǫh?
Pete: Né:ʔ gyę:ʔ tréhs degahǫhstǫ́ʔe:s.
David: Mmmm. Nę neʔ gwáʔyǫʔ, ohę́naęʔ dʔigę́ hne:ʔ?
Pete: Ó:, tę́ʔ hne:ʔ gwáhs a:yę́:ʔ dewadadehsęnaędí:.
Pete: Tę́ʔ sgahoʔdę́ʔ dʔeoihǫ́:t sgahoʔdę:ʔę a:yagwahsę́:nǫʔ.

SANAHSGWAĘʔ GĘH SGAHOʔDĘ:ʔĘH? (English) p. 317

David: Hi Pete.
Pete: Hi.
David: Well, is that your dog?
Pete: Yes, it is.
David: Do you have any other pets?
Pete: Yes, I also have a cat.
Pete: I also have a rabbit, too.
Pete: That's all I have, myself, the dog, cat, and rabbit.
David: So what is your dog called?
Pete: He is called Rover.
David: Mmm. Why is it a White name?
David: Does he have an Indian name?
David: What is his Indian name?
Pete: Tahdawę:nyeh, ('he wanders'), because, you know, he always wanders around here and there.
David: Oh. And the cat, what's its name?

Wadewayęstanih

Pete:	Ogǫhstǫʔaʔ (whiskers) is its name. Ogǫhstǫʔaʔ.
David:	Why is it called that?
Pete:	Because its whiskers are too long.
David:	Mmmm. And the rabbit, does it have a name?
Pete:	Oh, no, it doesn't know its own name.
Pete:	There is no reason for us to give it a name.

P. 320

Do: niya:gáʔ satse:nęʔ?
Ó:, gwáhs giʔ nę:há niyá:gaʔ.
Do: niya:gáʔ satse:nęʔ?
Ó:, niya:gú:ʔuh.
Dęʔ hoʔdęʔ nigayʔadoʔdę: satse:nęʔ so:wa:s?
Swęʔdʔáę nigayʔadóʔdę:.
Dęʔ hoʔdęʔ nigayʔadoʔdę: satse:nęʔ so:wa:s?
Gę:ʔgę: nigayʔadóʔdę:.
Swęʔdʔáę nigayʔadoʔdę: gę:ʔgę: owahgwáǫnyǫʔ.
Gę:ʔgę: nigayʔadoʔdę: swęʔdʔáę owahgwáǫnyǫʔ.
Dęʔ hoʔdęʔ snǫ:dę satse:nęʔ so:wa:s?
Onǫʔgwáʔ knǫ́:dęh.
Dęʔ hoʔdęʔ snǫ:dę satse:nęʔ gwaʔyǫʔ?
Awęnohgraʔshǫ́:ʔǫ knǫ́:dęh.
Ojiʔnǫwaheʔdáʔ o:gáʔs neʔ age:tse:nęʔ ojǫ́ʔdaʔ.
Ojǫʔdáʔ go:gáʔs neʔ age:tse:nęʔ dagu:s.
Ohe:tsáʔ ho:gáʔs neʔ age:tse:nęʔ só:wa:s.

p. 335 *(not part of the dialogue, but maybe you want to record it)*

Pete:	Hae!
Benchsitter:	Hae.
Pete:	Wadęganyahs gęh satse:nęʔ so:wa:s?
Benchsitter:	Tęʔ dʔehadęgá:nyahs.
Pete:	Dęʔ diʔ ni:yóht ǫge:gáiʔ satse:nęʔ?
Benchsitter:	Tęʔ giʔ gyę:ʔ í:ʔ dʔeagetse:nęʔ nę:gyę́ esá:gaiʔ.

Pete:	Hi.
Benchsitter:	Hi.
Pete:	Does your dog bite?
Benchsitter:	No, he doesn't bite.
Pete:	Why did your dog bite me?
Benchsitter:	That isn't my dog.

Chapter 24 OʔDRÉHDATGIʔ

OʔDRÉHDATGIʔ (Cayuga) p. 339

Neil:	Háe Sam.

Wadewayę́stanih

Sam:	Háe. Węhnisri:yó: ę:ʔ.
Neil:	Ęhę́ʔ ę:ʔ.
Sam:	A:yę́:ʔ sʔadrehdahetgʔęse:ʔ.
Sam:	Dęʔ hoʔdę́ʔ a:yę́:ʔ nʔa:węh?
Neil:	Dó:gaʔ. To tsǫ́: nhe:yóht ageʔdrę́ʔ atgá:daʔ.
Sam:	Ganadagǫ́: giʔ haʔgeʔ. Ęhsatnʔǫhdá: gęh?
Neil:	Haoʔ dʔęnyó, tga:go:t gyę́:ʔ ganadagǫ́: hę́:ge:ʔ.
Neil:	Ęhehnǫksáʔ neʔ haʔdrehdǫ́:nihs.
Sam:	Satnʔǫhdá: giʔ gyę́:ʔ.
Sam:	Sǫ: ní:s nʔaht gwahs? Tę́ʔ gwáhs ǫ:wé dʔegǫyędéi.
Sam:	Dave gę haya:sǫ neʔ hyʔanih?
Neil:	Tę́ʔ. Né:ʔ hné:ʔ knoʔsę́ neʔ Dáve hayá:sǫh.
Neil:	Néǫ hné:ʔ hayá:sǫ neʔ haʔnih. Hehsyę:dé:t gęh?
Sam:	Tę́ʔ dʔeheyędéi. Né:ʔ tsǫ́:.
Sam:	Heyę:déi neʔ Dáve hyanóʔsęh. Sgyędéi dʔigęʔ ni:ʔ?
Neil:	Tę́ʔ giʔ gwáhs ǫ:wé dʔegǫyędéi, né:ʔ tsǫ́: neʔ gǫhsęnaędí:.
Neil:	Heyędéi giʔ hne:ʔ neʔ hehshá:wahk. Gado:gę́: agyadadrihǫnę́:ni:.
Neil:	Nę:tó giʔ nhǫ́: ęgatnʔǫhdáhgoʔ.
Sam:	Tę́ʔ gyę́:ʔ hné:ʔ dʔehadʔidrehdǫ́:nihs nę:toh.
Sam:	A:yę́:ʔ hné:ʔ ǫtnegahní:nǫh.
Neil:	Né:ʔ gíʔ hné:ʔ dó:gęhs.
Neil:	Gyę:gwáʔ hne:waʔ sǫga:ʔá ęhe:gę́ʔ nʔetó neʔ haʔdrehdǫ́:nihs.
Neil:	Stǫ:hǫ́ gʔishę hwaʔ hniʔ hogyéʔsęh.
Sam:	A:yę́:ʔ giʔ gyę́:ʔ do:gę́hs desęnʔǫáesdǫh.
Sam:	A:ya:wę́ giʔ gyę́:ʔ do:gę́hs a:setséiʔ sǫgá:ʔa a:heyaʔdagé:nhaʔ,
Sam:	a:yesayʔadagenháʔ gʔishęh, gaeʔdrehdǫ:níhs gyę́:ʔ nę́ne:ʔ hęʔ hne:ʔ o:nę́ gá:gǫgweh.
Neil:	Haoʔ dʔisáh. O:nę́ giʔ hya:.
Neil:	Nya:wę́ giʔ gyę́:ʔ shę nyó: dasknʔǫ́hda:.
Sam:	Haoʔ.

OʔDRÉHDATGIʔ (English) p. 339

Neil:	Hi Sam.
Sam:	Hi. Nice day, isn't it.
Neil:	Yes it is, isn't it.
Sam:	You seem to have car trouble.
Sam:	What seems to have happened?
Neil:	I don't know. All of a sudden I'm driving along and it stops.
Sam:	I'm going to town. Do you want a ride?
Neil:	Well all right. I'll have to go to town anyway.
Neil:	I'll go get a mechanic.
Sam:	Well, get in then.
Sam:	Who are you, anyway? I don't really know you.
Sam:	Is Dave your father?
Neil:	No, that is my uncle; his name is Dave.

Neil:	Neil is my father's name. Do you know him?
Sam:	No, I don't know him.
Sam:	I just know your uncle Dave. Do you know me?
Neil:	No, I really don't. I just know your name.
Neil:	But I know your son. We go to school together.
Neil:	I'll get out here.
Sam:	They don't repair cars here.
Sam:	It looks like a bar.
Neil:	That is true.
Neil:	Maybe I might see someone in there who repairs cars.
Neil:	And then, too, he might be cheap.
Sam:	You sure seem to have been using your head.
Sam:	I sure hope you find someone who could help you,
Sam:	or perhaps a woman who could help you, because women also fix cars you know.
Neil:	All right. So long.
Neil:	Thanks for the ride.
Sam:	O.K.

Chapter 25 DĘ' HO'DĘ' NQHSA:GYE:'?

DĘ' HO'DĘ' NQHSA:GYE:'? (Cayuga) p. 349

Bessie:	Háe Pete!
Pete:	Háe Bessie!
Bessie:	Gwé:, sgę́nǫ'jih?
Pete:	Ęhę́', ne:' gi' á:yę:'. Nę́ di' ni:s?
Bessie:	Ęhę́'. Swe'ge tgǫ:gę́ hne:'.
Pete:	Ęhę́', swe'gé:hah.
Bessie:	Dę' di' ho'dę́' nihsagyeha'?
Pete:	Ó:, a:yę́:' gi' tę́' gwáhs sgaho'dę'.
Bessie:	Dę' di' ho'dę́' nęhsa:gyę́:' nę:gyę́ hwa' dejogęnho:di'?
Pete:	Ó:, a:yę́:' gahsga:né:s otow'egé há:ge:',
Pete:	a:gęnadáęhna'.
Bessie:	Ó:o:, do: nęyonishé' hęhse'se:g?
Pete:	Ó:, ahí:' gaęgwa'nhǫ́: ne' dekní: dęyaǫdadogęhtę' a:gagwé:ni'.
Pete:	Né:' gę:s gwáhs gahsga:né:s ne' a:gadáhnyo:'.
Pete:	Togyę'ǫ́ hne:' niyó: gwáhs ęyoyanrahsdǫhǫ́:k nę dęyogęnhǫ́:di'.
Pete:	Tga:gó:t hni' ęgadadekǫnyę́' í:' gwé:gǫh.
Pete:	Ojǫ'dá' gyę:ǫ́ hne:' tsǫ́: gw'ató ęgǫnhehgǫ́hǫ:k.
Pete:	Tę́' d'i gę́ d'esé: áekne:'?
Bessie:	Ó:, tę́' gyę́:'ǫh onen'ǫgé nigwa:dí ha'ge'.
Pete:	Ó:. Dę' ni:s ho'dę́' n'asagyeha'ne'?
Bessie:	I:wí: ní:' a:gahya:ksá' onén'ǫgeh.
Pete:	Do: d'i ní:s nęyonishé' ęsahdęgyǫhǫ:g?
Bessie:	Ó:, dewęhn'ida:gé: g'ishę́ hwa' nęyonishé' dętge'.

Pete:	Mmm. Dęˀ diˀ nęhsa:gyé:ˀ neˀ ęyoˀga:ˀ
Bessie:	Ó:, a:yę́:ˀ gˀi hne:ˀ tę́ˀ sgahoˀdęˀ.
Bessie:	Né:ˀ nę ęgegaohaehsǫ́:goˀ, tę́ˀ sgahoˀdęˀ taǫsagá:gye:.
Pete:	A:wa:dǫ́ˀ dˀigę neˀ gayaˀtáˀ aegyatgęˀsehaˀ?
Bessie:	Ęhę́ˀ, seˀ gyę́:ˀǫ hne:ˀ.
Bessie:	A:yę́:ˀ tę́ˀ sgahoˀdęˀ tá:gagye:.
Pete:	Haoˀ dˀęnyóh. Ętgǫhnǫkséˀ giˀ gyę́:ˀ gaęgwaˀnhǫ́: neˀ jadahkshǫ́:ˀǫh.
Bessie:	Haoˀ dˀęnyóh. Ędknigǫhá:k giˀ.
Pete:	Haoˀ dˀęnyóh. O:nę́ gˀihya:.

DĘˀ HOˀDĘˀ NǪHSA:GYE:ˀ? (English) p. 349

Bessie:	Hi Pete!
Pete:	Hi, Bessie!
Bessie:	Well, is everything going well?
Pete:	Yes, it seems like it. How about you?
Bessie:	Yes. It has been a long time since I've seen you.
Pete:	Yes, a long time.
Bessie:	What are you doing?
Pete:	Oh, it doesn't seem like too much.
Bessie;	What will you do when summer comes?
Pete:	Oh, I guess I want to go North.
Pete:	I might camp.
Bessie:	Oh, how long will you be away?
Pete:	Oh, I thought somewhere around two weeks would do it.
Pete:	What I really want to do is fish.
Pete:	It will be good, this summer.
Pete:	I'll have to do all of my own cooking.
Pete:	I'll just live on fish.
Pete:	Don't you think we should go together?
Bessie:	Oh, I don't think so. I am going South.
Pete:	Oh. What are you going to do?
Bessie:	I want to pick fruit in the South.
Pete:	How long will you be away?
Bessie:	Oh, I'll probably come back after two months.
Pete:	Mmm. What are you doing this evening?
Bessie:	Oh, nothing much, it seems.
Bessie:	When I have finished the dishes, I won't do anything more.
Pete:	Would it be possible for us to go see a movie?
Bessie:	Yes, it certainly would, I guess.
Bessie:	I don't seem to be doing anything.
Pete:	All right. I'll pick you up somewhere around seven-ish.
Bessie:	All right. I'll be waiting.
Pete:	All right. So long for now.

Chapter 26 DEGAHENÁʔTRAʔSE:ʔ

DEGAHENÁʔTRAʔSE:ʔ (Cayuga) p. 368

Georgina:	Háe.
Lila:	Sgę́:nǫʔ.
Georgina:	Dęʔ hoʔdę́ʔ n<u>i</u>hsagy<u>e</u>haʔ?
Lila:	A:yę́:ʔ giʔ hné:ʔ tęʔ gwáhs sgahoʔdę́ʔ.
Georgina:	Ní: gę:ʔ giʔ ahí:ʔ a:gęnháʔ sa:wę́ʔ degahenáʔtraʔse:ʔ.
Lila:	Ó:o.
Georgina:	Ętséʔ giʔ gyę́:ʔ waʔjí ętsáw<u>i</u>hdahk.
Georgina:	Ętsá:ʔ, tohgé hętsá:ʔ gwʔató nę ęgéhsd<u>a</u>hsiʔ.
Lila:	Haoʔ dʔęnyóh.
Georgina:	Waʔjí dʔitsǫ́: ętséʔ gęh?
Lila:	Ęhę́ʔ. Waʔjihshǫ́: hęgyǫʔ.
Georgina:	Haoʔ dʔęnyóh. Desaʔdraihę́ giʔ gyę:ʔ.

DEGAHENÁʔTRAʔSE:ʔ (English) p. 368

Georgina:	Hi.
Lila:	Hello.
Georgina:	What are you doing?
Lila:	It doesn't seem like much.
Georgina:	I thought I might borrow your scissors.
Lila:	Oh.
Georgina:	Come over after while and bring them along.
Georgina:	You can take them back when I have finished with them.
Lila:	All right.
Georgina:	You'll just come over after while, then?
Lila:	Yes. I'll be there pretty soon.
Georgina:	All right. Hurry up then.

Chapter 27 DAJǪH

DAJǪH (Cayuga) p. 376

Georgina:	Dajǫh!
Lila:	Sgę́:nǫʔ.
Georgina:	Sgę́:nǫʔ.
Lila:	Gwé:, dęʔ hoʔdę́ʔ n<u>i</u>hsagy<u>e</u>haʔ?
Georgina:	Gagyaʔdawiʔtrǫ́:nih.
Georgina:	A:yę́:ʔtsǫ́: waʔhé agęnihna:dó:k deyokyuʔkdaʔǫ́ neʔ degahenáʔtraʔse:ʔ.
Lila:	Ó:, nę:dá giʔ gyę́:ʔ, i:séhs neʔ í:ʔ aga:wę́ degahenáʔtraʔse:ʔ.
Georgina:	Há:oʔ. Né:ʔ giʔ gyę́:ʔ hya: aekninaʔdá:k agatnʔadáǫt degáhswaʔne:t.
Georgina:	Gwáhs waʔhé tsǫ: agatnʔadaǫdá:gwęh.
Georgina:	Onę́ʔǫ hné:ʔ onaʔn<u>u</u>hsdǫ́ stǫ́:hǫh.
Georgina:	Sagyę:.
Georgina:	Odi: gęh, ka:fí nigę́ʔǫ ęhsneg<u>e</u>haʔ?

Lila:	Odi: ęknégiha'.
Georgina:	Ne̜:dah.
Georgina:	Nawę'da' gęh, onǫ'gwá' hni'?
Lila:	Háo' d'ęnyó dó:gęhs, dejáǫ.
Georgina:	Ne̜:dah. Í:se:k.
Lila:	Ogá'ǫh!
Lila:	Agatsęnǫ:ní' nę:tó nǫdá:ge:'.
Lila:	O:nę gi' gyę́:'ǫ ęsgahdę́:di'.
Lila:	O:nę gyę́:' nę́ne:' hné:' ha'wa:j'áht degáhswa'ne:t!
Lila:	O:nę g'ihya:.
Georgina:	Dętsé' gi' gyę́:' é:'.

DAJǪH (English p. 376

Georgina:	Come in!
Lila:	Hello.
Georgina:	Hello.
Lila:	Well, what are you doing?
Georgina:	I am making clothes.
Georgina:	It seems like I just now noticed that my scissors are dull.
Lila:	Oh here, use my scissors.
Georgina:	Mmm. Before anything else, we should eat the pie I baked.
Georgina:	I just took it out of the oven.
Georgina:	It should have cooled a little by now.
Georgina:	Sit down.
Georgina:	Would you like tea or coffee?
Lila:	I'll drink tea.
Georgina:	Here.
Georgina:	Sugar or milk?
Lila:	Sure, all right, both.
Georgina:	Here. Eat.
Lila:	It is delicious.
Georgina:	I am glad you came.
Lila:	Well, I might as well go home now,
Lila:	because the pie is all gone, you know!
Lila:	So long.
Georgina:	Come back again.

Chapter 28 GAHÁ:GǪ:

GAHÁ:GǪ: (Cayuga) p. 386

Lila:	Háe háe!
Pete:	Háe.
Lila:	Sgę:nǫ' gęh?
Pete:	Ęhę́', gi' á:yę:'.
Lila:	Gaę di' nǫdahse:'?

Pete:	Ó:, gaha:gǫ́: hegéʔsgę̱hę̱:ʔ.
Lila:	Ó:o:, dę̱ʔ diʔ hoʔdę̱ʔ nisagyaʔnǫhg?
Pete:	Né:ʔ tsǫ́: shę haʔde:yǫ́: aonhiʔdrǫ:nyǫ́:ʔ gahá:gǫ:.
Lila:	Ó:o:. Dę̱ʔ diʔ hoʔdę̱ʔ nʔa:węh.
Pete:	Ó:, neʔ giʔ dawagyę:hdáhk agadade:ʔó:k gahsíʔdʔageh.
Lila:	Ó:o:, gahe:tgę̱ʔ dʔigęh, asa:dǫʔ? Asadade:ʔó:k gęh?
Pete:	Tę̱ʔ giʔ hné:ʔ gwahs á:yę̱:ʔ, tréhs gyę́:ʔǫ do:gę́hs wahdahgwadę́:s dewagę́:sǫ:.
Pete:	Shę niyó: nʔadǫ:da:gé:ʔ to hné:ʔ ohǫ:dáʔ nʔetoh, daga:ye:ná:ʔ agagyʔadawʔitráʔgeh.
Pete:	Atgadadahji:yó:ʔ nʔetoh.
Lila:	Atsadadahji:yo:ʔ?
Lila:	Tréhs giʔ gyę̱:ʔ do:gę́hs a:yę́:ʔ esadrʔaswahetgęʔnhéʔ shę nʔesayʔadá:węh.
Pete:	Agidagráʔ hniʔ shę nyó: nʔadǫ:dá:ge:.
Pete:	Né:ʔ gyę́:ʔǫ hné:ʔ nę agídagraʔ agadadwęʔnahsáik.
Lila:	Asadadwęʔnahsaig? Dę̱ʔ hne:ʔ hoʔdę̱ʔ nʔahsye:ʔ?
Pete:	Tę̱ʔ dʔeagęnǫ́hdǫʔ, tréhs gyę́:ʔǫ do:gę́hs agęnʔewá:ʔ neʔ nę̱ agídagraʔ.
Pete:	Dǫgahsiʔgyáʔk sʔegyę́:ʔ nę́ne:ʔ.
Lila:	Ó:o:. Tréhs giʔ gyę́:ʔ do:gę́hs sadraʔswahé:tgę̱ʔ, shę nʔesayaʔda:wę̱ wáʔne:ʔ.
Pete:	Do:gę́hs tó ne:ʔ.
Pete:	A:yę́:ʔ giʔ gyę́:ʔ ohdrǫ́ht a:hayę́dagoʔ.
Pete:	O:nę̱ giʔ gyę́:ʔǫ hyá: a:gadǫ́:goht.
Lila:	Sʔnigǫ:há:k giʔ gyę́:ʔ shę nyó: hętse:ʔ.
Lila:	Ahgwígwaʔ ęjisahnǫhnyáʔk é:ʔ!

GAHÁ:GǪ: (English) p. 386

Lila:	Hi.
Pete:	Hi.
Lila:	Are you all right?
Pete:	Yes, I seem to be.
Lila:	Where are you coming from?
Pete:	Oh, I've been in the bush.
Lila:	Oh, what did you go there for?
Pete:	There are just all kinds of mishaps in the bush.
Lila:	Oh. What happened then?
Pete:	Oh, the first thing was that I cut my foot with an axe.
Lila:	Oh, is it bad? You cut yourself with an axe?
Pete:	No, it doesn't really seem too bad, I guess, because I have really thick shoes on.
Pete:	As I was coming out, the bushes grabbed my coat.
Pete:	I scratched myself then.
Lila:	You scratched yourself?
Lila:	It sure seems like your luck turned bad, the way things happened to you.
Pete:	I also fell down along the way.
Pete:	I guess it was when I fell that I bit my tongue.
Lila:	You bit your tongue? How did you do that?
Pete:	I don't know, probably because I was really startled when I fell.

Pete:	I stubbed my foot, you see.
Lila:	Oh. It sure is amazing, how bad your luck turned, with all that happened to you today.
Pete:	True, mind you.
Pete:	It seems to be dangerous to go after wood.
Lila:	Well, I guess I'll go on now.
Lila:	Watch out as you go.
Lila:	Don't get hurt again!

Chapter 29 ĘYAGWAHDĘ:DI?

ĘYAGWAHDĘ:DI? (Cayuga) p. 402

Junior:	Sgę́:nǫ?.
Sam:	Sgę́:nǫ?.
Junior:	Gwé:, dę? ní:s hwa? ho?dę́? nęswa:gyé:? nę:gyę́ hwa? dęyogęnhǫ:di???
Sam:	Ó:. Ęgyagwahdę:dí? ni:? hwa?.
Junior:	Ó:o:, tę́? hwa? taeswayętwahsǫ: gęh?
Sam:	Tę́?. Ęyagwahdę:dí? ni:? hwa?.
Junior:	Gaę di? hęswe:??
Sam:	O:, otow?egé hęyá:gwe:?. Hęyogwagya? danúhsdǫhǫ:k.
Sam:	Hęyagwadahnyó:? hni?, nę hęya:gwá:yę?.
Sam:	Ęyǫgwadáhnyo:k, né:? gi? tsǫ́: gwahs ęyagyonhéhgǫhǫ:k,
Sam:	ojǫ?dá? ganyo?shǫ́:?ǫ ne? gyę:?ǫ́ hni?, dę? ho?dę́? ęyagwatsę́i? a:yagwadekǫ́:ni?.
Sam:	Ǫh, a:yę́:? i:wí: odǫtga:dé?ǫh.
Junior:	Hwę:dǫ́ eji:swa:yǫ??
Sam:	Ó:, gęnęn?agéhneh shę nyo:wé dędwa:to:wá:t to nyó:weh, o:nę́ dęgyagwahdę:di?, eja:gwá:yǫ?.
Sam:	O:nę́ ejgwagyę́:daę?, ęyagwadehsrǫnyahnǫ́:? o:nę́ é:? ejóhsra:t.
Sam:	Eswahdęgyǫ́he? d?igę́? ní:s?
Junior:	Tę́? ní:? ta:yagwahdę́:di?. Ęyagw?ędrǫ:dá?k ní:?. Ęyagwayętwahsǫ́:? é:?.
Junior:	Gyę:gwá? hne:hwá? ęwadohsrá:tgiht, ęyǫgwadęn?atrag?adé:k gi?.
Junior:	Sa:dǫ́ gyę:? ní:s tę́? ní:s taeswayętwahsǫ:.
Junior:	Gyę:gwá? gyę:?ǫ́ ęswadǫhswé:dę?, ędí:swe?...
Sam:	Do:gę́hs ę́:?.
Junior:	ęgwadęna?tranǫ́:t dę? ní:s ho?dę́? ęyǫgwayę́:da?k.
Sam:	Do:gę́hs ę́:?.
Sam:	O:nę́ gi? gyę:?ǫ́ hya:.
Junior:	Hao? d?ęnyóh.

ĘYAGWAHDĘ:DI? (English) p. 402

Junior:	Hello.
Sam:	Hello.
Junior:	Well, what are yous going to do this summer?
Sam:	Oh, we're going away this time.
Junior:	Oh, you're not going to plant this time?

Sam:	No, we're going away this time.
Junior:	So where will yous go?
Sam:	Oh, we'll go up North. We'll cool off up there.
Sam:	We'll fish up there too, when we get there.
Sam:	We'll be fishing, and that's all we'll live on,
Sam:	fish and game, I guess, whatever we will find to eat.
Sam:	Oh, it seems, I think, it will be fun.
Junior:	When will yous come back?
Sam:	Oh, when it gets to be fall, when it starts to get cold again, then we'll leave, we'll come back.
Sam:	Then we'll store wood, we'll get ready for winter.
Sam:	Are yous going away?
Junior:	No, we aren't going away, we'll stay here. We'll plant again.
Junior:	It might be a bad winter, so we'll have a lot of food.
Junior:	You say that yous aren't going to plant.
Junior:	Maybe you'll be hungry, and you'll come to us…
Sam:	True, isn't it.
Junior:	we'll give you food, what we have.
Sam:	True, isn't it.
Sam:	Well, so long for now.
Junior:	Goodbye.

Chapter 30 ĘSWAYĘTO' GĘH?

ĘSWAYĘTO' GĘH? (Cayuga) p. 420

Lila:	Ęswáyęto' gę' ní:s hwa' gagwid<u>e</u>hji:hah?
Georgina:	Ęhę́', né:' gi' agwe:.
Lila:	Dę' di' ní:s ho'dę́' gwahs ęswayętwahso:'?
Georgina:	A:yę́:' agwé: onęhę́' osahe'dá' ohǫn'adá'ǫ hni',
Georgina:	gwahs i:só:'a ęyagwayętwahso:', tréhs a:yę́:' o:nę́ do:gę́hs ganǫ́:' ohǫ́n'ada'.
Lila:	Swa<u>h</u>ǫn'adayętwę́ hne:' d'igę tsigę:nheh?
Georgina:	Tę́' tóne:' tréhs do:gę́hs agasda:nǫhwé' hne'.
Georgina:	Agetsahní'k a:y<u>o</u>hǫn'adá'tgęh.
Georgina:	Né:' tsǫ́: ne' onęhę́' osahe'dá' hni' ǫgwayętwę́ hne:'.
Georgina:	I:só' agwayę:twá:go'.
Junior:	O:nę́ gi' gwá' agatehdǫ́:ni:,
Junior:	gwe:gǫ́ sgagáhatwę shę nhǫ́: ǫgwayętwę hne:'.
Junior:	He'gę:'ę́ hohǫn'adátg'ade'.
Junior:	Ne' i:wí: ęshehni:nǫ́' do:gwá' ní:yǫ:.
Lila:	Do: di' ni:yǫ́: ęswayęto'?
Junior:	I:wí: ahsę́ nigaya:gé:'ǫ a:gagwé:ni'.
Sam:	Gaiho'dęhsrowa:nę́ gi' to:gyę́:' ní:yǫ:.
Junior:	Ó:, tę' gyę́:'ǫ hné:' ǫ:wí: agyę́' gyę́:' nęne:' ne' degahehdáwenyehs.
Junior:	Dají:ha gę́:s tsǫ́: i:só' adkehdawé:nye:'.
Junior:	Ganǫ́:' gi' tsǫ:.

554

Sam:	Do: di? niga:nǫ:??
Junior:	Géi n?adew?enyá:w?e: sigwa:dí:ha niga:nǫ:?.
Junior:	A:sni:nǫ́? gi? gyẹ:? hẹ́? ní:s.
Junior:	Sa̲hwihsdaga?dé? gyẹ́:? nẹne:?.
Sam:	Oga:ẹ? d?igẹ to ni:yǫ:?
Junior:	Ẹhẹ́?, ogá:ẹ?.
Georgina:	Sam!
Sam:	O:nẹ́ gi? ni? tga:gǫ́:t ẹsgahdẹ́:di?,
Sam:	tréhs ganadagǫ́: agẹ́? ní:? hẹyágya̲hge:t.
Sam:	O:nẹ́ g?ihya:.

ẸSWAYẸTO? GẸH? (English) p. 420

Lila:	Are yous going to plant this spring?
Georgina:	Yes, we think so.
Lila:	Just what are yous going to plant?
Georgina:	It seems like we think corn, beans, and potatoes,
Georgina:	we'll plant a lot, because it seems like potatoes are really expensive now.
Lila:	Did yous plant potatoes last summer?
Georgina:	No, in fact we didn't, because it rained so much.
Georgina:	I was afraid the potatoes would rot.
Georgina:	It was just corn and beans.
Georgina:	We harvested a lot.
Junior:	I have already prepared the earth.
Junior:	It is already plowed where we plant.
Junior:	My younger brother has a lot of potatoes.
Junior:	I'll buy some from him.
Lila:	How many will yous plant?
Junior:	I think about three bags should do it.
Sam:	That's a lot of work, that much.
Junior:	Oh, not really, because I have a cultivator, you know.
Junior:	In just a short time I plow a lot.
Junior:	But it is expensive.
Sam:	How expensive is it?
Junior:	It costs a little more than four hundred dollars.
Junior:	You should buy one too.
Junior:	You have a lot of money, you know.
Sam:	Is it worth that much?
Junior:	Yes, it is worth it.
Georgina:	Sam!
Sam:	Well, I have to go now,
Sam:	because I've heard we are going uptown.
Junior:	So long for now.

Chapter 31 DWĘNǪHSANEGAHǪˀ

DWĘNǪHSANEGAHǪˀ (Cayuga) p. 441

Lila:	Nę́: haˀsatgahtó o:yáˀ tganǫ́hso:t.
Lila:	A:yę́:ˀ sǫgwa nˀáht gonęnˀadíny'ǫdǫh.
Sam:	Do:gę́hs ę́:ˀ.
Sam:	Sǫ: diˀ hne:ˀ nˀaht?
Lila:	Dó:gaˀ.
Lila:	Sekdǫhná giˀ gyę́:ˀ.
Lila:	Ęgasehǫgáǫˀ hniˀ ętgaǫdekǫnyáhneˀ hwisǫ́:ˀǫh.
Lila:	O:nę́ hné:ˀ ęyǫgwado:gę́hs dę́ˀ hoˀdę́ˀ niyǫgwˀedoˀdę́:ˀ neˀ agaǫnádinyǫˀt.
Lila:	Háoˀ desaˀdráihęh, gǫdagyéˀ dętseˀ.
Sam:	Dewagˀedraihę́hs hęˀ ní:ˀ a:wagęnǫhdǫˀnhe:ˀ sǫ: hne:ˀ nˀaht.
Lila:	Gwéˀ a:yę́:ˀ gę ga:gǫgwéˀdi:yo:?
Sam:	A:yę́:ˀ tó ne:ˀ, agaǫtsę:nǫ:níˀ giˀ haˀgáhge:t.
Sam:	Ętgáęˀ giˀ gyę́:ˀ hwihsǫ́:ǫh.
Sam:	O:nę́ giˀ ní:ˀ ęsgadrihóˀdataˀ.
Sam:	A:snˀadaǫníˀ giˀ gyę́:ˀ, sgahoˀdę́:ˀę neˀ waˀjí ędwa:k.
Lila:	Ó: gyé: agadeteˀdroˀkdáˀǫh!
Lila:	A:yę́:ˀ hniˀ gwe:gǫ́ agadranawˀędoˀkdˀáǫ hniˀ.
Lila:	Wˀagyę́ diˀ seteˀtraníhahsah, nawę́ˀdáˀ hniˀ ętsęniha'ˀ.
Sam:	Haoˀ dˀęnyóh. Wˀagyę́ diˀ é:ˀ nˀetó hesge:.
Neighbour:	Dajǫh!
Sam:	Sgę́:nǫˀ.
Neighbour:	Sgę́:nǫˀ. Sˀesgęhę́:ˀ ę:ˀ gwˀató waˀjih?
Sam:	Ęhéˀ gyę́:ˀ. Ǫgęnihaˀǫhǫgyéˀ sˀetsǫ: neˀ kegę́hjih,
Sam:	geteˀtraníhahseˀ, nawę́ˀdáˀ agęˀ hniˀ ęgęniha'ˀ.
Neighbour:	Wˀají giˀ gyę́:ˀ hya:.
Neighbour:	Wˀahéˀ ęgíhsa:k. Tę́ˀ seˀ sǫ:gwáhs dˀeagatrehnagáˀtsǫ:.
Neighbour:	Ó:, nę:dá giˀ gyę́:ˀ wadá:nyǫˀ!
Neighbour:	Oˀnhǫhsáˀ hniˀ to í:wa:t.
Neighbour:	Tę́ˀ dˀigę́ hne:ˀ dˀeséˀ a:sˀenhǫhsanihaˀ hniˀˀ?
Sam:	Tę́ˀ giˀ hnéˀ dˀeagęnǫhdǫ́ˀ a:gˀenhǫhsanihá gę́ˀǫ hniˀ.
Sam:	A:yę́:ˀ hné:ˀ nę́:tó ǫ hne:ˀ naǫdáęˀ.
Sam:	Nę:to a:yotnˀadáǫdęˀ.
Sam:	Haˀde:yǫ́: seˀ a:yę́:ˀ godóˀkdˀaǫh.
Sam:	O:nę́ ǫ hné:ˀ gwé:gǫh.
Sam:	Tę́ˀǫ hnéˀ dˀaǫdaǫsagǫˀnigǫháęˀ ó:nęh.
Sam:	Ó:, wˀají hya:, sǫgˀnígǫhęh.
Sam:	Ohnáˀ nigeˀ hniˀ agęˀ ęgęniha'ˀ.
Neighbour:	Ó:, tę́ˀ hnéˀ dˀea:gyę́ˀ néˀ ohnaˀ.
Neighbour:	Tga:gǫ́:t gyé:ˀǫ hnéˀ o:nę́ ęhsní:nǫˀ.
Sam:	Háoˀ dˀęnyóh. O:nę́ gˀihya:. Hęsni:yǫ́ˀ giˀ gyę́:ˀ wˀají heségęhji hwisǫ́:ˀǫh.
Lila:	Gwé:, o:nę́ sahsyǫˀ.
Sam:	Agoneha:gǫ́ˀ gˀihnéˀ o:nę́ haˀde:yǫ́: sadóˀkdˀaǫh.
Sam:	A:yę́:ˀ gˀi ní:ˀ agádehęh.

Sam:	Agáę'ǫ hné:' tę' ní:' d'ǫgwadęn'atráę'.
Lila:	Oihwi:yó' gi' gyę:' hné:' sę ga:gǫgwe'dí:yo:.
Lila:	Gyagone̲hdahgǫ́ sę ni:yóht gyǫgwéhda̲hgǫh.
Lila:	Dęyǫgwadagy'adagenhęhę́:k ne' dwęnǫhsanékahǫ'.
Sam:	Desa'draihę di' satna'daǫdę́ ó:nęh.

DWĘNǪHSANEGAHǪ' (English) p. 441

Lila:	Say, have a look at the next house.
Lila:	It seems like somebody has moved in.
Sam:	It does, doesn't it.
Sam:	Who is it?
Lila:	I don't know.
Lila:	Go and see.
Lila:	And give them my invitation to come and eat around five-ish.
Lila:	Then we'll know what kind of people they are that have moved in.
Lila:	Come on, hurry, and come right back.
Sam:	I'm in a hurry too, to find out who they are.
Lila:	Well, do they seem like nice people?
Sam:	They certainly seemed glad that I went over.
Sam:	And they will come around five.
Sam:	I'm going back to work now.
Sam:	You should bake something for us all to eat later on.
Lila:	Oh, I've run out of flour!
Lila:	I seem to have completely run out of sugar, too.
Lila:	So why don't you go and borrow some flour from her, and borrow some sugar, too.
Sam:	O.K. Then I'll go back there again.
Neighbour:	Come in!
Sam:	Hello.
Neighbour:	Hello. Weren't you here a while ago?
Sam:	Yes, I was. It's just that my wife sent me on an errand,
Sam:	to come borrow flour, and she said to borrow sugar, too.
Neighbour:	Just a minute.
Neighbour:	I'll just look for it. I'm not really unpacked yet.
Neighbour:	Oh, here they are in this!
Neighbour:	There are eggs in here, too.
Neighbour:	Don't you think you should borrow some eggs, too?
Sam:	I don't really know whether I should borrow eggs too.
Sam:	It seems almost as if she might as well come here.
Sam:	She could bake here.
Sam:	She seems to have run out of all sorts of things.
Sam:	This must be everything now.
Sam:	I shouldn't bother you any more now.
Sam:	Oh, wait a minute, I forgot.
Sam:	She says I should also borrow lard.
Neighbour:	Oh, I don't have any lard.

Neighbour:	I guess now you'll have to buy that.
Sam:	All right. So long. Then you and your husband will come over later, around five.
Lila:	Well, you're back!
Sam:	She was surprised that you were out of so many different things.
Sam:	I felt embarrassed.
Sam:	They probably thought we don't have anything to eat.
Lila:	They sure seem to be nice people.
Lila:	They believe in what we believe in.
Lila:	Neighbors will help each other.
Sam:	Hurry up now and bake.

Chapter 32 OYĘHSRAʔ

OYĘHSRAʔ (Cayuga) p. 456

Georgina:	Sgę:nǫʔ.
Lila:	Sgę:nǫʔ.
Georgina:	Gaę heseʔsgehéːʔ te:dęʔ?
Georgina:	Dagatwęnódaː, tęʔ dʔesíʔdrǫʔ.
Lila:	Óː, agahdęgyǫ́ː hnéːʔ.
Lila:	Agagyʔǫsehǫ́hk gyéːʔ knóhaʔgeh.
Georgina:	Eʔdrǫʔ gęh?
Lila:	Ęhę́ʔ, gyʔedrǫ́ʔ giʔ. Néːʔ giʔ hoːníʔ to itgéːs węhnihsragwéːgǫh.
Georgina:	Óː, dęʔ diʔ hoʔdę́ʔ nʔeja:gyeːʔ?
Lila:	Óː, aknʔinikǫnyǫ́ːʔ gíʔ. Oyęhsráʔ aknihsrǫ́nyanǫːʔ. Gyʔagodʔedraːdǫ́ʔ giʔ tgayęhsraníːyǫːt neːʔ agʔiníkǫnyǫːʔ.
Georgina:	Óː. Esniwayęːnę́ːdaʔ diʔ gęh?
Lila:	Tę́ʔ gwahs dʔeǫkniwayęnę́dʔaǫʔ, stǫ́ːhǫ daonǫ́ːʔ.
Georgina:	Hwęːdǫ́ dʔigę́ ęsniwayęːnęːdaʔ?
Lila:	Óː, gyęːgwáʔ gęʔ gaęgwáʔ nęyónishéʔ to hęsgeːʔ,
Lila:	oːnę́ hęyakniwayęnę́ːdaʔ.
Georgina:	Oyáːnreʔ dʔi gę neʔ jagyęhsrǫːnih?
Lila:	Ęhę́ʔ, néːʔ giʔ neʔ gwáhs gęːs stǫːhǫ oyaːnréːʔa hóʔdęʔ.
Georgina:	Dęʔ diʔ hoʔdę́ʔ niyoyęhsroʔdęː jagyęhsrǫːnih?
Lila:	Óː, jʔidęːʔę giʔ, gadiyʔadáǫnyǫʔ.
Georgina:	Dęʔ hoʔdę́ʔ nʔagadiyaʔdʔodę́ʔ jʔidęːʔęh?
Lila:	Degaːgyaʔs giʔ gadiyʔadáǫnyǫʔ, degáːgyaʔs.
Lila:	Néːʔ gyéʔ aǫhęːʔę ohsohgwíːyoʔs.
Georgina:	Dęʔ diʔ hoʔdę́ʔ niyohsohgoʔdęʔs?
Lila:	Haʔdeyohsohgwagéː giʔ, ǫhyʔáęʔ, onrahdʔáęʔ, ojiʔtgwáːʔ, tgwęhjʔiáʔ, ojiʔtgwáːji hniʔ.
Lila:	Néːʔ giʔ nęːgyéʔ hwaʔ néːʔ niyohsohgoʔdęʔs neʔ gahsdúʔdrʔageh.
Lila:	Tohgé neʔ gahsinʔagéh hehsʔáęʔ hnéːʔ niyohsohgóʔdęː.
Lila:	Tohgé neʔ gajiʔohdʔagéh, swęʔdʔáęʔ hneʔ niyohsohgóʔdęː.
Lila:	Gęːʔgéː hneːʔ nigagahóʔdęʔs.

Lila:	A:yę́:ʔ degayehsdǫ́ neʔ deyodʔagę́hnyʔagǫh.
Georgina:	Ó:, oyęhsri:yó: giʔ gyę́:ʔǫh.
Lila:	Ęhę́ʔ ji giʔ aǫgohdǫ́ oyęhsrí:yoʔ, neʔ gwahs ǫ:wé á:gehs.

OYĘHSRAʔ (English) p. 456

Georgina:	Hello.
Lila:	Hello.
Georgina:	Where were you yesterday?
Georgina:	I called up, and you weren't home.
Lila:	Oh, I had gone away.
Lila:	In fact, I went to visit my mother.
Georgina:	Is she home?
Lila:	Yes, she is home. That's why I was there all day.
Georgina:	Oh, so what did yous do?
Lila:	Oh, she and I sewed, we made quilts. (Literally, 'the blanket is hanging on a frame, that is what we sewed.')
Georgina:	Oh. So did yous finish?
Lila:	Not quite we didn't. There was still a little more left to do.
Georgina:	When will yous finish it?
Lila:	Oh, in a certain length of time I will go back there,
Lila:	and we will finish it then.
Georgina:	So is it nice, the blanket you are making?
Lila:	Yes, it is one of the better ones.
Georgina:	What kind of a blanket are you making?
Lila:	Oh, there are pictures of birds on it.
Georgina:	What kind of birds are they?
Lila:	Parrots, pictures of parrots.
Lila:	They have the nicest colors.
Georgina:	What colors?
Lila:	All kinds of colors, blue, green, yellow, red, orange.
Lila:	Those are the colors of the feathers.
Lila:	And the legs are brown.
Lila:	And on the claws there is black.
Lila:	And the eyes are white.
Lila:	It seems to be mixed with gray.
Georgina:	Oh, then it must be a nice quilt.
Lila:	Yes, it is too good a quilt to really use.

Chapter 33 DĘDWAʔĘNÁĘʔ

DĘDWAʔĘNÁĘʔ (Cayuga) p. 481

Pete:	Sgę́:nǫʔ!
Sam:	Sgę́:nǫʔ!
Sam:	Gwé:, dędwaʔęnáęʔ agę́ʔ ęyó:hęʔ.
Sam:	Oyanrahsdǫ́ giʔ hne:ʔ shę i:sóʔ ográęʔ.

Sam:	Wʔaheʔ giʔ gyę:ʔ gę ędwagyadǫ:niʔ.
Sam:	O:nę́ giʔ ní:ʔ nʔetó haʔgeʔ.
Sam:	Ękné:ʔ gęh?
Pete:	Haoʔ dʔęnyó né:ʔ giʔ gyę:ʔ.
Sam:	O:nę́ giʔ to:há hękní:yǫh.
Sam:	Nę̨:. Tęnénǫgyeʔs. Háe, háe.
Three men:	Sgę́:nǫʔ.
Sam:	Gwé:, o:nę́ gę sǫgʔyagǫ́ neʔ ędwadǫdíʔdre:ʔ?
Junior:	Ó:nęh. Sigwa:dí tgá:yęʔ.
Sam:	Né:ʔ gʔigyę́:ʔ hya: ędwa:gyę́ht ęyagwʔagranhohsro:dę́ʔ nę́:toh.
Sam:	Tohgé né:ʔ ní:s ędiswa̱hsa:wę́ʔ, tó hęwahsawę́ʔ, ęswatahǫ́:niʔ.
Jimmy:	Gaę diʔ nyǫ:ʔ hęya:gwé:ʔ ęyagwatahǫ:niʔ?
Sam:	Ó:, ęga:gwe:níʔ gyę:ʔǫ hnéːʔ, shę nyo:wéʔ togyę́ gyonǫ:dȧheʔge:.
Sam:	Tę́ʔ gyę:ʔ nę́ne:ʔ neʔ dʔá:ǫ a:yę́:ʔ ęgadinédʔokdęʔ gęh?
Sam:	Háoʔ giʔ gyę:ʔ ní:ʔ nę:tó dwʔagranhohsró:dęh.
Sam:	A:yę́:ʔ do:gę́hs oyánragyeʔ.
Junior:	Ęhę́ʔ giʔ nę:gyę́ odęháiyo: stǫ́:hǫ awaʔgraná:wę́ʔ.
Pete:	Gwé:, o:nę́ gę ęga:gwe:níʔ shę niyo:ya:de:s?
Sam:	O:nę́ giʔ hné:ʔ a:yę́:ʔ ęga:gwé:niʔ.
Sam:	Degrǫ́ʔ sgaheʔ gyę́:ʔ nę́ne:ʔ niyowęyǫhgá:ge: niyo:wéʔ nęgayadáhaʔk.
Junior:	A:yę́:ʔ o:nę́ gwe:gǫ́ awadewayęnę́:daʔ.
Jimmy:	Né:ʔ tsǫ́: o:nę́ neʔ ędwaǫdiʔdré:ʔ ędwadagwáihsiʔ.
Sam:	Háoʔ giʔ gyę:ʔ dagwa:dí swaǫda̱hę oyádagǫ:.
Jimmy:	Háoʔ sǫgwaʔnʔáht gaǫdʔagé dęhá:daʔ.
Sam:	Háoʔ o:nę́ dajagyę̱hę́:toh!
Sam:	Heʔsniǫdiʔdré: o:nę́ shę niyó: heyó:doʔk.
Sam:	Neʔ o:nę́ hęsnóʔkdęʔ, dęjniyǫdʔidré:ʔ gwʔató nę:tó ęjísnʔokdęʔ.
Sam:	A:yę́:ʔ giʔ gyę́:ʔ o:nę́ edwawayę:nę́:daʔ!.
Jimmy:	Hó: oya:di:yó: giʔ!
Sam:	Ęyo:hę́ʔ giʔ gyę́:ʔǫ hné:ʔ dęjidwadá:tgęʔ,
Sam:	neʔ o:nę́ ętęna̱hsá:wę́ʔ, tęnʔáęnaęʔ.

DĘDWAʔĘNÁĘ́ʔ (English) p. 481

Pete:	Hello.
Sam:	Hello.
Sam:	Well, they say we're going to play snowsnake tomorrow.
Sam:	It is ideal because there is a lot of snow.
Sam:	Supposedly we are just now going to build the track.
Sam:	I'm going there now.
Sam:	Shall we go there together?
Pete:	All right, fine.
Sam:	We'll be there soon.
Sam:	Look. There they are. Hi! Hi!
Three men:	Hello.
Sam:	Well, have yous cut the log yet, the log that we're going to drag?
Junior:	Yes we have. It is laying over there.

Sam:	Well first, we'll pile some snow here.
Sam:	And yous will start making the track from here.
Jimmy:	So how far shall we go with the track?
Sam:	Oh, I suppose it should be enough to go up to the big hill.
Sam:	It doesn't seem like they're going to go up the hill, anyway.
Sam:	Come on, let's pile this snow here.
Sam:	It seems to be going well.
Junior:	Yes, with this bright sun, the snow melted a little.
Pete:	Well, is the hole deep enough now?
Sam:	It seems like this will do now.
Sam:	They say the track should be eighteen inches deep.
Junior:	It seems like everything is finished.
Jimmy:	All we have to do now is drag the log straight.
Sam:	All right, come and put the log in the track here.
Jimmy:	Come on, somebody stand on the log.
Sam:	Come on, you two pull.
Sam:	Drag the log now right to the end. Drag the log until it gets to the end.
Sam:	When you get to the end drag the log back here, this way, so you end up back here.
Sam:	We seem to be all finished.
Jimmy:	Oh, it is a good track.
Sam:	I guess we'll see each other again tomorrow
Sam:	when they start to play snowsnake.

Chapter 34 ĘKNIYĘTOʼ

ĘKNIYĘTOʼ (Cayuga) p. 494

Pete:	Háeʼ Sam!
Sam:	Háeʼ Pete!
Pete:	Agǫ:gę́ʼ sǫ:déʼ syętwáhsǫh.
Pete:	A:yę́:ʼ do:gę́hs desawayęnhá:ʼǫh.
Sam:	Do:gę́hs tó ne:ʼ. Dewagewayęnhaʼs gyętwáhsǫh.
Pete:	Tę́ʼ dʼigę dʼese: a:gǫyęnawáʼs aekniyętwahsǫ:ʼ?
Sam:	Haǫʼ dʼęnyó neʼ giʼ gyę:ʼ, gyę:gwáʼ saná:kdo:t.
Sam:	Ǫhnyaʼgé giʼ nhǫ́: ahsǫ́ hekǫnʼadáyętoʼ.
Pete:	Né:ʼ giʼ gyę:ʼ ęgǫyena:wáʼs ęknihǫnaʼdayé:toʼ.
Sam:	Haoʼ dʼęnyóh.
Pete:	Hęknéhdahk dʼigę́h, ękniho̱naʼdayętwasaʼ?
Sam:	Tę́ʼ. Hęgyę́ʼtsǫ:. Sedjí:ha ní:ʼ ęgahdę:díʼ gǫ́dagyeʼ.
Sam:	Ęgadehsrǫnyahnyǫ́: shę nhǫ́: ękníyętoʼ.
Pete:	Haoʼ dʼęnyóh.
Pete:	Hęgǫhawíhdęʼ gęh, neʼ atsókdǫhsraʼ?
Sam:	Haoʼ dʼęnyóh, né:ʼ gíʼ gyę:ʼ, hęskawi̱hdę́ʼ neʼ agatsokdǫ́hsraʼ.
Pete:	Sgahoʼdę́:ę dʼigę́h, o:yáʼ ihsé: hęgǫhawíhdęʼ?
Sam:	Haoʼ dʼęnyóh, né:ʼ giʼ gyę́:ʼ gyę:gwáʼ ęhságaę

Sam:	ohǫnʔadáʔ giʔ gyę́:ʔ hniʔ ętskáwihdęʔ.
Sam:	Tohgeh, í:ʔ hné:ʔ hęgǫhawihdę́ʔ sadę́nʔatraʔ.
Sam:	O:nę́ giʔ gyę́:ʔǫ hyá:.
Sam:	Ęsgǫ́ʔdrǫhnaʔ gęh?
Pete:	Haoʔ dʔęnyó dó:gęhs, dǫdasgʔidrǫhnah.
Pete:	O:nę́ giʔ gyę́: hne:ʔ sasgíʔdrǫ:ʔ.
Sam:	Ęyo:hę́ʔ ęsgǫ́:gęʔ.
Pete:	Haoʔ dʔęnyóh.

ĘKNIYĘTOʔ (English) p. 494

Pete:	Hi Sam!
Sam:	Hi Pete!
Pete:	I saw you planting last night.
Pete:	You really looked busy.
Sam:	I sure was. I was busy planting.
Pete:	Don't you think I could help you plant?
Sam:	All right, if you have time.
Sam:	I'll still plant some potatoes on the flats there.
Pete:	I'll help you, we'll plant potatoes together.
Sam:	All right.
Pete:	Shall we go there together, to plant potatoes?
Sam:	No, never mind, I'll go there right away, early in the morning.
Sam:	I'll get it ready where we will plant.
Pete:	All right.
Pete:	Shall I take the hoe for you?
Sam:	All right, you will carry the hoe for me.
Pete:	Do you think there is something else I could carry there for you?
Sam:	All right then, if you are willing,
Sam:	you can carry the potatoes for me too.
Sam:	Then I'll carry your lunch for you.
Sam:	So long for now.
Sam:	Shall I take you back?
Pete:	All right, sure, take me home then.
Pete:	Now you have brought me back.
Sam:	I'll see you tomorrow.
Pete:	All right.

Chapter 35 AǪHDĘGYǪHEʔ

AǪHDĘGYǪHEʔ (Cayuga) p. 508

Pete:	Sgę́:nǫʔ.
Helen:	Sgę́:nǫʔ.
Pete:	Eʔdrǫ́ʔgęˌsanoːhaʔ?
Helen:	Ęhę́ʔ, eʔdrǫʔ. Waʔhetsǫ́: jagó:yǫ:.
Pete:	Gaę diʔ heyęʔsgęhę:ʔ?

Helen:	O:, sganyada:digo:wá heyę́ʔsgęhę:ʔ.
Pete:	Gaę diʔ nhọ:wé neʔ sganayada:digo:wá heyę́ʔsgęhę:ʔ?
Helen:	Sę giʔ nhǫ́: tadinagréʔ neʔ ohwęʔgá:ʔ tonę:sowé:ksǫʔ.
Helen:	Néːʔ gyę́ːʔ gone:nǫ́hk neʔ ǫdádenhaʔs.
Helen:	Neʔ gyę́ʔ nʔaeyʔadóʔdę́ʔ neʔ ohwęʔgá:ʔ deyagonę:hsóweksǫʔ.
Pete:	Do: diʔ nʔaoniséʔ to he:yę́ʔs, hegaę́ʔs neʔ ǫdadenhaʔs?
Helen:	Dekní: agyaǫdadogęhtę́ʔ gonáhdęgyǫ:.
Pete:	Aęnǫhwéʔ diʔ gę sano:haʔ?
Helen:	Ęhę́ʔ, aʔenǫhwéʔ tó né:ʔ agę́ʔ.
Helen:	Do:gę́hs agę́ʔ sę ga:gǫgweʔdi:yó: neʔ nʔetó tgáenagreʔ.
Pete:	Gahǫwagǫ: gęh haʔgáęhdahk?
Helen:	Tę́ʔ. Degadęhné haʔgáęhdahk.
Pete:	Dó: diʔ gę nʔaoniséʔ to nyó: haʔgaę́ʔ?
Helen:	Hwíhs agę́ʔ tsǫ́: nʔagahwihsdáʔe:k to nyó: haʔgáę́ʔ.
Helen:	Hwíhs agę́ʔ niyohwihsdaʔé:ʔ gonahdęgyǫ́: neʔ Tyodró:wę:.
Pete:	Setji:há gę oʔga:sʔa nigę́ʔǫh?
Helen:	Setji:háh
Helen:	Gaǫhyʔáę agę́ʔ odǫgohdǫ́ heyagodí:yǫ:.
Pete:	Dęʔ diʔ hoʔdę́ʔ ni:yóht tréhs hnaʔ:gę:ʔ?
Pete:	Ahí: níːʔ sá:dǫ gęh hwíhs tsǫ́: nʔagahwihsdaʔé:k heyagodí:yǫ:.
Helen:	Nʔetó sʔehnéːʔ tsǫ́:, tgaíːʔ sʔehne:ʔ.
Helen:	Néːʔ gyę́ʔ tsǫ́: dewagyęonyǫ́ neʔ gahwísdʔaes hadíhsreʔ.
Pete:	Oihwi:yóʔ gʔigyę́:ʔ sę deyonʔidǫ:nyáʔt neʔ gahwisdʔáes hadísre.
Pete:	Ahoʔnigoháędaʔ diʔ gę hnéːʔ hyʔanih?
Helen:	Tę́ʔ néʔ sgahoʔdę́ʔ dehoʔnigǫhaędáʔs dęʔ hoʔdę́ʔ niyo:gyę́: neʔ gahwísdʔaes.
Helen:	Néːʔ tsǫ́: he:gę́ʔ neʔ ahatsęnǫ:níʔ neʔ o:nę saeyǫ́ʔ neʔ knó:haʔ.
Helen:	Haʔde:yǫ́: giʔ tsęhahwinǫ:gyéʔ ǫkihawí:sehéʔ.
Helen:	Ahdahgwi:yóːʔs neʔ ohwęʔgá:ʔ hoʔdę́ʔ sǫwahawiʔsehéʔ neʔ háʔnih.
Helen:	O:nę́ gʔigyę́:ʔ daheʔ!
Helen:	Tę́ʔ gę desa:tǫ́:deʔ, né:ʔ gyę́:ʔ nę́neːʔ dehǫęhsǫ́: neʔ ohwęʔgá:ʔ hóʔdę́ʔ.

AǪHDĘGYǪHEʔ (English) p. 508

Pete:	Hello.
Helen:	Hello.
Pete:	Is your mother home?
Helen:	Yes, she's home. She just got back.
Pete:	Where was she then?
Helen:	Oh, she was overseas (Europe).
Pete:	Where overseas was she?
Helen:	Where those people who wear wooden shoes live.
Helen:	She went with her employer.
Helen:	That's her nationality, Dutch (they wear wooden shoes).
Pete:	So how long was she there, she and her employer?
Helen:	They were away two weeks.
Pete:	Did your mother like it?
Helen:	Yes, she said she liked it.

Wadewayęstanih

Helen:	They sure are nice people, the ones that live there.
Pete:	Did they go by boat?
Helen:	No. They went by plane.
Pete:	How long did it take them to get there?
Helen:	They said it took only five hours to get there.
Helen:	They said they left Buffalo at five o'clock.
Pete:	In the morning or the evening?
Helen:	Morning.
Helen:	They said they got there at four in the afternoon.
Pete:	Why was it so late?
Pete:	I thought you said it only took them five hours to get there.
Helen:	That's all it was, that's right.
Helen:	It's just confusing the way they keep track of time.
Pete:	It sure _is_ confusing the way they keep track of time.
Pete:	Does your father understand it?
Helen:	No, he doesn't understand how time works.
Helen:	He's just happy that my mother is home.
Helen:	She brought back all sorts of things for us.
Helen:	She brought back some nice wooden shoes for my father.
Helen:	Here he comes now!
Helen:	Don't you hear it? He has on the wooden shoes.

Printed in Poland
by Amazon Fulfillment
Poland Sp. z o.o., Wrocław